Finding God

Our Response to God's Gifts

As I open this book, I open myself
to God's presence in my life.
When I allow God's grace to help me,
I see with truth, hear with forgiveness,
and act with kindness.
Thank you God, for your presence in my life.

Barbara F. Campbell, M.Div., D.Min.
James P. Campbell, M.A., D.Min.

LOYOLAPRESS.
A JESUIT MINISTRY
Chicago

Imprimatur	In Conformity
In accordance with c. 827, permission to publish is granted on March 10, 2011 by Rev. Msgr. John F. Canary, Vicar General of the Archdiocese of Chicago. Permission to publish is an official declaration of ecclesiastical authority that the material is free from doctrinal and moral error. No legal responsibility is assumed by the grant of this permission.	The Subcommittee on the Catechism, United States Conference of Catholic Bishops, has found this catechetical text, copyright 2013, to be in conformity with the *Catechism of the Catholic Church.*

Finding God: Our Response to God's Gifts is an expression of the work of Loyola Press, a ministry of the Chicago-Detroit Province of the Society of Jesus.

Senior Consultants
Jane Regan, Ph.D.
Richard Hauser, S.J., Ph.D., S.T.L.
Robert Fabing, S.J., D.Min.

Advisors
Most Reverend Gordon D. Bennett, S.J., D.D.
George A. Aschenbrenner, S.J., S.T.L.
Paul H. Colloton, O.P., D.Min.
Eugene LaVerdiere, S.S.S., Ph.D., S.T.L.
Gerald Darring, M.A.
Thomas J. McGrath, M.A.

Catechetical Staff
Jeanette L. Graham, M.A.
Jean Hopman, O.S.U., M.A.
Joseph Paprocki, D.Min.

Grateful acknowledgment is given to authors, publishers, photographers, museums, and agents for permission to reprint the following copyrighted material; music credits where appropriate can be found at the bottom of each individual song. Every effort has been made to determine copyright owners. In the case of any omissions, the publisher will be pleased to make suitable acknowledgments in future editions.
Acknowledgments continue on page 275.

Cover design: Loyola Press
Cover Illustration: Rafael López
Interior design: Loyola Press and Think Bookworks

ISBN-13: 978-0-8294-3171-1
ISBN-10: 0-8294-3171-3

Manufactured in the United States of America.

LOYOLAPRESS.
A JESUIT MINISTRY

3441 N. Ashland Avenue
Chicago, Illinois 60657
(800) 621-1008

www.loyolapress.com
www.ignatianspirituality.com
www.other6.com

Webcrafters, Inc. / Madison, WI, USA / 08-11 / 1st Printing

Contents

GRADE 3

Unit 1	God, Our Creator and Father	1
Session 1	Created to Be Happy	3
Session 2	Created to Be Together	9
Session 3	God Is Our Father	15
Session 4	Jesus Is with Us	21
Session 5	Celebrating Ordinary Time	27
Unit 2	**Jesus, Our Lord and Savior**	**31**
Session 6	Jesus' Good News	33
Session 7	Following Jesus	39
Session 8	Jesus Gathers Disciples	45
Session 9	Jesus Dies and Rises	51
Session 10	Celebrating Advent	57
Unit 3	**The Church, Our Community in the Spirit**	**61**
Session 11	Jesus Sends the Holy Spirit	63
Session 12	The Catholic Church	69
Session 13	The Church Prays	75
Session 14	Mary Is Holy	81
Session 15	Celebrating Christmas	87

Unit 4 Sacraments, Our Way of Life 91

Session 16	Sacraments of Initiation	93
Session 17	Celebrating Reconciliation	99
Session 18	Celebrating the Eucharist	105
Session 19	Christian Living	111
Session 20	Celebrating Lent and Holy Week	117

Unit 5 Morality, Our Lived Faith 121

Session 21	Faith, Hope, and Charity	123
Session 22	Making Good Choices	129
Session 23	Living as God's Children	135
Session 24	All Life Is Sacred	141
Session 25	Celebrating Easter	147

The Year in Our Church 151

Advent 153
Christmas 157
Lent 161
Holy Week 165
Easter 169
Pentecost 173
All Saints Day and All Souls Day 177

Prayers and Practices of Our Faith 181

Knowing and Praying Our Faith 184
Celebrating Our Faith 200
Living Our Faith 212
Songs of Our Faith 218

Art Print Pages 227

Unit 1 227
Unit 2 232
Unit 3 237
Unit 4 242
Unit 5 247

Glossary 253

Index 269

Acknowledgments 275

UNIT 1

God, Our Creator and Father

Saint Ignatius of Loyola

Saint Ignatius of Loyola recognized God in every living creature in the heavens and on earth. He saw God in plants, in animals, and especially in people.

Saint Ignatius of Loyola

Saint Ignatius of Loyola was born in Spain in 1491. He grew up in a noble family in the castle of Loyola. He was a soldier until he was wounded in a battle. He went home to get well. There he read about the lives of Jesus and the saints. He wanted to become a saint too.

From *The Spiritual Journey of St. Ignatius*

Ignatius traveled to a monastery in Spain at Montserrat. There he saw the mountain and many of God's wonderful creatures. He prayed at the shrine of Our Lady of Montserrat. He laid down his sword and pledged his life to God. He gave away his fine clothes and dressed as a poor man.

Later Ignatius wrote what he learned about God and Jesus. His book is called *Spiritual Exercises*. He wrote it to help people grow closer to God. He tells us that God cares for all the things he created. If we want to know God, we can begin by caring for the world God gives us. Ignatius's feast day is July 31.

The Montserrat monastery was built into the side of a mountain.

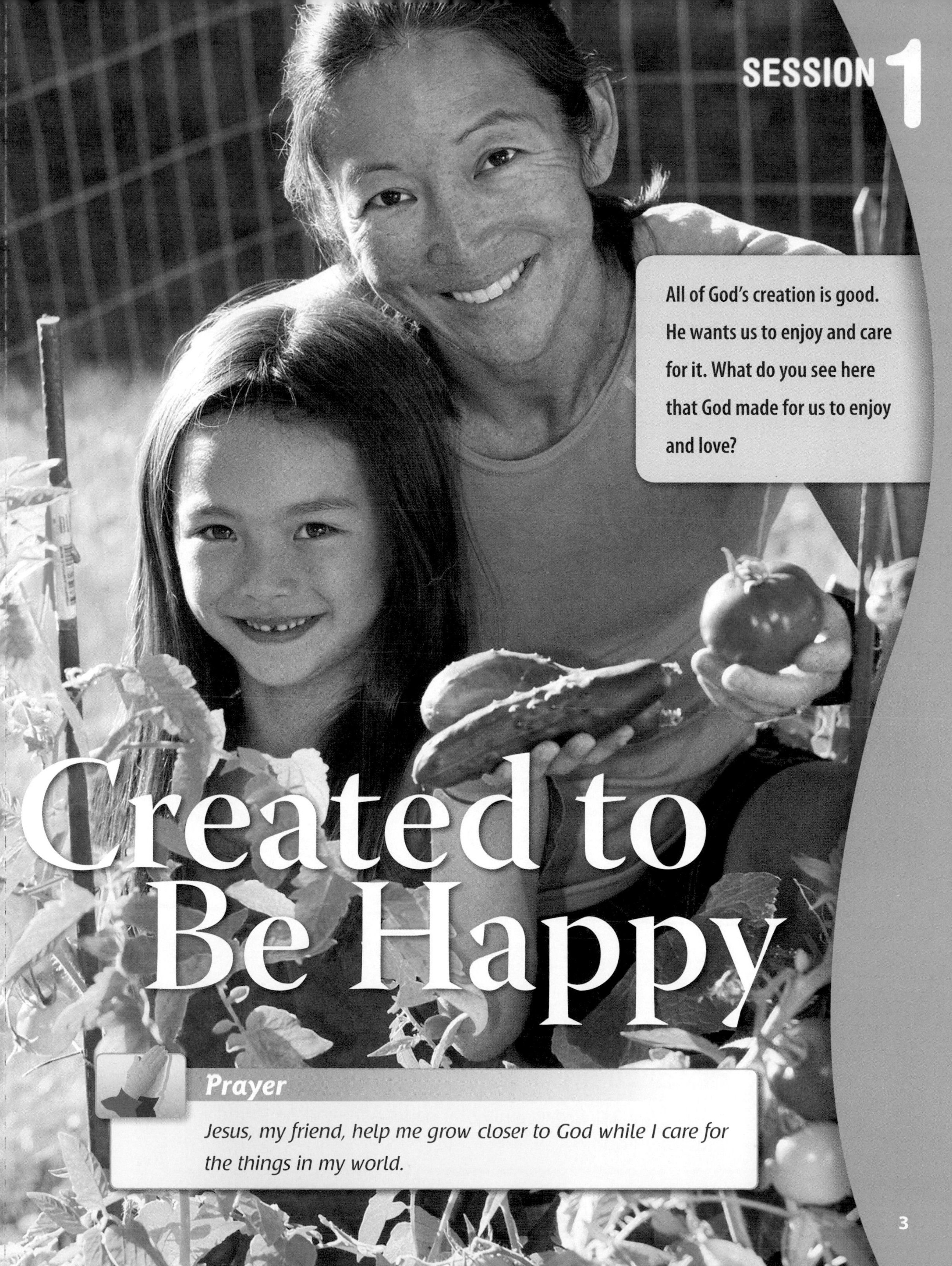

SESSION 1

All of God's creation is good. He wants us to enjoy and care for it. What do you see here that God made for us to enjoy and love?

Created to Be Happy

Prayer

Jesus, my friend, help me grow closer to God while I care for the things in my world.

We Believe in God

We see the world around us and know that God blesses us and cares for us. We depend on him. We praise God to show that we believe in him.

We pray a special prayer called the **Apostles' Creed** to show our faith. An **apostle** was a special follower of Jesus'. A **creed** tells us what people believe. The Apostles' Creed tells us what the apostles believed. It states the beliefs of our Catholic faith. This is how the Apostles' Creed begins. Learn this part and pray it often.

I believe in God,
the Father almighty,
Creator of heaven and earth,

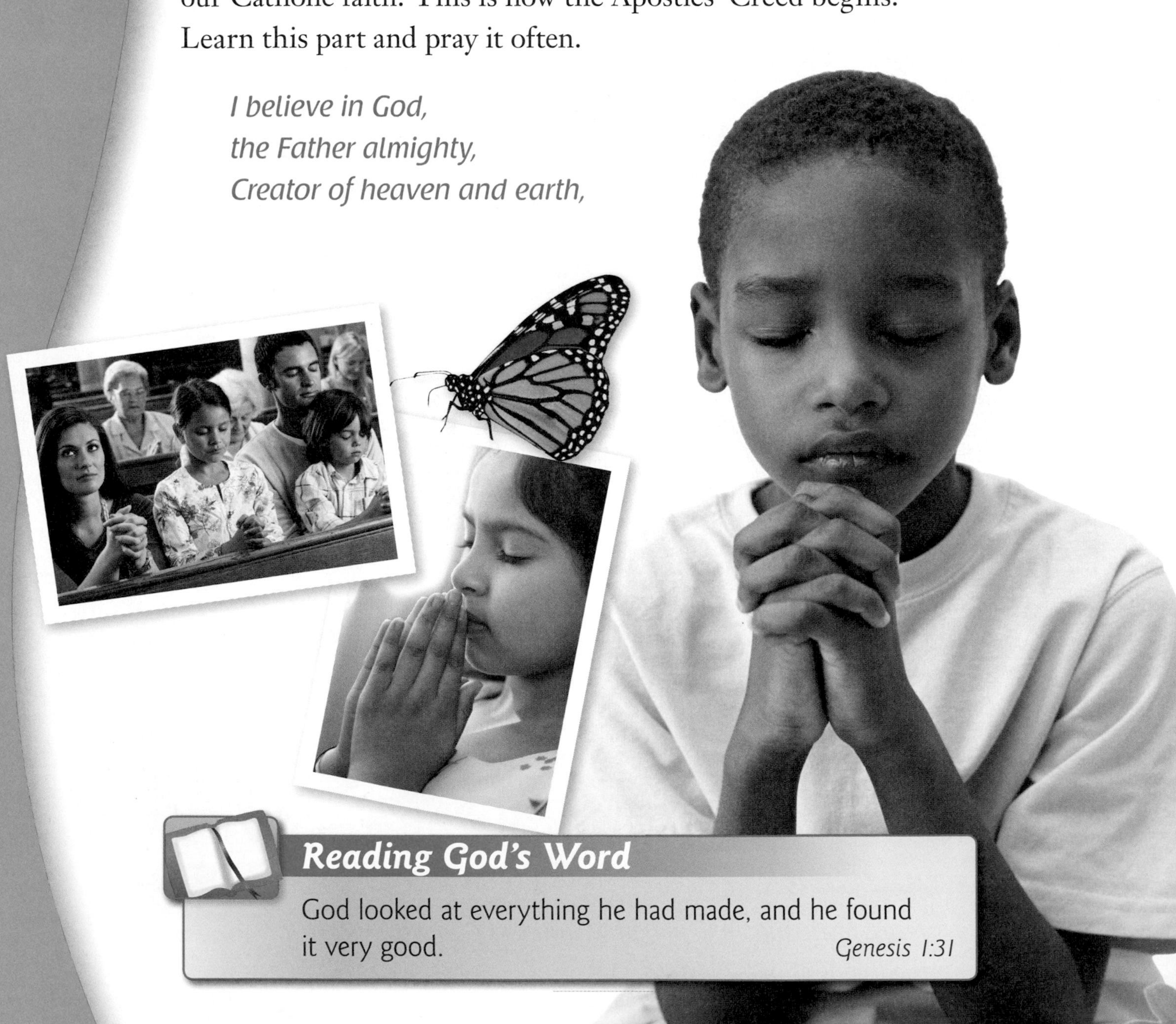

Reading God's Word

God looked at everything he had made, and he found it very good. *Genesis 1:31*

All Creation Praises God

We have a feeling of wonder when we see the things God made for us. We tell God that we believe in him and love him. We sing praise to God.

> Let all God's creation praise him, from the animals in the sea to the clouds in the sky. Mountains and trees, birds and animals praise God their creator. People young and old sing praise to God. His name alone is greater than heaven and earth.
>
> *adapted from Psalm 148:7–13*

Your Own Song of Praise

On the lines below, write a message to praise God for something beautiful you saw this week.

GO TO PAGE 227

Prayer

A Special Faith Prayer

These are the first words of the Apostles' Creed, our very special faith prayer. Pray these words often.

I believe in God,
the Father almighty,
Creator of heaven and earth,

Knowing that God is in your heart, think about him as the Father of Jesus and your Father too. Then think about God making everything in the universe. Tell God how awesome he is. Thank him for his gift of creation. Tell God how you will keep our world beautiful.

Knowing God

The beauty of the world helps us to know God. We see that God created all things because of his love. Because he created us and loves us, we make God important in our lives. We can know about God and creation by reading the Bible, which is the Word of God.

Loving God's Creation

We can love all of God's creation. Think of three people, animals, or parts of nature that you love, and write them on the lines. Draw pictures of them in the hearts.

Living My Faith

Faith Summary

We believe in God our Father, who created the world out of love for us. God wants us to know him and love him through the beauty of our world that leads us to him.

Words I Learned	Ways of Being Like Jesus
apostle	Jesus loves and cares for all God's people.
Apostles' Creed	*Be kind to people and animals around you.*
creed	

Prayer

Jesus, thank you for helping me to know and love God. Help me to care for God's world as he cares for me.

With My Family

Activity Work together as a family to keep your neighborhood neat. Take a walk around the block and pick up litter you find lying on the ground.

Faith on the Go Ask one another: *Think about our wonderful earth. What do you think is the most beautiful part of God's creation? Why?*

Family Prayer *Dear God, bless our family as part of your creation. Help us to show love for your creation by taking care of the world around us. Amen.*

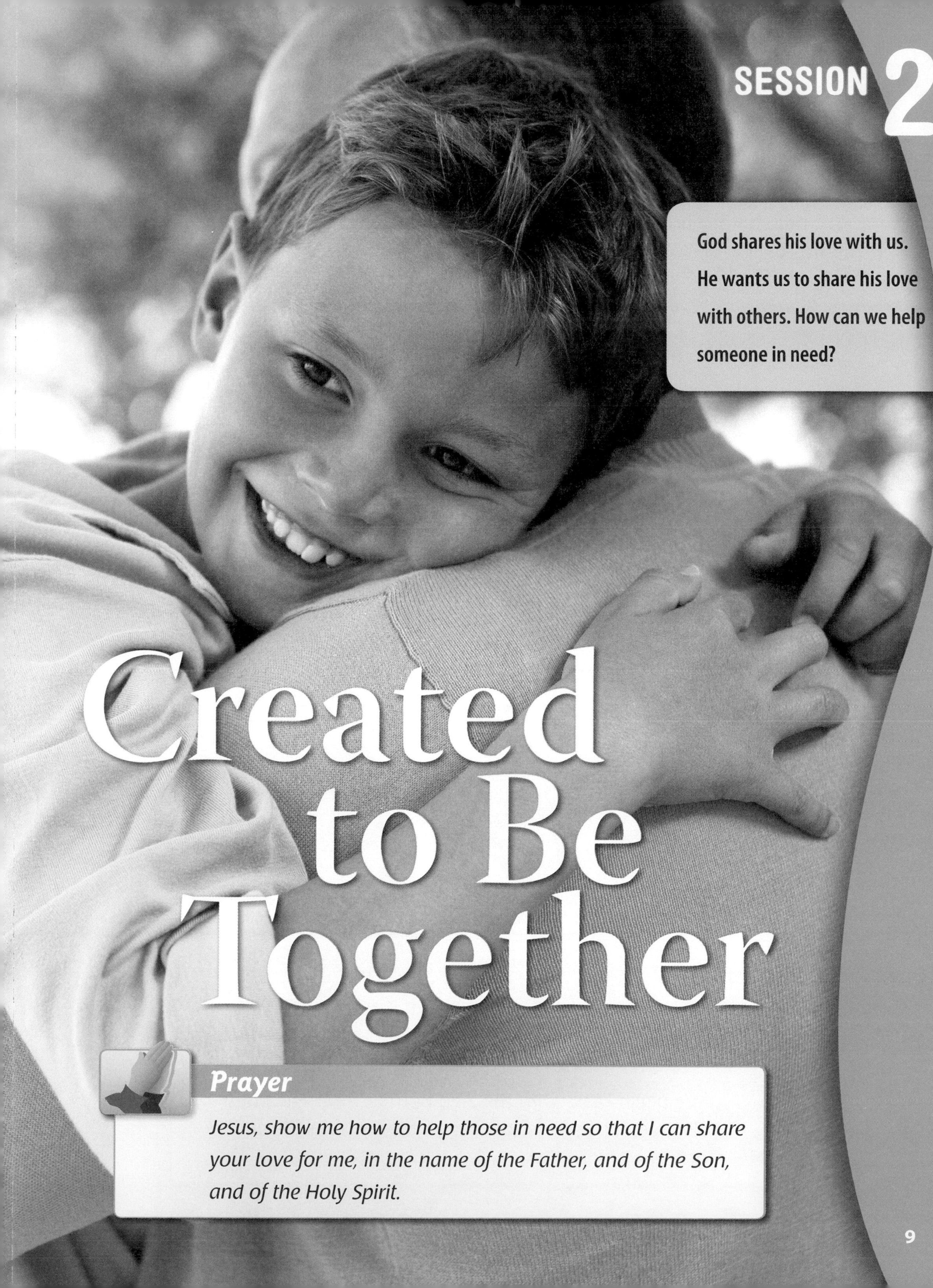

SESSION 2

God shares his love with us. He wants us to share his love with others. How can we help someone in need?

Created to Be Together

Prayer

Jesus, show me how to help those in need so that I can share your love for me, in the name of the Father, and of the Son, and of the Holy Spirit.

Sign of the Cross

Each night before bed, Katie prayed the **Sign of the Cross** as she began her evening prayers. Julia copied her older sister, but she did not understand what her sister was doing.

"Why do we make that sign when we pray?" Julia asked.

Katie explained that the Sign of the Cross reminds us of the Trinity. We pray to the Father, the Son, and the Holy Spirit.

We pray to God our Father. He created all things because he loves us. We pray to the Son, Jesus. Jesus, the Son of God who became man, came to tell us of the Father's love and to save us. We pray to the Holy Spirit. The Holy Spirit helps us to understand how much God loves us. The Spirit helps us show God's love to others.

Link to Liturgy

We begin Mass with the Sign of the Cross. The priest also blesses us with the Sign of the Cross at the end of Mass.

Another Prayer to the Trinity

Katie told Julia of another prayer that praises God as the Trinity. She said, "When we pray the Glory Be to the Father, we are praising God, who created us. He is with us now, and he always will be." Katie helped her sister pray this prayer.

Glory be to the Father, and to the Son, and to the Holy Spirit. As it was in the beginning, is now, and ever shall be, world without end. Amen.

As they closed their prayer with the Sign of the Cross, Julia smiled. From now on, when she prays these prayers, she will think of the Trinity: the Father, the Son, and the Holy Spirit.

Reading God's Word

We have come to know and to believe in the love God has for us. God is love, and whoever remains in love remains in God and God in him. *1 John 4:16*

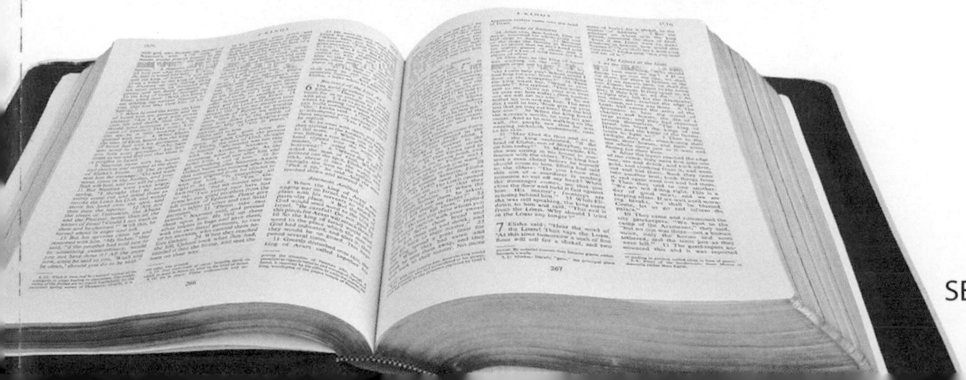

GO TO PAGE 228

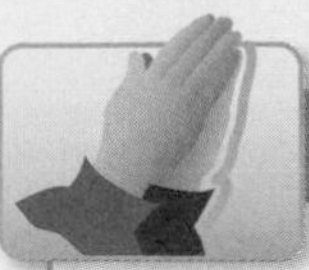

Prayer

A Reminder of the Trinity

Let the Sign of the Cross be our prayer today. Think about the meaning of the words as we pray them.

Sign of the Cross

In the name of the Father,

Bring to mind some of the wonderful things God the Father has created.

and of the Son,

Imagine that you are walking with Jesus. What is Jesus telling you about God?

and of the Holy Spirit.

Think about the kind and caring things you do for others. The Holy Spirit helps you do these things.

Amen.

Spend a few more minutes with Jesus. Tell him how you will follow the guidance of the Holy Spirit. Tell him something you will do for another person. Thank him for his love.

Gentle Jesus

Jesus showed us how to love others. He used gentle words when he talked to people.

What Would Jesus Say?

Read the sentences below. Make a smiling face in the circle next to each sentence that Jesus would like to hear you say. Make a frowning face in the circle next to the unkind sentences.

◯ You cannot have any of my candy.

◯ You can go first.

◯ Do you want to come to my house?

◯ I do not like you.

◯ Let's ask Michaela to play.

◯ You cannot join my team.

Kindness Counts

Draw a scene where two people are being kind to each other. Add balloons that show words they are saying to each other.

Living My Faith

Faith Summary

The love of the Trinity—Father, Son, and Holy Spirit—is the source of our love. God wants us to share his love with others.

Words I Learned

Sign of the Cross

Ways of Being Like Jesus

Jesus helped people when they were sick or in need. *Treat people kindly. Offer to help others, even when you are busy.*

Prayer

Jesus, thank you for showing me how to help others. Let me care for others like you did so I can grow closer to you.

With My Family

Activity Decide with your family what you can do together to help others. Some choices are making a food basket for a family in need, shopping for a wish-tree gift at Christmas, or helping a sick or elderly neighbor with chores around the house.

Faith on the Go Ask one another: *If you could help one person, whom would it be? Why?*

Family Prayer Pray the Sign of the Cross and the Glory Be to the Father with your family. Then spend a few minutes talking about the Trinity.

SESSION 3

God Is Our Father

Think about the last time you said a prayer. For whom did you pray? Why did you pray for that person?

Prayer

Jesus, my guide, teach me how to pray to God our Father so that I can grow in love for God and others.

Jesus Reveals God as Our Father

As God's Son, Jesus shows us what God is really like. He reveals that God is our Father, who cares for us as his children.

As God's children, we call God our Father, as Jesus did. *Father,* for Jesus, means the one who loves, forgives, and is good to his children. Sometimes Jesus called God **Abba.** That is a special name like Dad or Papa.

Children all over the world use Father in their own language when they call God. The word for father in Spanish is *padre;* in German it is *Vater.* Do you know the word for father in another language?

Padre

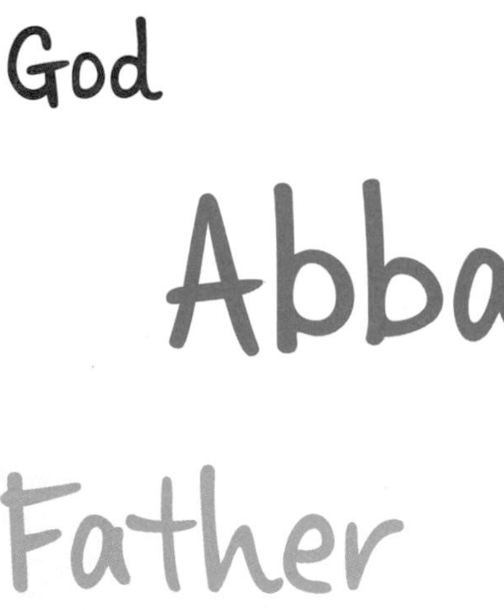

Did You Know?

When we pray, we raise our minds and hearts to God. We ask God for good things.

Jesus Teaches Us to Pray

Jesus went up the side of the mountain and sat down. His disciples gathered around him. Jesus began to teach them.

> This is how you are to pray:
>
> Our Father in heaven, hallowed be your name, your kingdom come, your will be done on earth as in heaven. Give us today our daily bread; and forgive us our trespasses as we forgive those who trespass against us; and lead us not into temptation, but deliver us from evil.
>
> If you forgive others for the wrongs they do, your heavenly Father will forgive you.
>
> *adapted from Matthew 6:9–14*

Forgive Each Other

Write about a time when you forgave someone or someone forgave you.

____

____

____

____

____

Link to Liturgy

We pray the Lord's Prayer as we prepare to receive Holy Communion.

GO TO PAGE 229

Prayer

Grow Closer to God

Jesus taught us the Lord's Prayer. He wanted to bring us closer to God the Father, to himself, and to one another. God is our loving Father, and we pray the Lord's Prayer to him.

Lord's Prayer

Our Father, who art in heaven,
hallowed be thy name;
thy kingdom come,
thy will be done
on earth as it is in heaven.

We give glory to God, whose name is holy. We pray that what he wants for us and for the world will happen.

Give us this day our daily bread,
and forgive us our trespasses,
as we forgive those who trespass against us;
and lead us not into temptation,
but deliver us from evil.
Amen.

We ask God for what we need to live. We tell him we will forgive others as he forgives us. We ask him to keep us from evil.

Imagine that you are with Jesus and his disciples on the mountain. You have a chance to talk to Jesus alone. Tell Jesus what the most important part of the prayer is for you. Listen in your heart for what he wants you to know.

Show Forgiveness

In the Lord's Prayer, Jesus tells us that God wants us to forgive others.

What Would You Do?

How would you show forgiveness in these situations? Write your answers on the lines. Then draw a picture of one of your answers.

1. You found your new souvenir from the museum in your sister's room. Earlier you told her that it was fragile and that she couldn't play with it.

 ____

 ____

2. Your good friend forgot to invite you to his laser tag birthday party. Later he said he was sorry he did not invite you.

 ____

 ____

Reading God's Word

Blessed be the God and Father of our Lord Jesus Christ. God the Father always shows us mercy. He encourages us. He supports us when we are troubled. He wants us to do the same for others who are suffering.

adapted from 2 Corinthians 1:3–4

Faith Summary

By teaching us the Lord's Prayer, Jesus reveals God as our Father. He tells us God wants us to forgive one another.

Word I Learned

Abba

Ways of Being Like Jesus

Jesus forgave others. *Ask God to help you learn forgiveness from him.*

Prayer

Jesus, thank you for showing us how to pray to God our Father. Help me forgive others so I can be more like you.

With My Family

Activity Take a walk with your family in a peaceful environment, such as a forest or a park. Enjoy each other's company.

Faith on the Go Think back to a time when you might not have been forgiving. Ask one another: *What happened? What would you do differently now?*

Family Prayer *Dear God, help us to ask for forgiveness when we hurt others. Help us to keep our hearts open to love others and forgive them when they hurt us. Amen.*

SESSION 4

Mary and Joseph prepared for Jesus to be born. How do you think they got ready for Jesus? If you had been there, how would you have helped Mary and Joseph?

Jesus Is with Us

Prayer

Jesus, Savior, help me to learn from your life so that I can live as God wants me to live.

Trust in God

A young woman named Mary was engaged to a good man named Joseph. An angel visited Joseph in a dream and told him that Mary would have a baby through the Holy Spirit. The angel said the baby's name would be Jesus, which means "God saves us." Jesus was to be our Savior. Jesus would also have the name Emmanuel, which means "God is with us."

adapted from Matthew 1:18–23

Joseph listened to the angel and trusted in God. He and Mary got married. Jesus, the Son of God, was born. Joseph cared for Mary and Jesus.

Did You Know?

The name Christ means "the anointed one." That means the one chosen by God to be our Savior.

trust in God

Listening and Trusting

In the **Scriptures** we learn that the angel visited Joseph in a dream. Joseph listened to the angel. He trusted in God and cared for Jesus and Mary.

We trust in God. Jesus, God's Son who became man, is with us always. Even when we are alone or afraid, Jesus is with us.

Sometimes we must listen to others. We trust our parents and teachers when we do not know what to do.

Can you think of a time when you listened and trusted what someone told you? On the lines below, share what happened.

____

____

____

____

listen and trust

Reading God's Word

The Lord leads you. He will always be with you. He will never disappoint you or abandon you. Do not be afraid or discouraged. *adapted from Deuteronomy 31:8*

GO TO PAGE 230

Prayer

We Believe in Jesus

Joseph believed and trusted the angel who appeared to him. We tell God we believe in Jesus when we pray this part of the Apostles' Creed.

[I believe] in Jesus Christ,
his only Son, our Lord,
who was conceived by the Holy Spirit,
born of the Virgin Mary,

Pray this part of the Apostles' Creed in the presence of Jesus. Spend some time talking with him. Invite him to be at home in your heart just as he was at home with Joseph and Mary. Think about how you will make Jesus at home in your heart. Talk it over with him. Remember to say "Thank you!"

Examples for Living

Jesus showed us how to live the way God wants us to live. Jesus spent his life teaching and healing others. Joseph also showed us ways of living a good life. He trusted in God and took care of Mary and Jesus.

Good Examples

People in our lives can show us good ways to live. Circle the pictures of the people below who set good examples for us.

Write a short prayer thanking God for people who show you how to live a good life. Use at least two of the following words in your prayer: *thanks*, *trust*, *lead*, *teach*, *God*.

RESPOND

Living My Faith

Faith Summary

We believe that God sent his Son to save us and to be with us at all times. Through his own life, Jesus reveals God's love for us and teaches us what it means to live as God wants us to live.

Word I Learned

Scriptures

Ways of Being Like Jesus

Jesus always helped others and was good to everyone. *Follow Jesus' example by looking for ways to help others.*

Prayer

Jesus, thank you for always being with me. Help me to reach out to others and treat them kindly, as you did.

With My Family

Activity Jesus reached out to people who were hurting. Try to notice when someone in your family seems sad. Do something to make that person happy.

Faith on the Go Ask one another: *Name a person that treats other people with love. What does that person do for others?*

Family Prayer *Dear God, help us to know when other people need us. Teach us how to care for them. Amen.*

Celebrating Ordinary Time

Each year the Church celebrates special feasts and seasons that help us remember the great things God has done to save us and how much he loves us.

The liturgical year is the Church's calendar. Ordinary Time is celebrated two times during each liturgical year—between Christmas and Ash Wednesday, and between Easter and Advent.

Prayer

Dear Jesus, I know you are with me during each day of Ordinary Time. As you walk with me, help me to serve others the best I can.

We Grow in Community During Ordinary Time

Ordinary Time is a time to be grateful that we belong to our church **community.** Together we work to serve others as Jesus did. We grow in community by being Christ to the world.

What is one way that your church community is Christ to the world?

Be Like Christ

During Ordinary Time how can you be more like Christ at home and in your school? Write your idea on the lines.

____

____

____

grow in your community

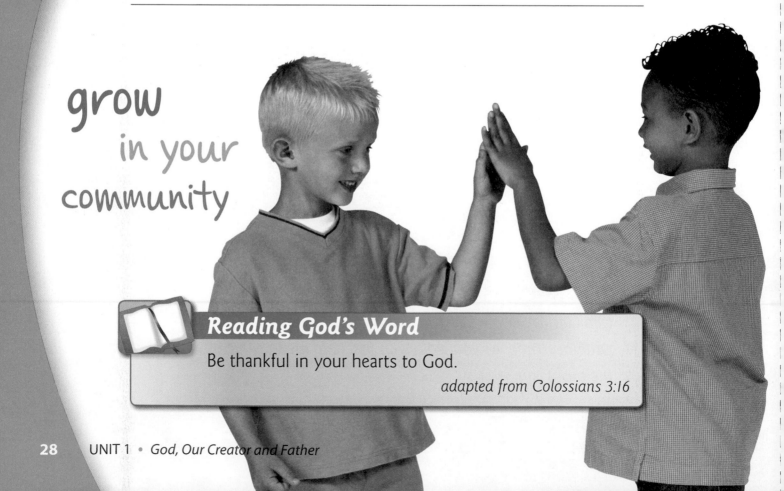

Reading God's Word

Be thankful in your hearts to God.

adapted from Colossians 3:16

Mass During Ordinary Time

When you go to Mass during Ordinary Time, you often receive a parish bulletin that tells about the life of the church.

As you read the bulletin, you will learn about opportunities to love and serve others in your community and around the world.

What We Experience

When you look around your church, you will see parish members praying and singing together as a community. Watch closely as they share in a sign of peace.

My Parish

Write a word on each line in the cross that tells something about your parish.

Did You Know?

Each Sunday you can find out which liturgical season or feast we are celebrating by looking in your parish missal or in your parish bulletin.

Faith Summary

Ordinary Time is celebrated twice during each liturgical year. It is a time to grow in community by being Christ to the world. We are grateful that we belong to our church community.

Word I Learned

community

Ways of Being Like Jesus

Jesus served those in need.
Spend time visiting with an elderly neighbor.

Prayer

Dear God, thank you for giving us the Church. Help us to grow in community by showing your love to the world.

With My Family

Activity When you go to Mass during Ordinary Time, bring home a church bulletin and discuss the information you read.

Faith on the Go Ask one another: *How can I become more involved in my church community?*

Family Prayer Use Ordinary Time to invite family members to grow in faith together by making a prayer box for special prayer intentions or requests.

UNIT 2

Jesus, Our Lord and Savior

Saint Scholastica and Saint Benedict

Saint Scholastica and her twin brother Saint Benedict lived in the hills of northern Italy. As adults, they each started a religious community.

Saint Scholastica and Saint Benedict

Saint Scholastica and her brother Saint Benedict grew up together in the hills of northern Italy. They were best friends. When they moved apart, they missed each other very much.

Benedict went to study in Rome. Scholastica stayed close to home. She loved to study and to take care of people who were poor or sick.

Saint Scholastica and her brother Saint Benedict.

Later, Scholastica started a community of nuns. It was about five miles from the monastery where Benedict had started a community of monks. Scholastica and Benedict met once a year in a little house nearby. They prayed and talked about their love of God.

At the end of one visit, Scholastica asked her brother to stay longer. When he refused, she prayed that he would stay. A powerful storm started, and Benedict could not leave. Scholastica explained that since he would not listen to her, she had asked God. She said God had heard her prayer. They talked and prayed all night. Scholastica's feast day is February 10. Benedict's feast day is July 11.

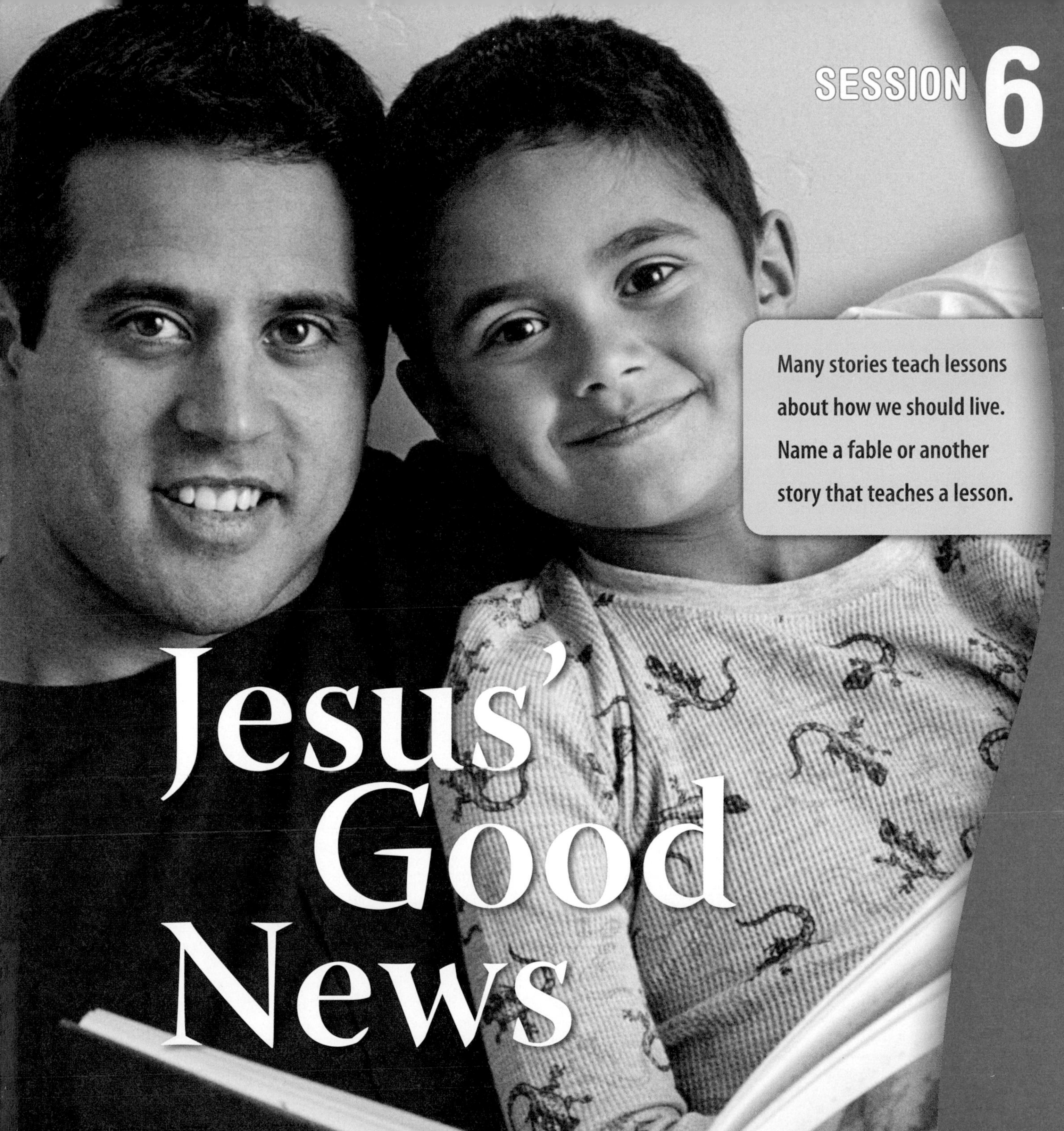

SESSION 6

Jesus' Good News

Many stories teach lessons about how we should live. Name a fable or another story that teaches a lesson.

Prayer

Jesus, my teacher, help me to understand your stories so that they can help me to know and love God and others.

The Kingdom of God

Many people gathered around to hear Jesus speak. Jesus wanted them to understand what the Kingdom of God is like. He told them this parable, or story.

> The Kingdom of God is like a mustard seed that is planted in a field. It is the smallest of all seeds, but it grows to be the largest of plants. It becomes a bush so large that birds come and nest in its branches. *adapted from Matthew 13:31–32*

Jesus used this parable to show how, with God's help, a great, welcoming kingdom can grow from small beginnings. Small acts of kindness can help many people feel welcomed by God.

We Serve God's Kingdom

When we love one another and live according to God's rule and direction, we serve the Kingdom of God just like Jesus did. During his life in Nazareth, Jesus worked hard and observed the rules of the Jewish faith. He loved all people. Jesus showed that we can serve God's kingdom in our daily lives.

A Small Act of Kindness

Here is an example of what Jesus meant. Anna, a third grader, goes to Mass on Sunday mornings with her family. One Sunday the priest said there were children in the parish who needed hats and gloves for winter. Anna went home and returned with a pair of warm mittens. Her friend Tara saw her and did the same thing. Soon many others did too. Anna's actions grew into something that served many people. Her small beginning served God's kingdom.

Random Acts of Kindness

Think about acts of kindness that you can do for others in your family or community. Pick someone you know, such as your little sister, your grandfather, or a neighbor, and write something you can do to make that person feel welcome in God's kingdom.

____

____

____

____

GO TO PAGE 232

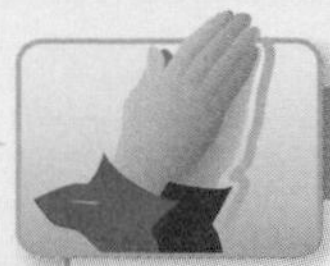

Prayer

Thanking Jesus for His Parables

Jesus' parables are like puzzles. When Jesus told the parables, people sometimes asked for help to understand them. Think about the parable of the mustard seed.

Imagine that you are there when Jesus is telling this parable. Who is with you? Do people look puzzled as Jesus tells the story?

Do you understand what Jesus is saying about the Kingdom of God? How does the parable help you understand what he means?

Now spend some time with Jesus. Thank him for telling parables to help you understand God's direction in your life. Tell him one thing you will do to serve God's kingdom.

Yeast Is Like the Mustard Seed

Jesus told the people a parable about yeast.

> He said the Kingdom of God is like yeast that a woman mixes with wheat flour to make dough rise. Even though the amount of yeast is small, it can make the dough rise. *adapted from Matthew 13:33*

When we make a loaf of bread, we add just a little yeast to make the dough rise. Yeast is like the mustard seed—a little bit makes a big difference.

Can You Be Like Yeast?

Small things we do can be like yeast. By doing small things, we can serve God's kingdom. On the lines below, write one small thing you can do to serve the kingdom. Explain how this act helps the kingdom grow.

____

____

____

____

____

____

Faith Summary

Jesus' parables teach us that we can serve the Kingdom of God in our own lives. Jesus teaches us that small acts of kindness can make a big difference.

Word I Learned

monastery*

Ways of Being Like Jesus

Jesus served the Kingdom of God by doing small things to help others. *Say something nice to a classmate and offer your help at home when it is needed.*

Prayer

Thank you, Jesus, for teaching me the importance of all the things that I do. Help me as I try to make a difference.

With My Family

Activity Bake some bread with your family. As you bake, talk about the yeast parable.

Faith on the Go Ask one another: *What is your favorite parable? What does it teach?*

Family Prayer *Dear God, help us to see ways that we can show kindness to other people. Lead us in finding ways to serve your kingdom. Amen.*

* This word is taught with the Art Print. See page 232.

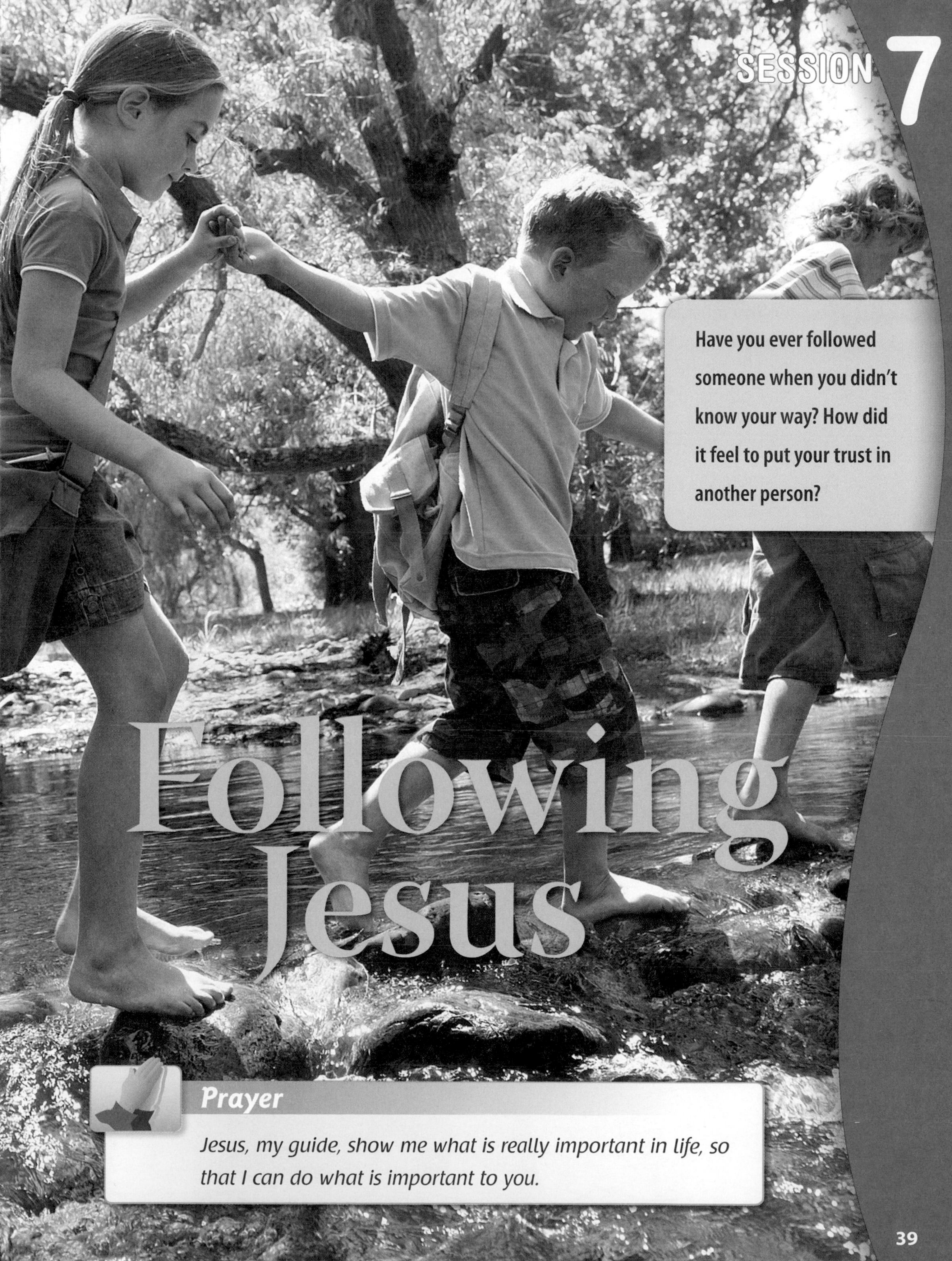

SESSION 7

Have you ever followed someone when you didn't know your way? How did it feel to put your trust in another person?

Following Jesus

Prayer

Jesus, my guide, show me what is really important in life, so that I can do what is important to you.

The Rich Young Man

In the story below, Jesus meets a rich young man and talks about choosing God's kingdom.

One day a young man stopped Jesus. "Good teacher," he asked, "what must I do to gain eternal life?"

You must keep the Ten Commandments," Jesus replied.

The young man smiled. "That is easy. I have kept the Commandments since I was a child," he said.

Jesus looked at the young man with love. "There is one more thing you should do, " he said. "Sell everything you own and give the money to the poor. Then come, follow me."

The young man frowned. He went away, for he was very rich.

Jesus said to his disciples, "It is not easy for people with wealth to choose God's kingdom!"

adapted from Mark 10:17–23

What do you think the rich young man will do next?

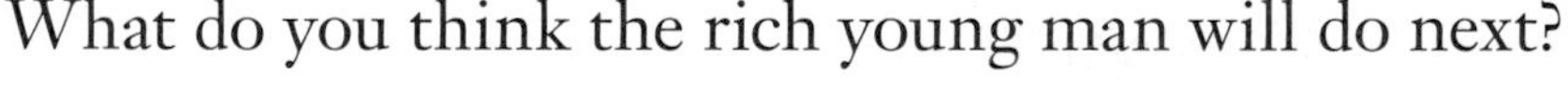

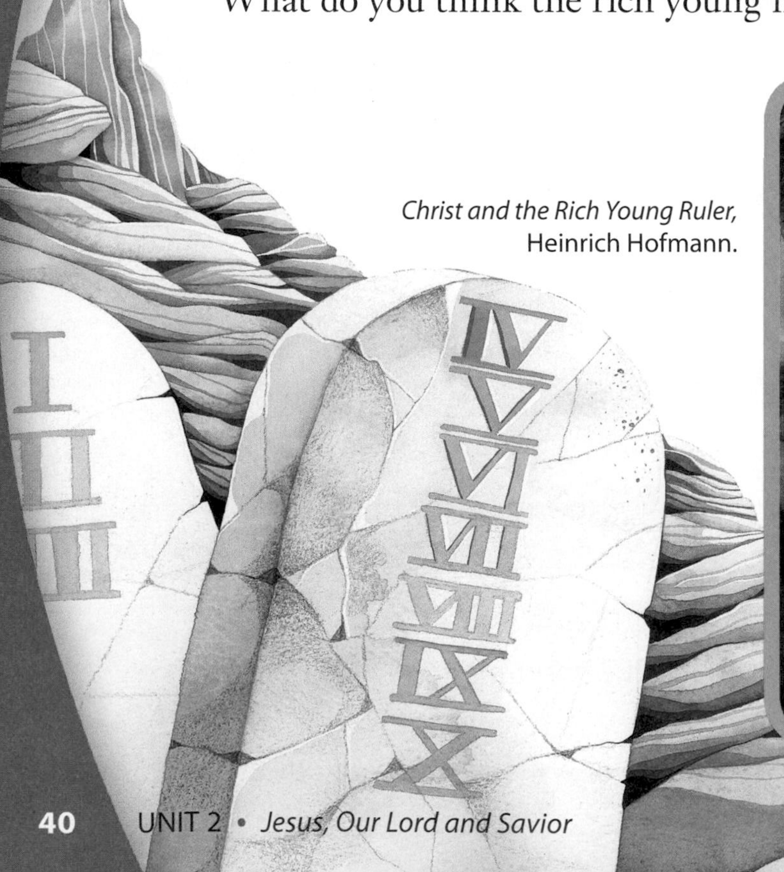

Christ and the Rich Young Ruler, Heinrich Hofmann.

Choosing God

God does not expect us to give up everything we have, but he does call us to change. He wants us to love him above all else. He wants us to love one another as much as we love ourselves.

God gave us the Ten Commandments to show us how to love him and one another. When we make wrong choices, we turn away from God and others. These choices lead us into sin. God calls us to be sorry for our sins. The Holy Spirit gives us the grace to turn back to God. We then mend our relationships with God and others. This is called **conversion.**

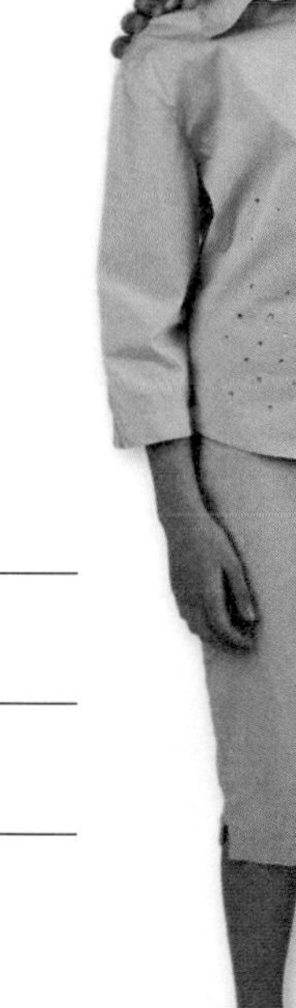

Every day we make choices about how to act toward God and others. The Ten Commandments help us to follow God and to care for others. On the lines below, share a recent choice that you made that brought you closer to God.

____

____

____

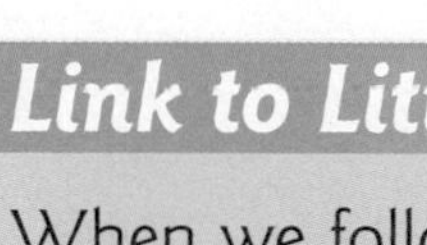

Link to Liturgy

When we follow the Ten Commandments, we live peacefully with one another. During the Sign of Peace at Mass, we share the peace of Christ with one another.

GO TO PAGE 233

Prayer

A Quiet Walk with Jesus

Imagine you are there when Jesus is talking to the rich young man. You see and hear everything. You see how sad Jesus is as he watches the young man walk away. If you could talk with the young man, what would you say?

After Jesus watches the young man leave, you and Jesus take a walk. When he looks at you, what do you tell him? What do you ask him? Walk quietly with Jesus, glad to be together.

Obey the Ten Commandments

By obeying the Ten Commandments, we show respect to God and others and live our lives without harming anyone. Jesus teaches us that this is a good thing. But Jesus asked the rich young man to do more. He asked him to give up all that he owned and follow him. The rich young man was not willing to do this.

What I Want and What I Need

Sometimes we are called to give up things we want but do not need. Draw an X through the things you may want but do not need.

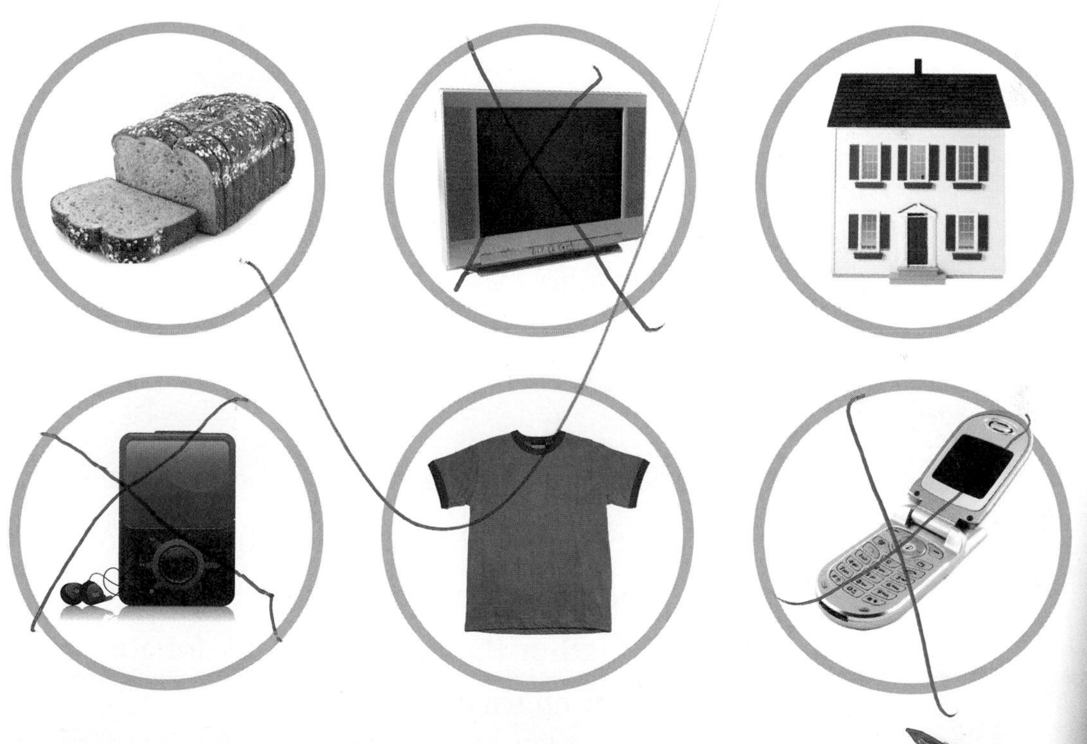

Did You Know?

The world is full of people in need. One of every seven people in the world does not get enough food to eat. Think of what you can do to help one person who doesn't get enough to eat.

RESPONDK

Living My Faith

Faith Summary

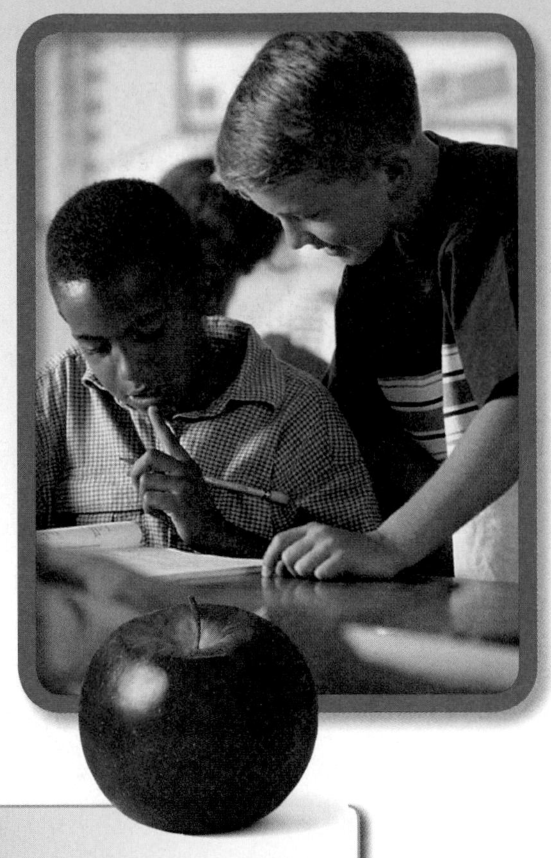

The Ten Commandments tell us how to love God and others. God gives us the grace to change and to cooperate with him.

Word I Learned

conversion

Ways of Being Like Jesus

Jesus helped those in need. *Do things for others cheerfully, even if it's not easy, to be like Jesus.*

Prayer

Thank you, Jesus, my friend, for showing me how to love you so much. I will follow you.

With My Family

Activity Find items around your home that someone else could use, such as clothes or toys that are in good condition. Gather them in a box and donate them to a shelter or charity.

Faith on the Go Ask one another: *If you were rich, who would you help with your money? Why?*

Family Prayer *Dear God, help us to use our free will to obey the Ten Commandments and follow you in all things. Amen.*

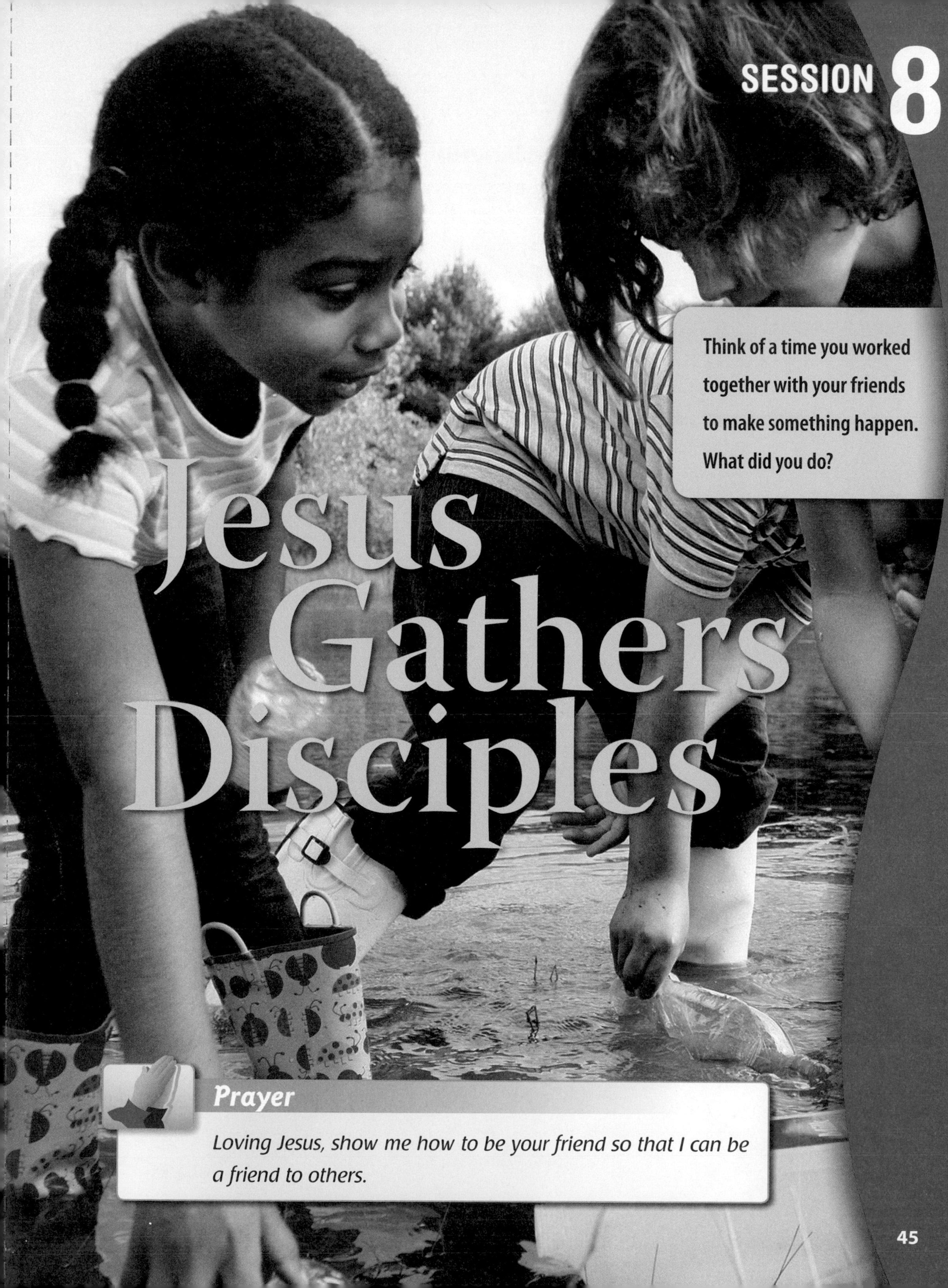

SESSION 8

Jesus Gathers Disciples

Think of a time you worked together with your friends to make something happen. What did you do?

Prayer

Loving Jesus, show me how to be your friend so that I can be a friend to others.

Jesus Calls Peter

The **Gospels** are parts of the Bible that tell the good news of Jesus' life. In the Gospel of Luke, we learn how Jesus called Peter to follow him.

> Jesus was near a lake, sharing the word of God with many people. He saw two boats with fishermen washing their nets. Jesus got into Peter's boat and asked him to move the boat away from the shore. Jesus taught the crowd from the boat.
>
> Later, he asked Peter to move the boat into deeper water and to lower the fishing nets. Peter answered, "We have worked all night long without catching anything. But if you tell me to, I will lower the nets.
>
> *adapted from Luke 5:1–5*

Would you trust Jesus as Peter did?

Peter Answers the Call

Peter knew he could do more with Jesus' help than by himself.

He trusted Jesus and lowered the nets into the water. The fishermen caught so many fish that their nets were tearing. They called to their partners on the other boat to come and help them.

Soon both boats were so full of fish that they almost sank. The fishermen were amazed. Peter knelt in front of Jesus and said, "Leave me, Lord, for I am a sinful man."

"Do not be afraid," Jesus said to him. "From now on you will be catching people instead of fish." When they reached the shore, Peter and the others left everything behind and followed Jesus.

adapted from Luke 5:6–11

Jesus accepted Peter as he was. He called Peter to help him bring others to God.

GO TO PAGE 234

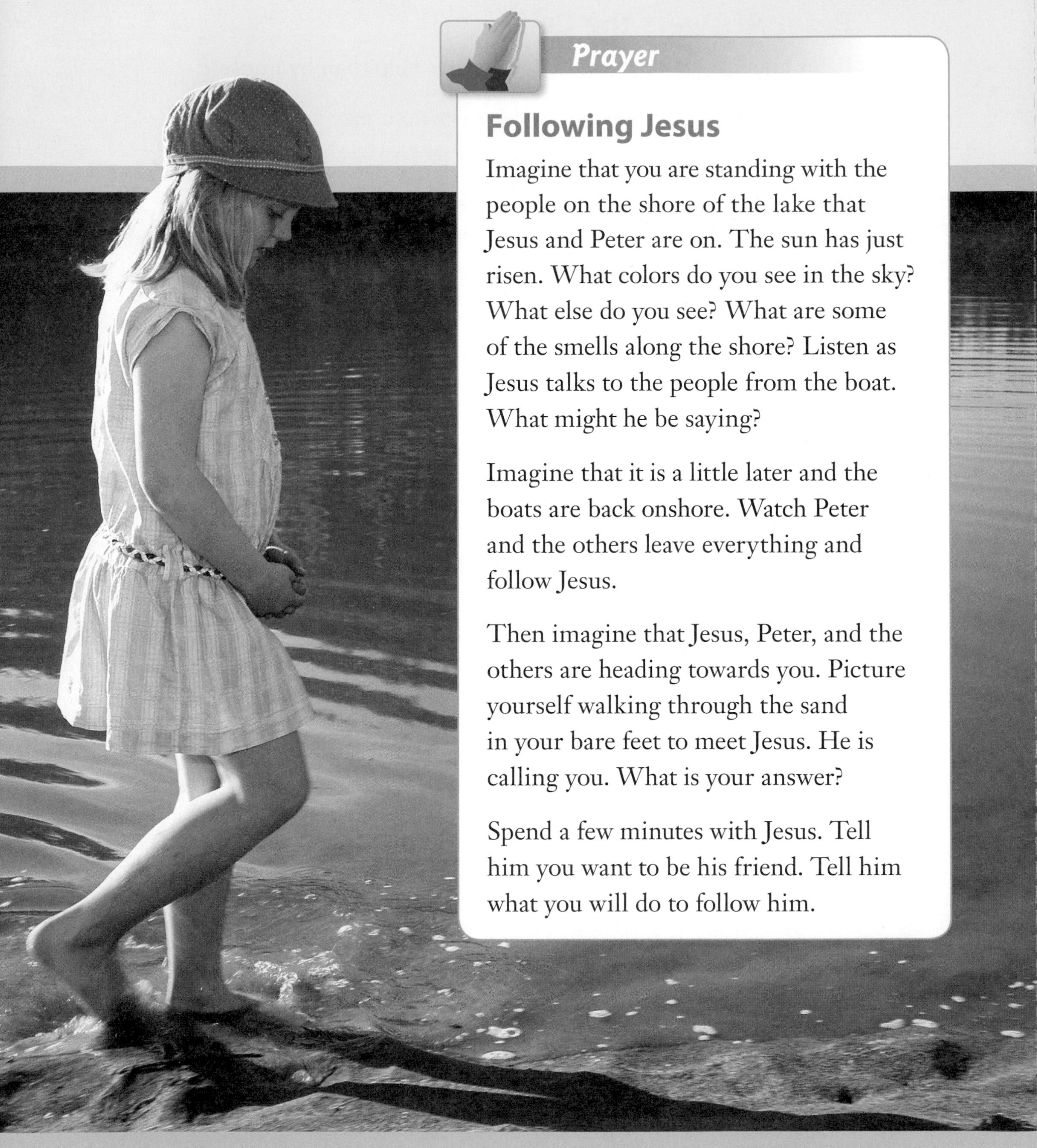

Prayer

Following Jesus

Imagine that you are standing with the people on the shore of the lake that Jesus and Peter are on. The sun has just risen. What colors do you see in the sky? What else do you see? What are some of the smells along the shore? Listen as Jesus talks to the people from the boat. What might he be saying?

Imagine that it is a little later and the boats are back onshore. Watch Peter and the others leave everything and follow Jesus.

Then imagine that Jesus, Peter, and the others are heading towards you. Picture yourself walking through the sand in your bare feet to meet Jesus. He is calling you. What is your answer?

Spend a few minutes with Jesus. Tell him you want to be his friend. Tell him what you will do to follow him.

Working Together to Follow Jesus

Sometimes it takes many people working together to do a job. Jesus' apostles learned to work together when they went out to proclaim God's Word. Write how you could work with others to follow Jesus' path.

Reading God's Word

Jesus told his disciples to gather followers. He said they would be like workers during a harvest. He said, "There is a large crop but few workers. More workers are needed to bring in the crop." *adapted from Luke 10:2*

RESPOND

Living My Faith

Faith Summary

Jesus chose apostles and sent them on a mission to preach the Word of God. He also chose disciples to help him. Jesus wants us to proclaim the Kingdom of God.

Words I Learned

Gospel
mission*

Ways of Being Like Jesus

Jesus chose special people to help him. *When you work in a group, listen to others and respect their ideas.*

Prayer

Dear Jesus, like Peter, I trust you to guide my life. Thank you for calling me to follow you.

With My Family

Activity Jesus called Peter personally. As a family, choose a relative or a friend who lives alone. Phone or visit that person.

Faith on the Go Ask one another: *What do you think life was like for Peter when he decided to follow Jesus? Why?*

Family Prayer *Dear God, help us to answer Jesus' call to follow him every day. Amen.*

* This word is taught with the Art Print. See page 234.

SESSION 9

Have you ever handled a new baby? Have you taken care of a puppy, a kitten, or another young animal? What did you do?

Jesus Dies and Rises

Prayer

Jesus, our risen Lord, help me to be a faithful disciple so that I can share in your new life.

We Proclaim Jesus' Death and Resurrection

After he died, Jesus opened the gates of Heaven for the just people who had died before him. Then he rose from the dead and appeared to Peter and the apostles. We call Jesus' passage from Death to Resurrection the **Paschal Mystery.**

The Holy Resurrection, Nana Quparadze.

Because Jesus Christ is God, we call him Lord. He was raised by the Father through the power of the Holy Spirit. Jesus Christ shares his life with us by sending the Holy Spirit to us. From the Holy Spirit, we receive the grace to be faithful to God and serve others. Jesus is with us today and awaits us at the end of life.

Reading God's Word

Jesus said, "I am the resurrection and the life. Everyone who lives and believes in me will never die."

adapted from John 11:25–26

We Believe in the Paschal Mystery

In this part of the Apostles' Creed, we proclaim our belief in the Paschal Mystery. Pray this part of the Creed.

[He] suffered under Pontius Pilate,
was crucified, died and was buried;
he descended into hell;
on the third day he rose again from the dead;
he ascended into heaven,
and is seated at the right hand of God the Father almighty;
from there he will come to judge the living and the dead.

Jesus is with us.

Link to Liturgy

At Mass we pray: "We proclaim your Death, O Lord, and profess your Resurrection until you come again."

GO TO PAGE 235

Prayer

A Special Faith Prayer

You have learned more of our special faith prayer, the Apostles' Creed. Pray these words now. Pause after each line to tell Jesus what the words mean to you.

[He] suffered under Pontius Pilate,
was crucified, died and was buried;
he descended into hell;
on the third day he rose again
from the dead;
he ascended into heaven,
and is seated at the right hand
of God the Father almighty;
from there he will come to judge
the living and the dead.

Spend a few quiet moments with Jesus. He loves being with you. You are content in each other's company. If there is something you want to ask Jesus or tell him, do it now. Listen to him.

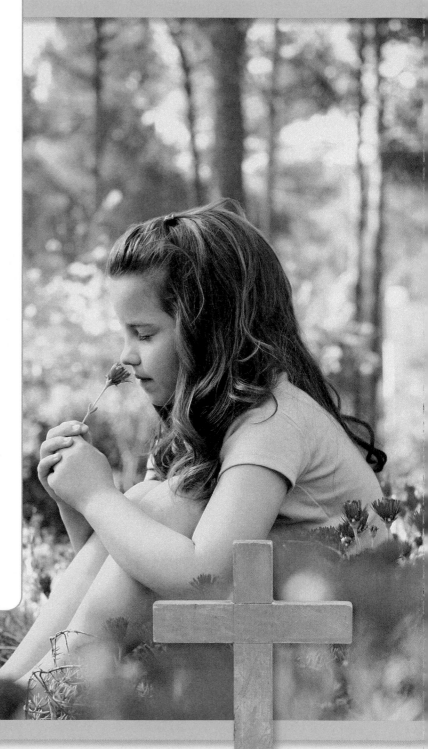

Celebrating New Life

Liliana and Rosa peeked excitedly into their butterfly box. They had seen the eggs hatch into caterpillars. The caterpillars ate so many leaves that they outgrew their skins several times. Then each caterpillar spun a silky chrysalis around itself and rested.

Two weeks later, the girls wondered if this would be the day the former caterpillars would fly off and start their new lives as butterflies.

Liliana told Rosa that she learned in church that the butterfly is a symbol of Jesus' Resurrection. When the butterfly comes out of the chrysalis and begins a new life, we are reminded of Jesus' Resurrection.

Color the Butterfly

Color this butterfly that is ready to fly off to a new life.

Living My Faith

Faith Summary

Jesus suffered and died for us. By the power of the Holy Spirit, he rose from the dead. Through his Death and Resurrection, we are saved.

Words I Learned

Paschal Mystery

Ways of Being Like Jesus

Before Jesus died, he asked the Father to forgive his enemies. *Forgive those who hurt you.*

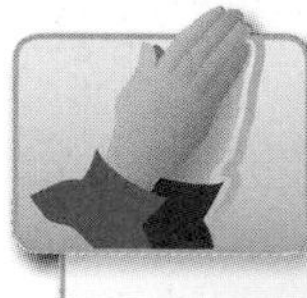

Prayer

Jesus, Lord, thank you for giving your life to save me. Help me to live my life to help others.

With My Family

Activity As a family, decide to help one another with chores that family members usually do alone.

Faith on the Go Ask one another: *Do we help out each member of the family as much as we can? If not, what prevents us?*

Family Prayer *Dear God, thank you for the gift of your Son, Jesus Christ. Help us to remember that Jesus suffered and died for us. Amen.*

SESSION 10

Celebrating Advent

The Church's liturgical year begins with Advent. Advent is the season before Christmas. It begins four Sundays before December 25 and ends at Christmas Mass.

Advent is a time to prepare our hearts and our homes to celebrate the birth of Jesus. We use this season to pray and to prepare ourselves to welcome him into our lives.

Prayer

Dear Jesus, on each day of Advent, I am preparing to celebrate your birth. Fill my heart with love and joy.

EXPLORE

We Prepare During Advent

Advent is a time to seek Jesus and to make room for him in our lives. We open our hearts by helping others. We also remember how faithful Mary and Joseph were to God's plan. Decorating our homes is another way we prepare for celebrating Jesus' birth. One way you can prepare your home for Advent is by setting up an Advent wreath or hanging up an Advent calendar.

We Prepare, We Remember

Think about what you will do this Advent to prepare to celebrate the birth of Jesus. Then finish each sentence on the lines below.

1. During Advent I prepare for Christmas by ______________

   ____.

2. During Advent I remember that ______________________

   ____.

3. During Advent my family and I ______________________

   ____.

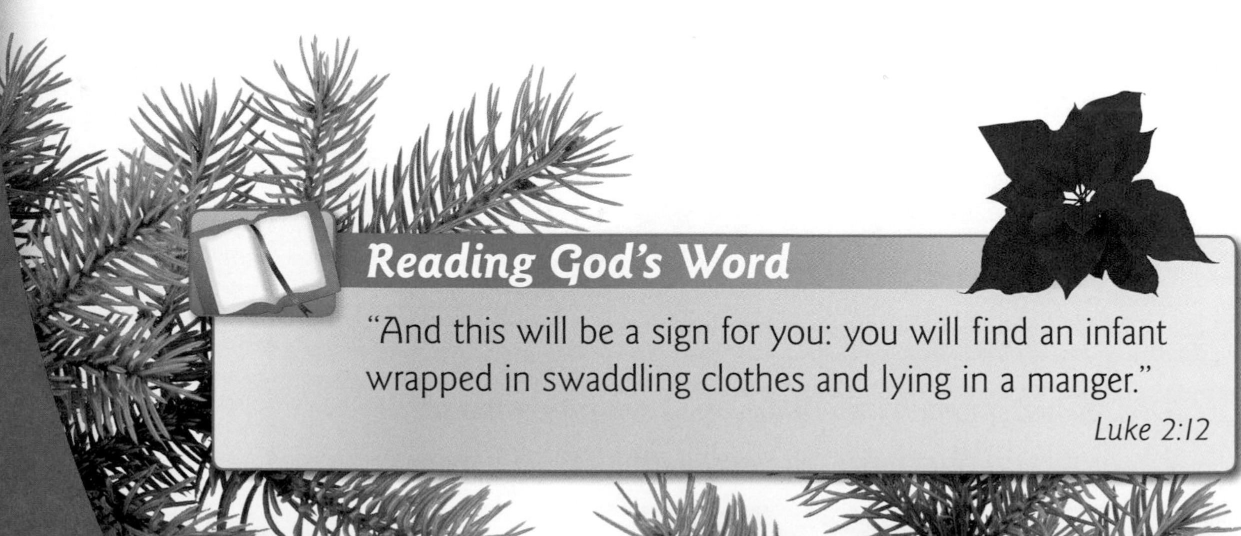

Reading God's Word

"And this will be a sign for you: you will find an infant wrapped in swaddling clothes and lying in a manger."

Luke 2:12

Mass During Advent

During Advent we long for Jesus, and we look forward to the celebration of his birth on Christmas Day. When you go to Mass during Advent, you might hear hymns such as, "O Come, O Come Emmanuel." Songs like this help us recognize how much we long for Jesus.

What We Experience

When you look around your church during Advent, you might see an Advent wreath with candles, which reminds us that we are preparing the way for Jesus, the Light of the World. You will also see the color purple on the altar cloth or priest's vestments. The color purple reminds us that Advent is a time of preparation.

My Advent Hymn

Imagine you are writing an Advent hymn. Write some of the words or phrases that you might include below.

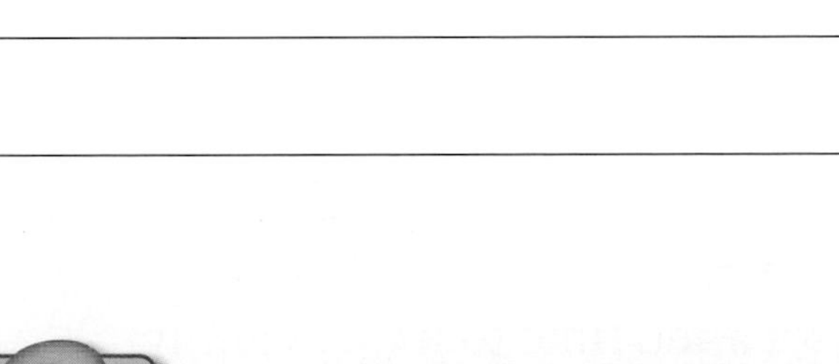

Did You Know?

The word *Advent,* from the Latin *adventus,* means "coming" or "arrival."

GO TO PAGE 236

RESPONDING

Living My Faith

Faith Summary

Advent is a season of preparing and remembering. We prepare our hearts and our homes to celebrate the birth of Jesus.

Ways of Being Like Jesus

Jesus was always thinking of others before himself. *This Advent I will put someone else's needs before my own.*

Prayer

Dear Jesus, as I prepare for the celebration of your birth, I know you are with me. Help me to remember to spread the joy of the Advent season to those I meet.

With My Family

Activity When you go to Mass during Advent, look around your church. Talk about the ways your church shows that it is celebrating Advent.

Faith on the Go Ask one another: *What more can we do to prepare our home for Christmas?*

Family Prayer Display an Advent wreath in your home. Each week, set aside time to have a family prayer service, using the wreath. Read from the Bible, light the Advent candles, and pray for those in need.

UNIT 3

The Church, Our Community in the Spirit

Saint Katharine Drexel

Katharine Drexel followed the path of Jesus. She gave away her wealth to help Native Americans and African Americans.

Saint Katharine Drexel

Katharine Drexel was born to a wealthy family in Pennsylvania in 1858. Her parents taught her to use her wealth to help others.

St. Katharine Drexel,
Robert Lentz, 2012.

After Katharine's parents died, she traveled around the country. She saw the suffering of the Native Americans and African Americans. She decided to use her fortune to help them.

Katharine asked Pope Leo XIII to send missionaries to help people in need. The pope replied, "Why don't you become a missionary?" She knew the pope was challenging her to do more. She started the Sisters of the Blessed Sacrament.

Mother Katharine Drexel began about 60 schools and missions in the United States. She spent many millions of her own money to help others. Katharine Drexel accepted Jesus' mission by giving up her wealth and following him. Her feast day is March 3.

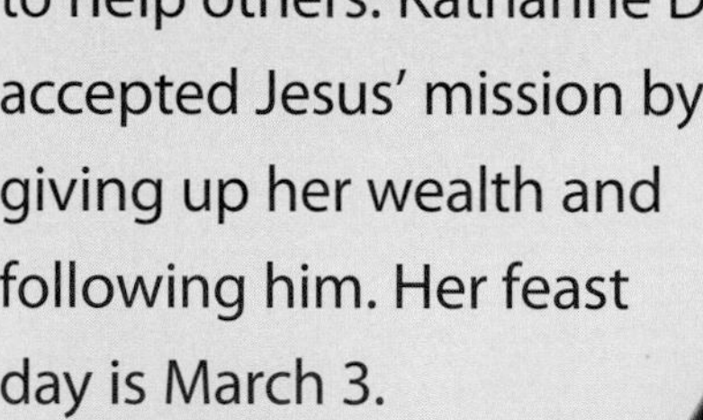

SESSION 11

Think of the special celebrations and activities in your life. What events have filled you with energy and excitement?

Jesus Sends the Holy Spirit

Prayer

Jesus, open my heart to receive the grace of the Holy Spirit. Help me to use the gifts he brings.

A Wind from Heaven

After Jesus' life on earth ended, his disciples gathered in Jerusalem during the celebration of Pentecost. Suddenly the sound of a strong wind filled the house. Tongues of fire appeared over each person's head. Jesus' disciples were filled with the Holy Spirit and began to speak in different languages.

Pentecost, El Greco.

Hearing the noise, a crowd gathered and began talking and shouting. They were confused. People from all over the world were there. They spoke many different languages. Yet each heard the disciples' message in his or her own language. They asked one another, "What does this mean?"

adapted from Acts of the Apostles 2:1–12

Accepting Jesus' Mission

The disciples realized that the Holy Spirit had come to them, just as Jesus had promised. They were excited. The Holy Spirit gave them strength to continue Jesus' mission. The disciples were ready to tell people all over the world about Jesus. Each disciple would be a **witness** to Jesus.

The Holy Spirit Builds the Church

At Pentecost the Holy Spirit gave the disciples the strength to continue Jesus' mission. The Holy Spirit began building the Church. Today the Spirit builds the Church through us, filling the Church with life. The power of the Holy Spirit is like the wind—though we cannot see it, we can feel its strength. The Holy Spirit gives us strength to continue Jesus' mission in our lives by being witnesses to him.

Jesus' Mission in Our Lives

Share your ideas about how you can continue Jesus' mission in your life.

____

____

____

____

Link to Liturgy

The Feast of Pentecost is celebrated seven weeks after Easter Sunday.

Prayer

Thankful for the Holy Spirit

People all over the world have prayed this prayer for a very long time. Invite the Holy Spirit into your heart. Think about what you are praying as you say these words.

Prayer to the Holy Spirit

Come, Holy Spirit, fill the hearts of your faithful.
And kindle in them the fire of your love.
Send forth your Spirit and they shall be created.
And you will renew the face of the earth.
Let us pray.

Lord,
by the light of the Holy Spirit
you have taught the hearts of your faithful.
In the same Spirit
help us to relish what is right
and always rejoice in your consolation.
We ask this through Christ our Lord.
Amen.

Now take a few minutes to thank Jesus for sending the Holy Spirit to you.

The Fruits of the Holy Spirit

Just as the Holy Spirit came to the disciples at Pentecost, he also comes to us. The Holy Spirit gives us the help we need to follow Jesus and to serve God and others. When the Spirit guides our actions, we can see the results of the Fruits of the Holy Spirit. The nine fruits are shown below.

The Spirit in Our Actions

Read each of the Fruits of the Holy Spirit and think about its meaning. Then choose one of them. Write how it can be seen in your actions by finishing this sentence.

The Fruit of ______________________ can be seen in my actions when I ______________________________________

____.

Reading God's Word

The Fruits of the Spirit are love, joy, peace, patience, kindness, generosity, faithfulness, gentleness, and self-control. *adapted from Galatians 5:22–23*

RESPONDE

Living My Faith

Faith Summary

On Pentecost Jesus sent the Holy Spirit to help his disciples continue his work. The Holy Spirit gives us strength and helps us to be witnesses to Jesus and to lead prayerful lives. The Fruits of the Holy Spirit can be seen in our actions.

Word I Learned

witness

Ways of Being Like Jesus

Jesus served the Kingdom of God by showing kindness to others. *Be kind to someone who needs a friend by eating together during lunch.*

Prayer

Jesus, my helper, thank you for sending the Holy Spirit to support me on my journey. Help me to appreciate the presence of the Spirit in my life.

With My Family

Activity Have everyone draw a family member's name from a box. Discuss how that person shows a Fruit of the Holy Spirit.

Faith on the Go Ask one another: *Is it easy for you to be patient? Why or why not?*

Family Prayer *Dear God, help us to see the ways that the Holy Spirit guides us. Grant us patience when dealing with others. Amen.*

SESSION 12

The Catholic Church

Think about the community where you live. Then think about your church. How would you describe your church community?

Prayer

Jesus, my Savior, show me how to follow you. I want to grow closer to you.

EXPLORE

Serving the World in God's Name

The Church is the sign that we are one with the Father, Son, and Holy Spirit. Jesus chose Peter and the other apostles to lead the Church. Today the pope, who is the **Vicar of Christ,** leads the whole Church. The bishops, the successors to the apostles, teach, guide, and lead the Church. They appoint **pastors** to lead each parish. These leaders serve the Church by helping us grow in our faith.

Leading the Church

Write the name of your parish. Then write the names of your church leaders. Ask for help if you need it.

My Parish ______________________

Pastor ______________________

Bishop ______________________

Pope ______________________

Reading God's Word

Jesus asked Peter for the third time, "Do you love me?" Peter was hurt that Jesus had asked him three times. He said to Jesus, "Lord, you know everything. You know that I love you." Jesus answered, "Feed my sheep."

adapted from John 21:17

Our Holy Catholic Church

The Church can be seen on earth and felt in our hearts. This is why we call the Church the **Mystical Body of Christ.** The Church has four important qualities, or marks:

- The Church is **one.** We have one Lord, and we share one faith. We receive one life in the Holy Spirit.
- The Church is holy. The Father, Son, and Holy Spirit are holy. In the sacraments, we receive all we need to make us holy.
- The Church is catholic. *Catholic* means "universal." Jesus told the apostles to teach all nations. The Church reaches out to all.
- The Church is **apostolic.** Jesus founded the Church with the apostles. The pope and bishops continue their mission today.

The Church is one, holy, catholic, and apostolic. These are the **Marks of the Church.**

Link to Liturgy

At Mass we pray for the Church and for our leaders, the pope and our bishop, during the Eucharistic Prayer. Listen for the names of your church leaders during this prayer.

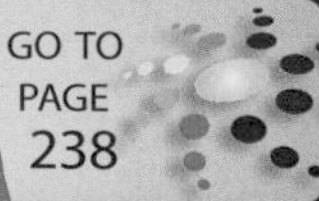
GO TO PAGE 238

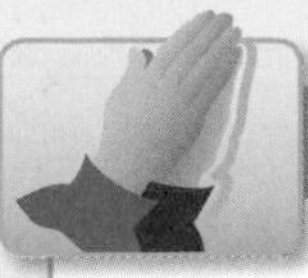

Prayer

We Believe

This last part of the Apostles' Creed states more of our beliefs. Think about them as you pray.

I believe in the Holy Spirit,
the holy catholic Church,
the communion of saints,
the forgiveness of sins,
the resurrection of the body,
and life everlasting. Amen.

Jesus knows what is in your heart. Be still with him for a few moments. Tell him that you believe. Ask him to strengthen your belief.

Who Am I?

There are many helpers to guide us as we grow in faith and love as Christians. Choose a word below to answer each question.

Holy Spirit   pope   pastor   Jesus Christ   Mary   bishop

1. I am the mother of Jesus. I love him, and I love you.

   Who am I? ____________________

2. I came to Jesus' followers on Pentecost. I bring life to the Church. Who am I? ____________________

3. I am a leader of the Church. I watch over many parishes.

   Who am I? ____________________

4. I am the leader of a parish. I help the people in my parish grow closer to God. Who am I? ____________________

5. I am the leader of the Catholic Church today. I am the Vicar of Christ. Who am I? ____________________

6. I give myself to my followers in the celebration of the sacraments. Who am I? ____________________

Now write the name of someone who is a special helper to you in becoming a better Christian and describe how that person helps you.

____

____

____

Faith Summary

Jesus chose Peter and the apostles to be the leaders of the Church. The bishops and pastors, with the pope as their head, are today's leaders. The Church is one, holy, catholic, and apostolic.

Words I Learned

apostolic
Marks of the Church
Mystical Body of Christ
one
pastor
Vicar of Christ

Ways of Being Like Jesus

Jesus asked the disciples to spread God's love through the Church.
Take part in parish activities to spread God's love in your church community.

Prayer

Jesus, thank you for calling me to your Church. Support me as I follow the example of my church leaders to serve others.

With My Family

Activity As a family talk about ways you can be active in your parish community. Then choose a parish event or service project in which to participate.

Faith on the Go Ask one another: *How can we support our church leaders?*

Family Prayer *Dear God, thank you for the gift of your Church. Lead us in being a part of our parish community. Amen.*

SESSION 13

The Church Prays

Signs of God are all around us. What signs do you see? What do they tell you about God?

Prayer

Jesus, Lord, help me to be aware of your presence in the sacraments. Help me to grow in my love of God.

EXPLORE

Jesus Is Present in the Sacraments

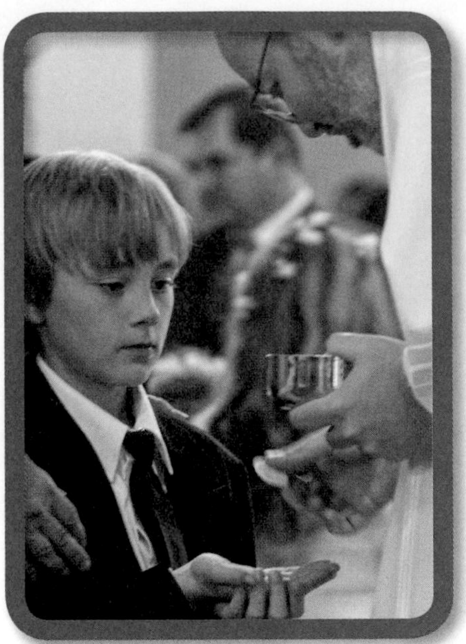

Jesus reaches out to be with us at Mass. He is present in the priest, in the people gathered, and in the Scriptures. Jesus Christ is especially present in the Eucharist.

Jesus Christ also reaches out to us through all the sacraments. They help us grow in faith and live as God wants us to. Through the Holy Spirit, Jesus Christ is present to us in the sacraments.

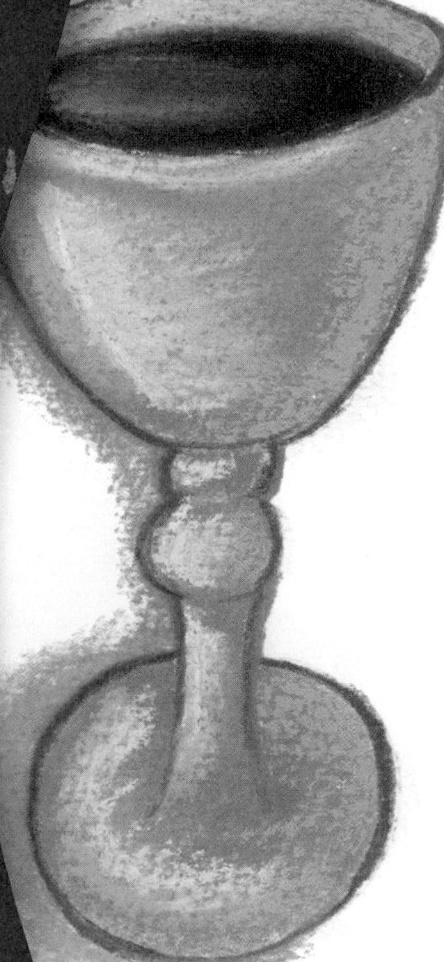

My First Holy Communion

Think back to when you celebrated your First Holy Communion. How does receiving Holy Communion feel during Mass now? How does this sacrament help you grow in faith? On the lines below, write your thoughts about the sacrament.

The first time I celebrated Holy Communion,

I felt ______________________________

______________________________.

This sacrament helps me grow in faith by

____

______________________________.

Signs of Grace

The sacraments are outward signs of the grace we receive from God. We are immersed in water or have it poured on us as a sign of Baptism. Bread and wine are signs of the Eucharist.

The Church gives us other signs, called **sacramentals.** They are not sacraments, but they help us grow in faith. Sacramentals can be objects, such as crosses or holy water. They can also be actions or a prayer, such as the **blessing** of a person or place.

A Sacramental at Your House

Describe a sacramental that you have at home. How does it help you grow in your faith?

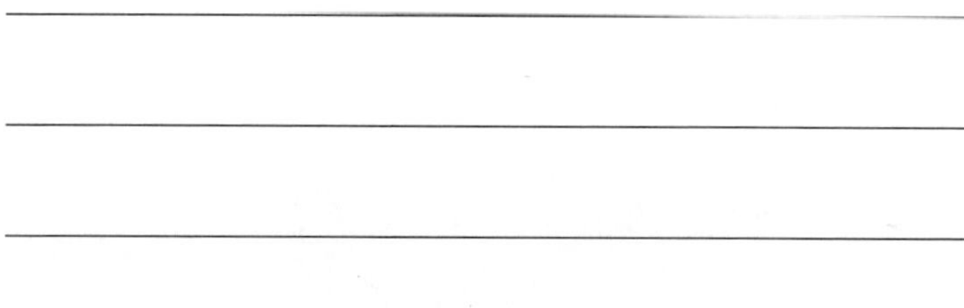

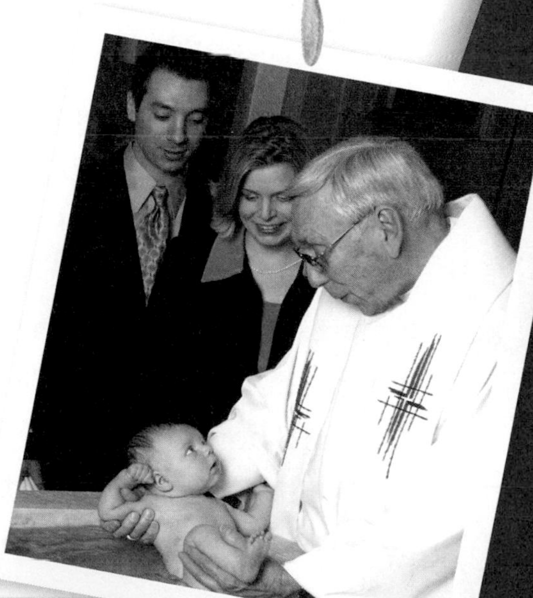

Did You Know?

Sacramentals are sacred signs established by the Church to help us become more prayerful people. Some objects that are sacramentals are holy water, crosses, crucifixes, rosaries, and medals honoring Mary or the saints.

GO TO PAGE 239

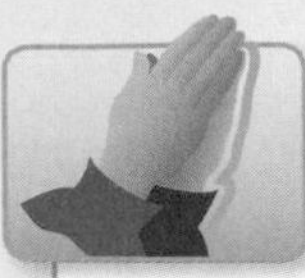

Prayer

Thanking Jesus for the Sacraments

Think about the day Jesus healed the Roman officer's servant. Imagine that you are with the people following Jesus that day. You watch and listen as men approach Jesus and speak to him. What are they saying to him? What are the people around you saying?

Imagine Jesus turning toward you after he hears the officer's reply. What does he tell you? What do you say to Jesus?

Now spend a few moments with Jesus. Ask him to strengthen your faith through the sacraments. Thank him for his presence in the sacraments. Thank him for caring for you. Tell him how you will help him to care for others. Ask Jesus to help you remember he is always with you.

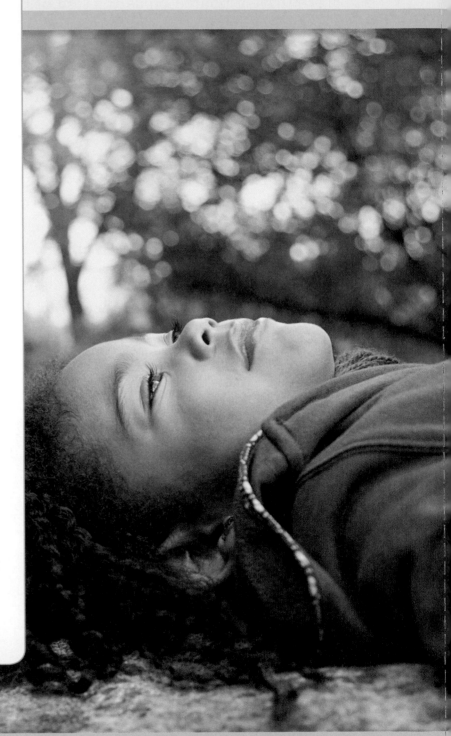

Gifts from God

God has given us many special gifts. Finish each sentence and fill in the puzzle with the missing words. Then unscramble the circled letters to find another special gift from God. Write that word in the sentence next to the puzzle.

1. Sacramentals help us grow in ____________________.
2. At Mass Jesus is ____________________ in the priest, in the people, and in the Scriptures.
3. The ____________________ of a person or place is one type of sacramental.
4. Bread and wine are signs of the ____________________.
5. A ____________________ is an outward sign of the grace we receive from God.

God's gift of

____

helps us to live as Jesus did.

Reading God's Word

Jesus was asked when the Kingdom of God would come. He answered, "No one will announce, 'Look, here it is,' or 'There it is.' For behold, the Kingdom of God is among you." *adapted from Luke 17:20–21*

RESPONDE

Living My Faith

Faith Summary

Jesus gives us the sacraments to help us grow in faith. Through the Holy Spirit, Jesus Christ is present in the sacraments. The Church gives us signs of grace called sacramentals.

Words I Learned

blessing

sacramental

Ways of Being Like Jesus

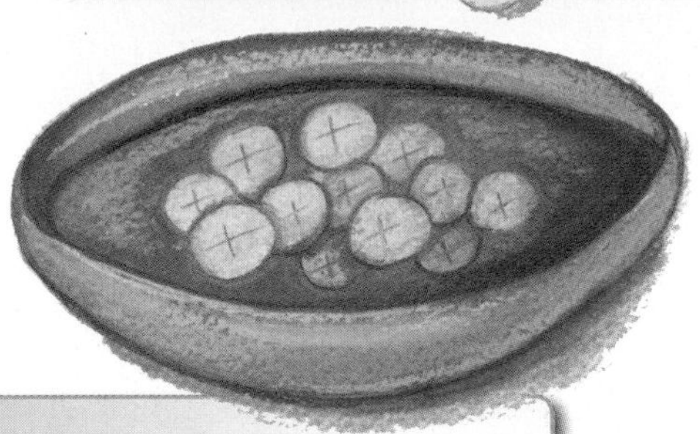

Jesus reached out to all people, not just those who were like him. *Reach out to someone who is different from you.*

Prayer

Dear Jesus, thank you for giving me the sacraments. Help me to be open to the grace of the Holy Spirit so that I can show my love for God and for others.

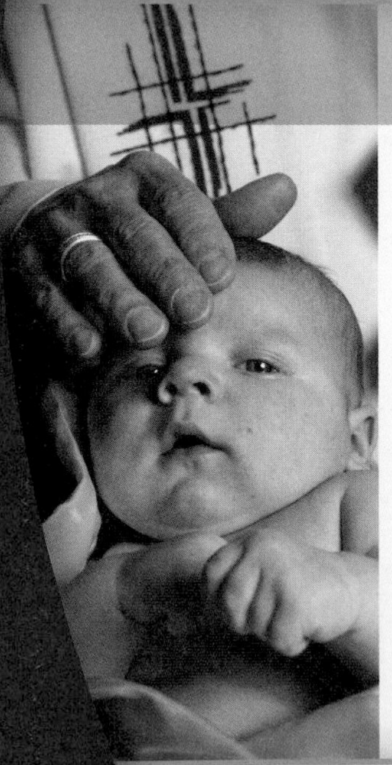

With My Family

Activity At dinner reach out to your family by talking to them about yourself and your day. Show your interest in them by listening about their day.

Faith on the Go Ask one another: *Which sacramental in your home is your favorite? Why?*

Family Prayer *Dear God, thank you for blessing us with the gift of your Son, Jesus. Help us to grow in faith through his presence in the sacraments. Amen.*

SESSION 14

Mary Is Holy

Mothers are very special people. They protect us and guide us. What are some things mothers do for their children?

Prayer

Jesus, help me to follow the example of Mary, your mother, so that I can grow in faith and love.

The Church Celebrates Mary

Becoming the mother of Jesus was the greatest thing that could happen to Mary. She praises God for blessing her. Just as Mary praises God, the Church honors Mary. She is the Mother of God and the Mother of the Church, which means she is the mother of all of us. Mary shows us how to truly listen to God. She teaches us how to trust and believe. Mary is the best example of what it means to be a saint.

We Are All One

Each of us is also called by God to be a saint. We pray together as the Church, especially in the Eucharist. Together with those who have died, we are one body, united before God. We call this one body the **Communion of Saints.**

Link to Liturgy

There are 19 feast days honoring Mary, Mother of God, in the liturgical year.

EXPLORE

We Pray the Rosary

Praying the **Rosary** is one way to honor Mary. The rosary is a string of beads and a crucifix. We hold the crucifix as we pray the Sign of the Cross and the Apostles' Creed.

We use the first five beads to pray one Lord's Prayer, three Hail Marys, one Glory Be to the Father, and conclude with another Lord's Prayer. Then we pray using the five sets of ten beads, called a decade, remembering an event in the life of Jesus and Mary. We begin each decade with the Lord's Prayer, then pray ten Hail Marys, and end with a Glory Be to the Father.

An illustration of the Annunciation

When we pray the Rosary, we reflect on the lives of Jesus and Mary as the Joyful, Sorrowful, Glorious, and Luminous Mysteries. A mystery is an event in the life of Jesus, Mary, and the Church. The first set of events we remember are the Joyful Mysteries. We remember the **Annunciation**, as Mary learned she was to be the mother of Jesus. The **Visitation** tells of when Mary visits her cousin Elizabeth. These are followed by the Nativity, the Presentation of Jesus in the Temple, and Finding Jesus in the Temple.

Did You Know?

The Church named October the month of the Rosary.

GO TO PAGE 240

Prayer

Events in the Lives of Jesus and Mary

Let us pray together, reflecting on these special events in the lives of Jesus and Mary.

The Annunciation The angel Gabriel tells Mary she will be Jesus' mother.

The Visitation Mary visits her cousin Elizabeth.

The Nativity Mary and Joseph go to Bethlehem, where Jesus is born.

The Presentation Mary and Joseph bring Jesus to Jerusalem to be presented to God.

The Finding of Jesus in the Temple Joseph and Mary find Jesus in the Temple, talking with the teachers.

We thank God for giving us Mary, who loves us and prays for us.

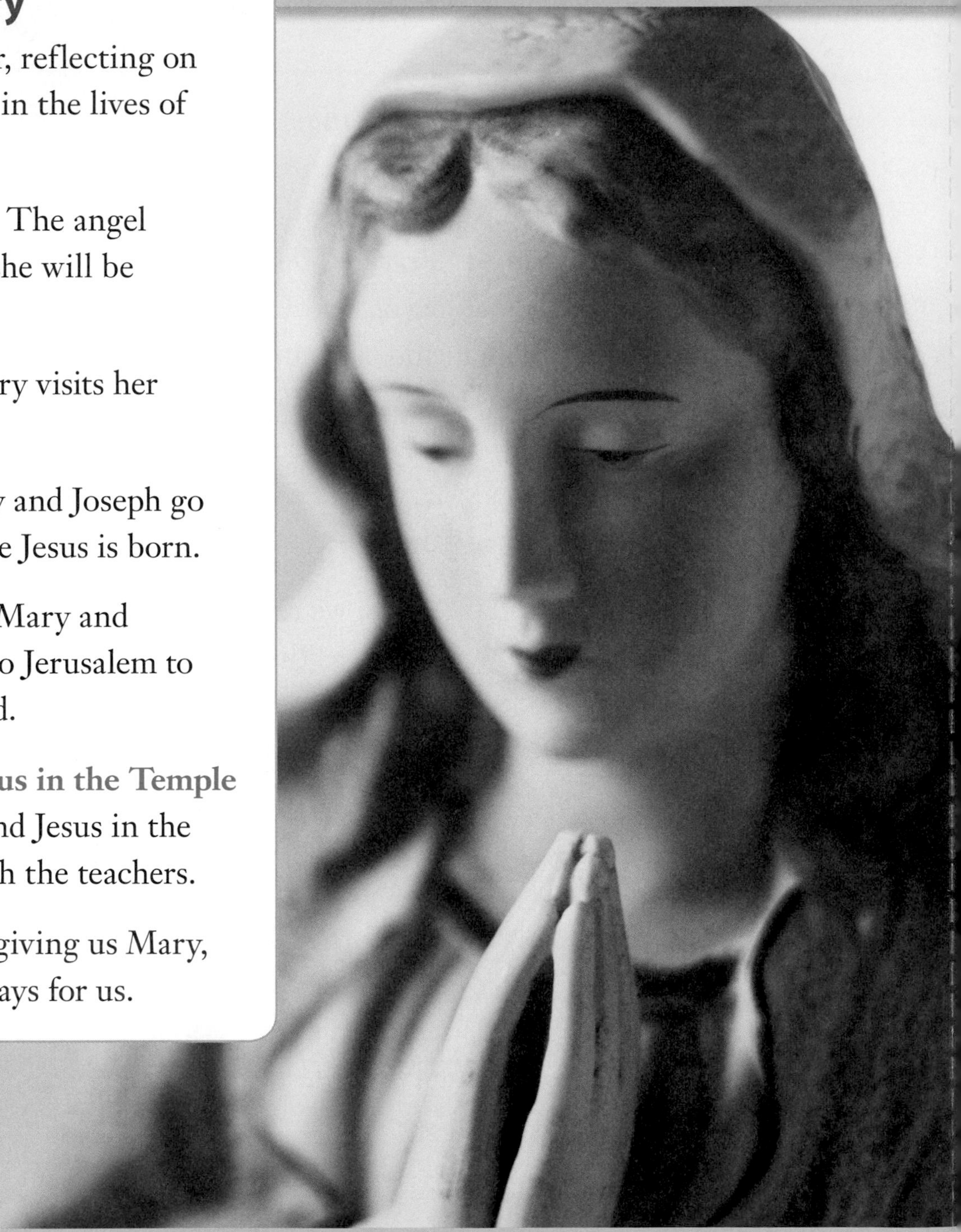

Mary's Song of Praise

Mary and Elizabeth were overjoyed. They would both be blessed with special children. Elizabeth's child would be John the Baptist. Mary's child would be Jesus, the Son of God. Mary praised God by praying these words:

> My soul praises the greatness of the Lord. My spirit finds joy in God my Savior. He has chosen and blessed me. God has done great things for me, and holy is his name! God helps the poor and feeds the hungry. He lifts up the lowly. He shows mercy to those who love him.
>
> *adapted from Luke 1:46–54*

We call this prayer the Magnificat. Like Mary, you can pray these words to thank God for all he has done for you.

I'm Thankful for . . .

Mary was thankful for all that God had given her. Make a list of people and things in your life for which you are thankful.

____

____

____

____

____

RESPONDED

Living My Faith

Faith Summary

The Church is united through the Eucharist in the Communion of Saints. We follow Mary's example of faith and love. We pray the Rosary to honor her.

Words I Learned

Annunciation
Communion of Saints
Rosary
Visitation

Ways of Being Like Jesus

Jesus loved his mother very much. *Show your love for Mary and follow her example of faith and love.*

Prayer

Jesus, my guide, thank you for sharing your mother with me. Watch over me as I listen to God and trust in him as Mary did.

With My Family

Activity As a family pray the Rosary together. Talk about the mysteries and the importance of each in Jesus' life.

Faith on the Go Ask one another: *What are you most thankful for? Why?*

Family Prayer *Dear God, thank you for blessing Mary as the mother of Jesus. Help us to praise and honor her. Amen.*

SESSION 15

Celebrating Christmas

During the Christmas season, we celebrate the birth of Jesus. It is one of the most beautiful seasons in the liturgical year. This season begins with the celebration of Mass on Christmas Eve and lasts until the Feast of the Baptism of the Lord. The Baptism of the Lord is celebrated on the first Sunday after the Epiphany.

On the Feast of the Epiphany, we celebrate Jesus' revelation to the whole world, which is represented by the Magi, or three Wise Men.

Prayer

Dear Jesus, thank you for the Christmas season. Help me to bring joy to my family and friends as we celebrate your birth.

EXPLORE

We Celebrate During Christmas

Christmas is a time to celebrate. We celebrate the gift of Jesus, God's Son, who was born in Bethlehem. At home we can celebrate God's love at Christmas by giving gifts and cards to one another. At church we celebrate by joining our parish community for Mass. The Eucharist is our joyful celebration that Jesus is with us. We remember Jesus' life and all the ways he shows us how to love God by loving other people.

Christmas Meaning

Read the words below and think about their meaning during Christmas. Then use each word in a sentence and underline it.

Jesus	Christmas	parish
community	joy	Eucharist

____

____

____

____

____

____

Reading God's Word

But from you, Bethlehem, shall come forth for me one who is to be ruler in Israel. *adapted from Micah 5:1*

Mass During Christmas

When you go to Mass during Christmas, you will hear about Bethlehem, the city of David. The Hebrew meaning for *Bethlehem* is "house of bread." We call Jesus the Bread of Life because he came to bring bread to all who hunger.

What We Experience

When you look around your church, you may notice symbols of Christmas. The priest wears white or gold vestments, and a white altar cloth is used. White, the liturgical color of the season, reminds us of purity and joy. You may also see a Nativity scene that shows Jesus' birth in Bethlehem.

Your Nativity Scene

Draw a Nativity scene. Imagine yourself being present at the birth of Jesus. Include yourself in the scene.

Did You Know?

The word *Christmas* means "Mass of Christ."

GO TO PAGE 241

Faith Summary

Christmas is a time to celebrate as a Church the birth of Jesus. It is also a time that parish communities gather to celebrate the Eucharist. Jesus, the living bread, comes to bring bread to all who hunger.

Ways of Being Like Jesus

As the Bread of Life, Jesus nourishes us. *Help others who have less than you do.*

Prayer

Dear Jesus, during the Christmas season, remind me to take time to pray for others who have less than I do.

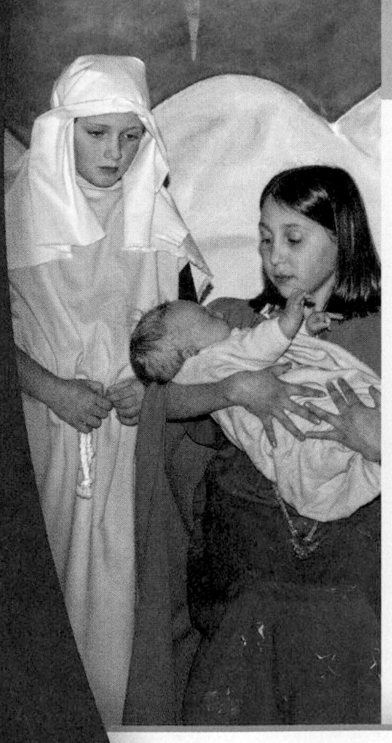

With My Family

Activity When you go to Mass during Christmas, look around your church. Find examples of Christmas decorations and talk about what you see.

Faith on the Go Ask one another: *How can I become more involved in my church during Christmas?*

Family Prayer Invite family members to think of one friend who needs a prayer. As a family pray for these friends this Christmas season.

Sacraments, Our Way of Life

Saint Paul the Apostle

Saint Paul was called to be a follower of Jesus'. He traveled to many countries to spread the Christian faith. In his writings he teaches us to love God and one another.

Saint Paul the Apostle

Saint Paul of Tarsus announcing the Holy Gospel

Paul was born in Tarsus, in what is now the country of Turkey. He went to school in Jerusalem and studied Jewish law. Paul did not believe that the followers of Jesus were faithful to Jewish tradition. Paul wanted to destroy the Church.

Paul was there when Stephen, a follower of Jesus', was killed because he was a Christian. Paul then went to Damascus to help arrest more Christians. On the way a bright light blinded him. He heard the voice of Jesus, who had chosen him to become a follower. Paul changed his ways, regained his sight, and was baptized.

Paul made long journeys to places around the Mediterranean Sea to tell people about Jesus. He started churches in many cities. He wrote letters to the people to help them become better Christians. These letters are found in the Bible. When we read them, we learn of Paul's love for Jesus. In addition to the letters, we can learn more about Saint Paul in the Acts of the Apostles. The feast of Saint Paul is June 29.

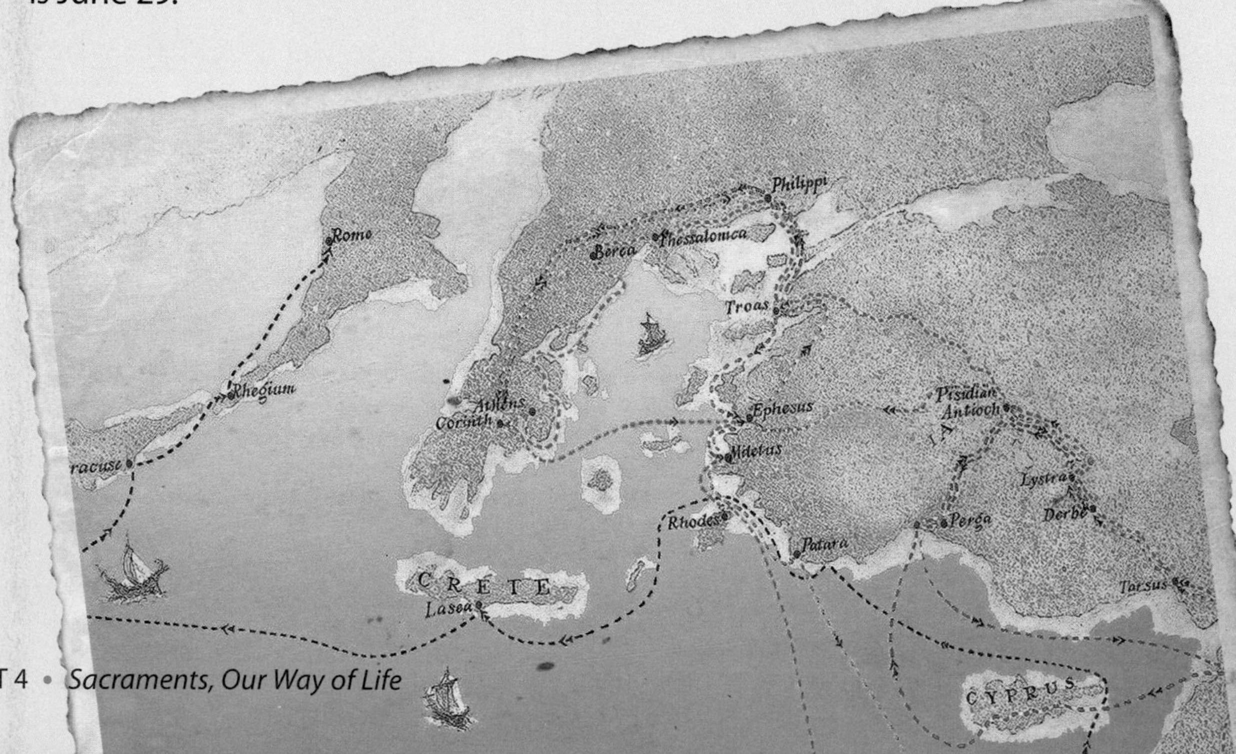

SESSION 16

Think of a time you were welcomed to a new place. How did you feel? How did people welcome you?

Sacraments of Initiation

Prayer

Jesus, Son of God, open my heart to the gift of faith I have received.

We Belong

We are called to accept joyfully the gift of faith and to form one family in Christ as members of the Church. We become part of the Church community, the **People of God,** by faith and Baptism. Through Baptism, Original Sin is forgiven. We receive sanctifying grace, the grace that fills us with Jesus' life and helps us to be his friend. We begin a new life when we are baptized.

Baptism is a gift from God. All people, no matter what their age or background, can enter God's family through Baptism. We trust in God's mercy and, as members of God's family, we pray for those who have died without Baptism.

Link to Liturgy

On special days the priest invites us to renew our baptismal promises at Mass. Easter is one time we do this. On Easter we think about rising with Jesus to new life. When we renew our baptismal promises, we recommit our lives to God.

Christian Initiation

Through the Sacraments of Initiation—Baptism, Confirmation, and the Eucharist—we receive the Holy Spirit. Each Sacrament of Initiation marks a special day in the life of a member of the Church.

Through the waters of Baptism, we begin a new life in Jesus. Our commitment to Jesus is symbolized through a candle. The white garments represent the purity of being freed from Original Sin.

At Confirmation we are anointed with holy oil. The laying on of hands symbolizes the gifts of the Holy Spirit. The Holy Spirit strengthens us and helps us to be witnesses to Jesus.

In the Eucharist the bread and wine are consecrated and become the Body and Blood of Jesus Christ. When we receive the Eucharist, we become one with him.

Together the three sacraments—Baptism, Confirmation, and the Eucharist—complete our initiation into the Church.

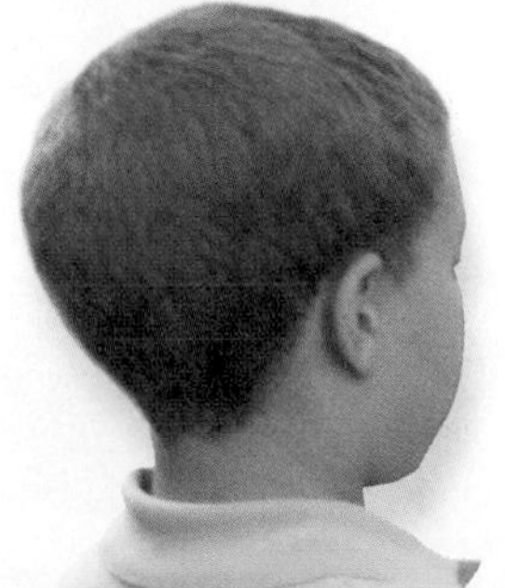

Reading God's Word

You have been called to live in hope as one body with one Spirit. *adapted from Ephesians 4:4*

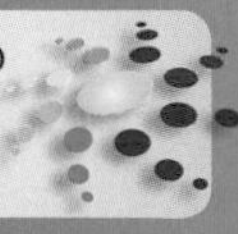

GO TO PAGE 242

Prayer

Prayer of Our Beliefs

Leader: *We read in the letter to the Ephesians that we are called to live as one body and one Spirit. Let us answer God's invitation to be part of his family by expressing our belief in him.*

Do you believe in God, the Father almighty, creator of heaven and earth?

All: *I do!*

Leader: *Do you believe in Jesus Christ, his only Son, our Lord?*

All: *I do!*

Leader: *Do you believe in the Holy Spirit?*

All: *I do!*

Leader: *Thank God for making you part of the People of God. Ask him to keep making your faith stronger as you grow older. Thank him for making you one with him. Then spend a moment just loving him.*

Sacraments in My Life

Each Sacrament of Initiation is celebrated using sacramentals. Think back to the day you first received the Eucharist or when you attended a Baptism or a Confirmation. Write the name of the sacrament for which each sacramental is used.

1. white garments ______________________
2. holy oil ______________________
3. water ______________________
4. bread and wine ______________________
5. laying on of hands ______________________
6. baptismal candle ______________________

Remembering a Special Day

What do you remember about the day you participated in or witnessed a Sacrament of Initiation? In the box below, draw a picture of yourself or someone you know who received that sacrament. Include the priest who celebrated the sacrament.

Faith Summary

Through the Sacraments of Initiation—Baptism, Confirmation, and the Eucharist—we complete our initiation into the Church. We belong to the People of God.

Words I Learned

People of God

Ways of Being Like Jesus

Jesus welcomed everyone. *Help children who are new to your class feel welcome by talking to them and offering your help.*

Prayer

Jesus, thank you for welcoming me to the People of God. Walk with me as I follow your example and spread your Word.

With My Family

Activity With your family, visit new neighbors and welcome them to your neighborhood.

Faith on the Go Ask one another: *When you meet a new person at school or work, do you introduce yourself? Why or why not?*

Family Prayer *Dear God, thank you for welcoming us into the Church when we were baptized. Please help us to treat all in our parish with respect. Amen.*

SESSION 17

Think of a time you asked for forgiveness for something you did wrong. How did you feel when you were forgiven?

Celebrating Reconciliation

Prayer

Jesus, my Savior, help me accept your gift of forgiveness. I want to be at peace with myself and others.

Peace Be with You

After the Resurrection, Jesus Christ visited the disciples.

> The disciples were gathered in a room. Suddenly the risen Jesus Christ came to them. He said, "Peace be with you." He showed them the marks from his Crucifixion. The disciples were filled with joy at seeing Jesus. Jesus said to them again, "Peace be with you. As the Father has sent me, so I send you."
>
> Then he breathed on them and said, "Receive the Holy Spirit. Those sins you forgive will be forgiven."
>
> *adapted from John 20:19–23*

Jesus gave the disciples two special gifts. He gave them peace to live happily together. He also gave them the authority to forgive sins. The priests who hear our confessions share these gifts. Through them, Jesus gives us peace and forgives our sins in the Sacrament of Penance and Reconciliation.

Jesus forgives our sins.

The Peace of Forgiveness

People have been tempted to disobey God ever since Adam and Eve. After Baptism takes away Original Sin, we can still reject God by disobeying him and being self-centered. We call this **personal sin.**

There are two kinds of personal sin. When we totally reject God, we commit a mortal sin. Sins that are less serious are venial sins. God asks us not to form a habit of committing sins, even venial sins. But when we do sin, the Holy Spirit helps us to be sorry. Then we can confess our sins in the Sacrament of Reconciliation, do penance, and be at peace with God and ourselves.

Jesus' Words of Forgiveness

Fill in the words of Jesus. Look back in this session for help.

1. ____________________ be with you.
2. As the ____________________ has sent me, so I send you.
3. Receive the ____________________ ____________________ .
4. Those sins you ____________________ will be forgiven.

Link to Liturgy

To remind us at Mass of Jesus' words, we turn to one another and offer a sign of peace.

GO TO PAGE 243

Prayer

Prayer of Forgiveness

Today let us reflect on Jesus' call to forgiveness. Think of times when you have sinned. Tell Jesus that you are sorry. Then pray the Act of Contrition.

Act of Contrition

My God,
I am sorry for my sins with all my heart.
In choosing to do wrong
and failing to do good,
I have sinned against you
whom I should love above all things.
I firmly intend, with your help,
to do penance,
to sin no more,
and to avoid whatever leads me to sin.
Our Savior Jesus Christ
suffered and died for us.
In his name, my God, have mercy.

During the rest of this week, ask Jesus to help you stay on the right path.

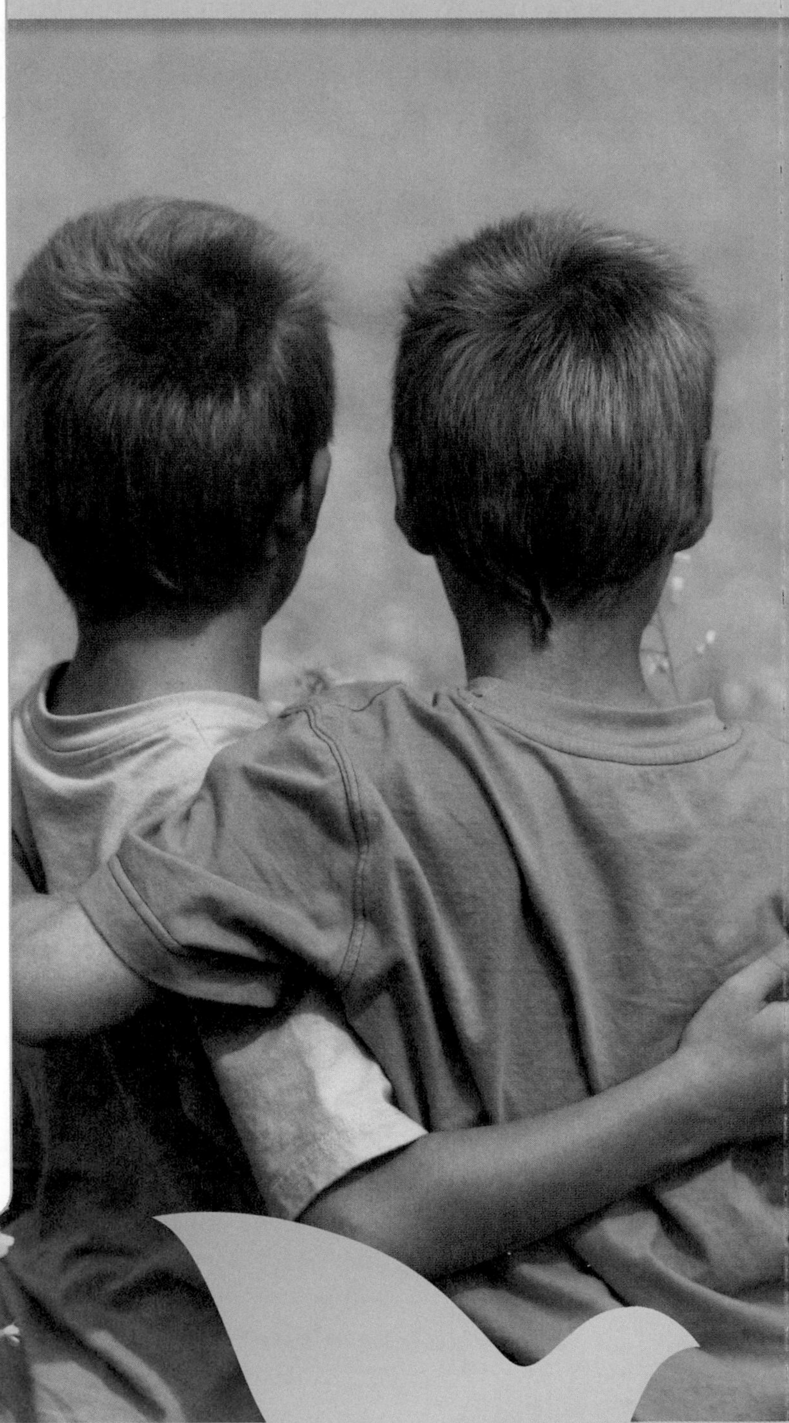

Bringing Peace to Others

In the Sacrament of Reconciliation, we tell God that we are truly sorry for our sins. He forgives us, and we feel peaceful and loved. When others hurt our feelings and then tell us they are sorry, we offer them forgiveness so that they can have peace as well.

Choose Peace

For each situation below, choose what you would do to bring peace to another person.

1. You and your brother start to argue about who will hold the remote control as you watch TV. He yells at you, and then says he is sorry for yelling. You feel angry at him. You:
   a. yell back at your brother.
   b. run from the room with the remote.
   c. take a deep breath and say, "It's OK. I'm sorry too. We'll take turns using the remote."
2. Your best friend borrowed your favorite book and lost it. You really miss the book and wish you had never loaned it to her. She tells you that she is really sorry. You:
   a. tell her that you will never loan her anything again.
   b. tell her you forgive her and discuss the book together.
   c. ask her to replace the book.
3. Your mom says she will take you to a movie tonight. Then she remembers that she has already made plans. She tells you that she is sorry but will take you tomorrow instead. You:
   a. ask her to change her plans.
   b. tell her you're angry and that you don't want to go.
   c. tell her that you know she would take you if she could and that you're happy to go tomorrow.

RESPOND

Living My Faith

Faith Summary

Jesus gave his disciples peace and the authority to forgive sins. When we turn away from God through personal sin, Jesus calls us to forgiveness in the Sacrament of Reconciliation. We confess our sins, say we are sorry, and do penance for our sins. God always forgives us, and we feel peaceful.

Words I Learned

personal sin

Ways of Being Like Jesus

Jesus forgave others. *Forgive others, and when you do wrong, be willing to say you're sorry.*

Prayer

Jesus, my friend, thank you for the gift of forgiveness. Help me to forgive others as you forgive me.

With My Family

Activity Family members can make "second chance" cards. When you accept an apology, offer the card to that person to show that you are ready to move on.

Faith on the Go Ask one another: *Did you forgive the last person who hurt your feelings? Why or why not?*

Family Prayer Practice the Act of Contrition with your family. Try to say it from memory.

SESSION 18

Celebrating the Eucharist

We gather with our family and friends for special celebrations. How does enjoying a meal with your family make it more special?

Prayer

Jesus, my guide, help me to celebrate the Mass with love and reverence.

Do This and Remember Me

Saint Paul told many people about Jesus' life. This is what he told the Church in a special letter, or **epistle,** about the Eucharist.

> On the night when Jesus was betrayed, he took bread and gave thanks. Then he broke it and said to his disciples, "This is my body that I give to you. Do this and remember me."
>
> After supper Jesus took the cup of wine. He said, "This cup is the new agreement made in my blood. As often as you drink it, remember me."
>
> As often as you eat this bread and drink the cup, you proclaim the death of the Lord until he comes again.
>
> *adapted from 1 Corinthians 11:23–26*

Reading God's Word

I am the bread of life. *John 6:48*

We Imitate Jesus

At the Last Supper, Jesus gave us a promise of his love. He called upon us to commit ourselves to God and to one another. The priest repeats Jesus' words at Mass. When we imitate Jesus in our lives, God's love is brought into the world.

At Mass Jesus Christ is present with us. He is present in the people gathered, in the priest who leads, in the Scriptures, and especially in the Eucharist, the consecrated Bread and Wine that becomes Jesus' Body and Blood.

The Mass is the central celebration of parish **worship.** It is the heart of the Church's life. It is offered for everyone, the living and the dead. An ordained priest leads us in the celebration of the Mass. We give thanks and praise to God for Jesus' life, Death, and Resurrection.

Link to Liturgy

The Eucharistic Prayer opens with joy in the words of the Preface. Everyone joins in by singing or saying, "Holy, Holy, Holy."

GO TO PAGE 244

Prayer

Thanking Jesus

Jesus said, "I am the bread of life." Think of how much love is in these simple words. Jesus loves us so much that he gives us himself so that we may live.

Now think of Jesus' love in giving us the Sacrament of the Eucharist. Jesus is truly present in the consecrated Bread and Wine. Thank Jesus for giving himself to you in the Eucharist. Tell him what the gifts of his Body and Blood mean to you.

Think of how close you are to him, especially when you receive Holy Communion. Thank Jesus for the wonderful gift of himself. Tell him how you will care for and share yourself with others as he does. Be still with Jesus in your heart.

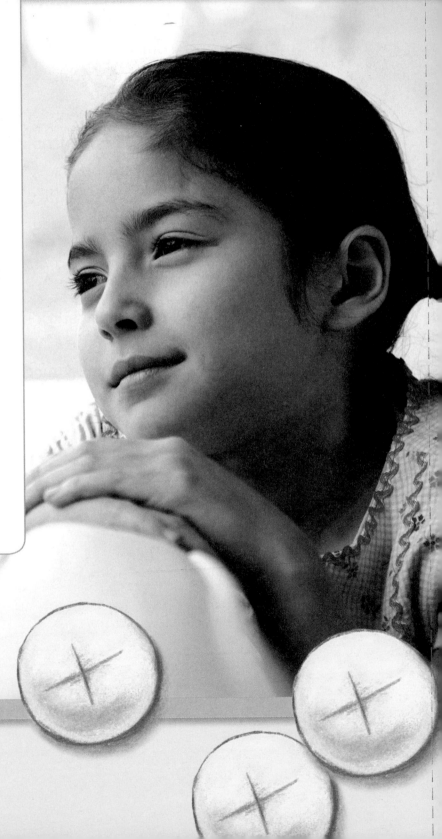

We Celebrate the Lord's Day

Sunday is the day on which we remember the Resurrection. It is the Lord's Day. The Church celebrates by gathering for Mass and resting from work. We remember that we are all part of God's family. We are rich and poor, old and young. We come from all over the world, but we gather at God's eucharistic table as brothers and sisters.

Days of Celebration

As Catholics, we are called to celebrate the Eucharist on Sundays and Holy Days of Obligation. The Church asks us to receive Holy Communion as often as possible.

Holy Days Matching

Draw a line from the dates to the holy days below. Then write about how your parish celebrates these special days.

1. December 25 ●   ● a. Mary, Mother of God
2. November 1 ●   ● b. birth of Jesus
3. January 1 ●   ● c. All Saints Day

RESPOND

Living My Faith

Faith Summary

The Mass is the most important celebration in the Church and is the central place where we worship. In the Eucharist we remember Jesus' life, Death, and Resurrection. We celebrate the Eucharist on the Lord's Day and on the Holy Days of Obligation.

Words I Learned

epistle
worship

Ways of Being Like Jesus

Jesus shared bread and wine with his disciples. *Imitate Jesus by gathering for Mass and celebrating the Eucharist.*

Prayer

Jesus, thank you for giving me yourself in the Eucharist. Thank you for making me one with God's family as I celebrate this sacrament.

With My Family

Activity After celebrating Mass as a family, share a special meal. Have each member help prepare for the meal, such as setting the table or pouring drinks.

Faith on the Go Ask one another: *How do you prepare yourself to receive the consecrated Bread and Wine when we celebrate the Eucharist?*

Family Prayer *Dear God, thank you for Mass so that we can celebrate the Eucharist with our brothers and sisters. Amen.*

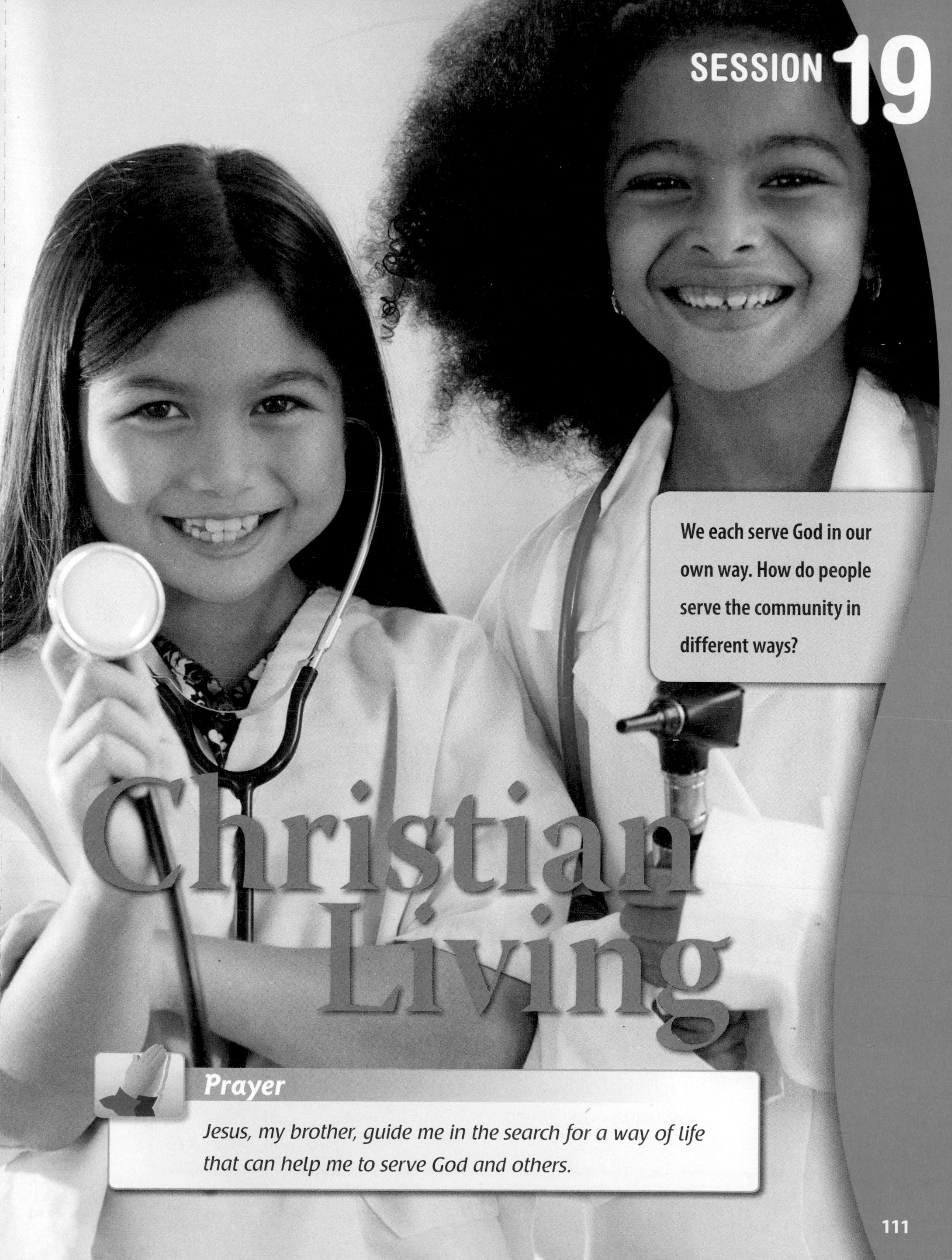

SESSION 19

Christian Living

We each serve God in our own way. How do people serve the community in different ways?

Prayer

Jesus, my brother, guide me in the search for a way of life that can help me to serve God and others.

The Call to Share Our Gifts

God gives us many wonderful gifts. These are our special talents and abilities. The Holy Spirit calls us to share our gifts with the Church and community. We share Jesus' mission and act in his name. We each are called to a special **vocation,** or way of life.

Sacrament of Holy Orders

Some men become priests. Other men serve the Church by being ordained as deacons. They celebrate the Sacrament of **Holy Orders.**

Some men and women publicly dedicate their lives to serving God and the Church. Can you name someone you have learned about in this book who has done this?

Reading God's Word

Each one of you has received a gift. Share God's grace by using your gift to serve one another.

adapted from 1 Peter 4:10

Sacrament of Matrimony

The Holy Spirit calls some men and women to be married. They agree to live in faithful love in the Sacrament of **Matrimony.** Other people choose to remain single. Single people serve God in their lives and in the work they do in the world. No matter what our vocation in life may be, we are each called to God's service.

Your Vocation

Have you imagined what your vocation may be as an adult? Write how you could share God's love through your choice.

____

____

____

____

Meet a Saint

Saint Andrew Kim Taegon was the first Korean person called to serve God as a priest. Andrew Kim was born to a noble family and became a Christian. When he was 15 years old, he went to a seminary in southern China. He returned to Korea and began spreading God's Word as a priest. Years later he and many others were martyred for their faith. The feast of Andrew Kim Taegon and his companions is September 20.

GO TO PAGE 245

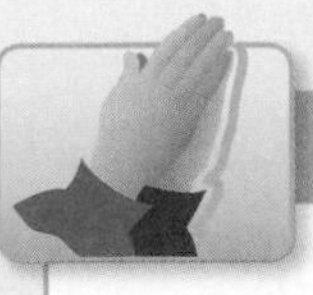

Prayer

Praying About Gifts and Talents

God has given each of us special gifts and talents. Think about your special talents. What things do you do very well? Do you use your talents at school? Do you use them to help at home?

Spend a few minutes talking with Jesus about your talents. Tell him what you think your special abilities are. Thank him for giving these gifts to you. Tell him how you will share your gifts. Ask Jesus to help you to choose a vocation that will allow you to serve others.

Be still with Jesus for a few moments. Trust that Jesus will help you use your gifts and talents to do things well and to help others.

What Will I Do?

The Holy Spirit has given each of us gifts and talents that we should use to help others and to make our world better for everyone. Think about your own gifts and talents and how you can use them when you grow up. Then fill in the following sentence.

When I am older, I will help others by____________________________.

Sharing Gifts and Talents with Others

Complete the sentences below. Look back in this session for help.

1. God gives us gifts, which are our special ____________________

   and ____________________.

2. The ____________________ ____________________ calls us to share our gifts with the Church and community.

3. We are each called to a special ____________________, or way of life.

4. Men who become priests celebrate the Sacrament of

   ____________________ ____________________.

5. The Holy Spirit calls some men and women to be married. They agree to live in faithful love in the Sacrament

   of ____________________.

RESPONDING

Living My Faith

Faith Summary

God gives us special talents and abilities. The Holy Spirit calls us to share these gifts. We each are called to a way of life that will help us share God's love.

Words I Learned

Holy Orders
Matrimony
vocation

Ways of Being Like Jesus

Jesus served others. *Share your gifts and talents with someone who is struggling or could use your friendship.*

Prayer

Jesus, thank you for helping me to recognize my gifts and talents. Support me as I try to use them to serve others.

With My Family

Activity Use your gifts and talents to contribute to your family. You could use your talents to help cook, clean, or cheer up someone.

Faith on the Go Ask one another: *If you could have any talent you wanted, what would you choose? How would you use this talent to help others?*

Family Prayer *Dear God, thank you for giving us special talents. Help us to use them to contribute to our family and our parish. Amen.*

SESSION 20

Celebrating Lent and Holy Week

The season of Lent begins on Ash Wednesday, 40 days before Easter Sunday, and ends on the evening of Holy Thursday. During this time we prepare for the celebration of Jesus' Resurrection at Easter by praying and thinking about how to follow Jesus more closely.

The last week of Lent is Holy Week. Holy Week begins on Palm Sunday and includes Holy Thursday, Good Friday, and Holy Saturday. During this important week, we remember the suffering, Death, and Resurrection of Jesus.

Prayer

Dear Jesus, I know you will be with me during each day of Lent and Holy Week. Help me to think of others' needs and ways to help them.

We Grow In Virtue During Lent and Holy Week

Lent is a time to think about how we treat others. We look beyond our own wants and desires. Lent is a time to be aware of the needs of others and to respond with help, just as Jesus did.

What are some ways I treat others with respect?

Almsgiving

Jesus had a special love for people who were poor.

> People were putting money into a collection box. Jesus noticed a poor widow put in two coins. He said, "This poor widow put in more than the rich. She gave all the money she had, but the rich people gave from their extra supply." *adapted from Luke 21:1–4*

During Lent we practice **almsgiving,** when we give money to people who are poor.

Earn Money for Almsgiving

Instead of asking your parents, what are three ways you could "earn" some extra money for those in need?

1. ______________________________

2. ______________________________

3. ______________________________

Reading God's Word

Graciously give alms. *adapted from Tobit 4:7*

Mass During Lent and Holy Week

When we go to Mass throughout the year, we pray the General Intercessions. During these prayers we pray for the needs of the Church, the world, and the local community. On Good Friday traditional ancient intercessions are prayed. The priest invites us to pray for the Church, the pope, the leaders of the Church and government, for those preparing to celebrate Baptism, and for people who do not believe in God and Jesus. We can include our own needs with the prayers of others.

What We Experience

When you look around your church during Lent, you will notice that the church looks very simple and plain. You do not see flowers or decorations in the sanctuary because this is a season of penance. The priest wears purple vestments.

Let Us Pray to the Lord

Finish the following prayers with the needs of your community or the needs of the world.

For ____________________, may God ____________________.
Let us pray to the Lord. Lord, hear our prayer.

For ____________________, may God ____________________.
Let us pray to the Lord. Lord, hear our prayer.

Did You Know?

The number 40 occurs frequently in both the Old and New Testaments of the Bible. It is a symbolic number.

GO TO PAGE 246

Living My Faith

Faith Summary

During Lent we prepare for the celebration of Jesus' Resurrection. It is a time to think about how we can love others as Jesus did. We are encouraged to look beyond our own wants and desires. We strive to be aware of others' needs and respond with help.

Word I Learned

almsgiving

Ways of Being Like Jesus

Jesus treated others with kindness.
Reach out to others by being a good listener.

Prayer

Dear Jesus, during Lent I will work hard to treat others with kindness and respect. I know you will guide me and help me to do the right thing.

With My Family

Activity Make a family alms jar. Use the jar to collect the money saved from a Lenten promise, such as giving up candy or renting DVDs. Donate the money to a charity of your family's choice.

Faith on the Go Ask one another: *What is one way that our family can help those in need this Lent?*

Family Prayer *God, help us to be aware of others' needs and think of ways we can help them. Amen.*

UNIT 5

Morality, Our Lived Faith

Saint Monica

Saint Monica was a Christian, but her son, Augustine, was not. She loved her son and prayed for him. Shortly before she died, her son was baptized. He later became Saint Augustine.

Saint Monica

Monica was a Christian who wanted her family to share in Jesus' love. She patiently prayed for her husband, Patricius, and his mother, who were not Christians. Her prayers were answered when they were baptized. Her son, Augustine, however, did not accept Jesus.

Monica loved Augustine very much. She never stopped praying for him, even though he grew up and moved away. She continued to hope, even when he made sinful choices. Her prayers were finally answered when Augustine was baptized at the age of 33. He later became a great bishop and teacher.

Monica is the patron saint of married women. She is a model for Christian mothers. She is our model when we pray for others to know Jesus. Her feast is August 27. The next day, August 28, is the feast of her son, Augustine.

Monica and Augustine were born in Tagaste, which is now Souk Ahras, Algeria.

SESSION 21

Faith, Hope, and Charity

We show our love for others by helping them. Think of a time you helped someone. How are you living like Jesus when you help someone?

Prayer

Jesus, my guide, show me how to live for others as you did. I trust in you, and I want to be like you.

Saints Who Showed Hope in God

Even when her son, Augustine, was far away, Saint Monica never stopped praying for him. She had **hope**, or trust, in God. She believed that her son would one day choose to follow Jesus.

When Saint Paul was far away from members of his Christian family, he trusted in God too. He wrote letters to his friends to praise them and to keep their faith strong. Here is part of a letter Saint Paul wrote.

> We thank God always for all of you. We pray for you. We tell God about your faith, love, and hope in our Lord Jesus Christ. Know that God loves you and has chosen you to be his people.
>
> *adapted from 1 Thessalonians 1:2–4*

Like Saint Monica, Saint Paul worked hard to keep his Christian family on the right path. He praised them for their faith, hope, and love. List two ways your family has helped you follow Jesus.

____

____

Sacred Site

Many people visit the Church of St. Augustine in Rome. Saint Monica is buried in this church. On the walls are pictures from the lives of Augustine and Monica.

Stained glass of Saint Paul

EXPLORE

faith

hope

charity

Important Virtues

God gives us gifts called **virtues** to help us live good lives. Faith, hope, and **charity** are three of the most important virtues.

Faith helps us to believe in God. We need faith to be saved and to live as God wants. Hope helps us to trust that God will always be with us. With hope we can be happy with God now and forever. We show charity when we love God above all things and love our neighbor as ourselves. Saint Paul tells us that charity, or love, is the most important virtue.

A Person of Virtue

Think of someone you know who is blessed with one of these virtues. Finish the sentence below by writing who that person is, what virtue he or she shows, and an example of how it is shown.

_________________________ shows the virtue of

____

____

____

____

____.

Reading God's Word

Faith, hope, and love each bring us closer to God;
but the greatest of these is love.

adapted from 1 Corinthians 13:13

GO TO PAGE 247

Prayer

Thanks for Faith, Hope, and Charity

Spend a minute quietly thanking God for the virtues you have been given. Thank him for your faith that helps you believe in him and all that he has told you.

Tell Jesus how hope helps you to trust in God's promises. Tell him how your faith and hope give you the strength to live a good life.

Now tell Jesus how you will show the virtue of charity. Tell him what you will do to help others.

Thank Jesus for guiding you. Ask Jesus to always help you remember he is with you.

She Lived Like Jesus

Saint Jeanne Jugan was blessed with the virtue of charity. She was born into a poor family in France in 1792. Her father died at sea when she was a child. Her mother taught her children to live with faith and love for God.

Tapestry of Saint Jeanne Jugan displayed on the facade of St. Peter's Basilica in the Vatican

In a local hospital, Jeanne learned how to help those who were even poorer than she was. She begged to raise money to help those who needed care. Jeanne and her friends formed a religious community to help people who were poor. Others joined and they became the Little Sisters of the Poor. This community still serves the needs of those who are poor and the elderly who cannot care for themselves.

Living Like Saint Jeanne Jugan

Think how you have practiced the virtues of faith, hope, and charity in your everyday life. Complete the sentence and then draw a picture of yourself showing that virtue.

I am showing ________________ when I ____________________.

RESPOND

Living My Faith

Faith Summary

Saints Monica and Paul were examples of hope, and Saint Jeanne was an example of charity. Faith, hope, and charity are virtues. These gifts from God help us lead good lives.

Words I Learned

charity hope virtues

Ways of Being Like Jesus

Jesus showed charity, or love, for others. *Be friendly to a child who seems lonely. Say hello and start a conversation.*

Prayer

Jesus, my example, thank you for sharing your life with me. Walk with me as I live my life with faith, hope, and charity.

With My Family

Activity As a family, visit residents at a nearby home for those who are elderly. Play a game with them or offer to help them write letters to loved ones.

Faith on the Go Ask one another: *If you found money on your front porch with a note saying that you had to give it away, who would you give it to? Why?*

Family Prayer *Dear God, thank you for the gifts of the virtues. Help me to practice the virtue of charity and think of others' needs every day. Amen.*

SESSION 22

Making Good Choices

Every day we make choices. Sometimes we need help to know what is right. What difficult choice did you make this week? How did you decide what to do?

Prayer

Jesus, my helper, give me the grace to make good choices. I want to live for God and others like you did.

How to Make a Moral Choice

The devil tempted Jesus three times. Jesus overcame these temptations by following his Father's will. Sometimes we must make hard choices too. With the help of the Holy Spirit, we can examine our choices. We can ask ourselves three questions that can help us make good choices. Read the questions below. Then read how a girl named Ana acted when she asked herself these questions. If we can answer yes to each question as Ana did, we know we have made the right choice.

1. **Is the thing I'm choosing to do a good thing?**
   Ana finds a hat on the school playground. She likes the hat very much but decides to bring it to the Lost and Found.
2. **Am I choosing to do it for the right reasons?**
   Ana knows that the hat is not hers and that the owner will be looking for it.
3. **Am I choosing to do it at the right time and place?**
   Ana turns in the hat to the Lost and Found right away. Ana made a good moral choice. She feels happy because she did the right thing. The owner will be happy too because she will get her hat back.

Reading God's Word

Whatever you do, in word or by your actions, do it in the name of Jesus, giving thanks to God the Father through him.

adapted from Colossians 3:17

The Ten Commandments Teach Us

God our loving Father gave us the Ten Commandments. They teach us how to live for God and others. They help us follow the **moral law,** rules that help us to do good and avoid evil.

Obeying God

The first three commandments teach us to honor God. This is what they tell us:

1. I am your God; love nothing more than you love me.
2. Use God's name with respect.
3. Keep the Lord's Day holy.

Think about these commandments. What are some ways you can obey them?

Loving Our Neighbor

While the first three commandments teach us about our relationship with God, the next seven commandments teach us how to live in peace with our neighbor. This is what they tell us:

4. Honor and obey your parents.
5. Treat all human life with respect.
6. Respect married life.
7. Respect what belongs to others.
8. Tell the truth.
9. Respect your neighbors and your friends.
10. Be happy with what you have.

GO TO PAGE 248

Prayer

Live Our Lives for God

Each day we remember to live our lives for God. Each morning we can tell God we will live for him by praying the Morning Offering. As you slowly pray this prayer, think of what you will give to God.

Morning Offering

My God, I offer you my prayers, works, joys, and sufferings of this day in union with the holy sacrifice of the Mass throughout the world.

I offer them for all the intentions of your Son's Sacred Heart, for the salvation of souls, reparation for sin, and the reunion of Christians. Amen.

Now spend a few moments with Jesus. Tell him that you want to offer everything you do to God. Ask Jesus to help you make good moral choices each day. Know that Jesus is with you.

Follow the Commandments

When we follow the commandments and make good moral choices, we become more loving disciples of Jesus.

And the Correct Commandment Is . . .

Choose a word from the box to complete each sentence. Then write the number of the commandment the person in the sentence is obeying.

God happy Mass mother respect return truth

1. Antonio obeyed his ________________ when she said it was time for bed. _____
2. Mara goes to ________________ with her family each Sunday. _____
3. Finn told the ________________ when the teacher asked if he had done his homework. _____
4. Sam likes Owen's new bike, but he doesn't want one. He is ________________ with his old one. _____
5. Isabella loves God and says his name only with ________________. _____
6. Jack forgot to take his skateboard home from Ben's house. Ben knew that he had to ________________ it to Jack. _____
7. Julia has friends who say they "worship" movie stars, but Julia worships only ________________. _____

RESPONDEND

Living My Faith

Faith Summary

We can make good moral choices by considering them closely. God gave us the Ten Commandments to teach us how to live for God and others. The commandments help us to follow the moral law. With the help of Jesus and the Holy Spirit, we can live our lives for God and others.

Words I Learned

moral law

Ways of Being Like Jesus

Jesus followed the Ten Commandments. *Make good moral choices by following the Ten Commandments.*

Prayer

Jesus, my brother, thank you for showing me how to be a good person. Help me to follow your example of making good moral choices.

With My Family

Activity As a family decide on a few house rules that will help your family, such as don't go to bed angry. Display them on the refrigerator.

Faith on the Go Ask one another: *Do you ever find it difficult to make a good choice? Why or why not?*

Family Prayer Practice the Morning Offering with your family. Try to learn the prayer so that you can say it by heart.

SESSION 23

Living as God's Children

Playing, laughing, and just being together are some of the great things to do with your family. What is one thing you do as a family to try to make your home a happy place?

Prayer

Jesus, my friend, teach me how to share love and joy with my family and with others in God's family.

EXPLORE

Our Call to Care

God calls us to care for one another. We start at home with our family. With the grace of the Holy Spirit, we can live together in peace and harmony. We obey and respect our parents, as Jesus did. We treat our family and others with **justice** by treating them fairly.

The Holy Spirit helps us live in peace, harmony, and justice with others. We can share the Spirit's love with one another by helping the members of our family. We can also help those who cannot help themselves.

My Letter of Thanks

We can tell our families how blessed we are to have them. Think of why you are thankful to belong to your family. Fill in this letter. Tell your family members why they are special to you.

Saint Louise de Marillac Cared

Louise de Marillac lived in France during the 17th century. When her husband died, she devoted her life to God. She began by visiting people who were poor and giving them clothes she had sewn and knitted. She met Vincent de Paul, and she helped him care for people who were poor or sick.

Vincent put Louise in charge of a new order of women, the Sisters of Charity. Louise decided this religious order would actively serve people in need. She and her community spent their lives working in homes, orphanages, hospitals, and schools. Today the Sisters of Charity of St. Vincent de Paul continue to serve people in need all over the world. March 15 is the feast of Saint Louise de Marillac.

St. Louise de Marillac,
Robert Lentz, 1991.

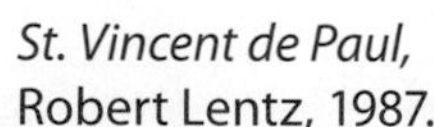

St. Vincent de Paul,
Robert Lentz, 1987.

Reading God's Word

Bear one another's burdens,
and you will fulfill Jesus' law of love.

adapted from Galatians 6:2

GO TO PAGE 249

Prayer

A Prayer for Family Members

Think of Saint Paul's letter to his friends. He prays for them and holds them in his heart. Close your eyes and picture the members of your family for a moment. Think of how much you love them. Thank God for the gift of your family. Pray that you will continue to grow in love with them.

Now spend a few minutes talking with Jesus. Tell him the good things you enjoy in your family and parish. Tell Jesus how you will show your love to your family and others you meet. Tell how you will try especially to help those who cannot help themselves.

Thank Jesus for being with you. Be still and remember Jesus loves you very much. Ask Jesus to bless you and everyone in your family and in your parish.

Peaceful Families

In peaceful homes children obey and respect parents, and family members show one another how they care. Members of peaceful families help in other ways as well, such as sharing work in the family or helping one another with problems. With the grace of the Holy Spirit, we live in peace and joy with our family.

Working Together

For each situation below, write what you can do to help a member of your family.

1. Your parents have planned your little sister's birthday party for this afternoon. Many people are coming. How can you help?

   ____

   ____

2. Your grandmother, who lives with you, has misplaced her glasses. What can you do to help her?

   ____

   ____

3. You and your older brother both want to play a video game at the same time. How do you work out this problem?

   ____

   ____

4. This is your brother's first day of kindergarten, and he is afraid because he doesn't know his way around. How can you help?

   ____

   ____

Faith Summary

With the help of the Holy Spirit, we can live in peace, harmony, and justice with others. We share God's love by caring for others. Saint Louise de Marillac cared for those who were poor through the Sisters of Charity. Obeying and respecting your parents is a way to show that you care about your family.

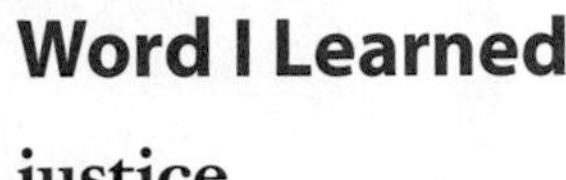

Word I Learned

justice

Ways of Being Like Jesus

We can share God's love by helping others. *Offer to do a chore, such as shoveling snow or raking leaves for someone who needs your help.*

Prayer

Jesus, help me always to be aware of those who need me so that I can serve others as you did.

With My Family

Activity As a family meet together once a week to share plans and to discuss anyone's concerns.

Faith on the Go Ask one another: *When you have differences, what is a good way to work them out?*

Family Prayer *Dear God, help our family to always be fair and respectful to one another. Amen.*

SESSION 24

All Life Is Sacred

We witness the beauty of God's creation when we enjoy nature. Where have you seen the beauty of nature? How would you describe it to someone who hasn't seen it?

Prayer

Jesus, Son of God, teach me to respect and care for God's wonderful world and all who live in it.

A Life of Caring

Every human life is sacred. Blessed Frederic Ozanam understood the worth of every person.

While Frederic was in college in 1832, a terrible disease broke out in Paris. Many people became sick and died. People who were poor suffered greatly. Each day Frederic would walk past the homes of these families. His parents had raised him to help others. His conscience told him he should help these people.

Frederic Ozanam, Fearghal O'Farrell.

Six of Frederic's friends decided to help him by giving their wood supply to a widow. Soon they were helping the less fortunate people of Paris in many ways. Some people asked, "How can seven men make a difference?" But they did. They kept working, and more people joined them. They called themselves the Society of St. Vincent de Paul after the patron saint of Christian charity. In 1997 Frederic was named Blessed.

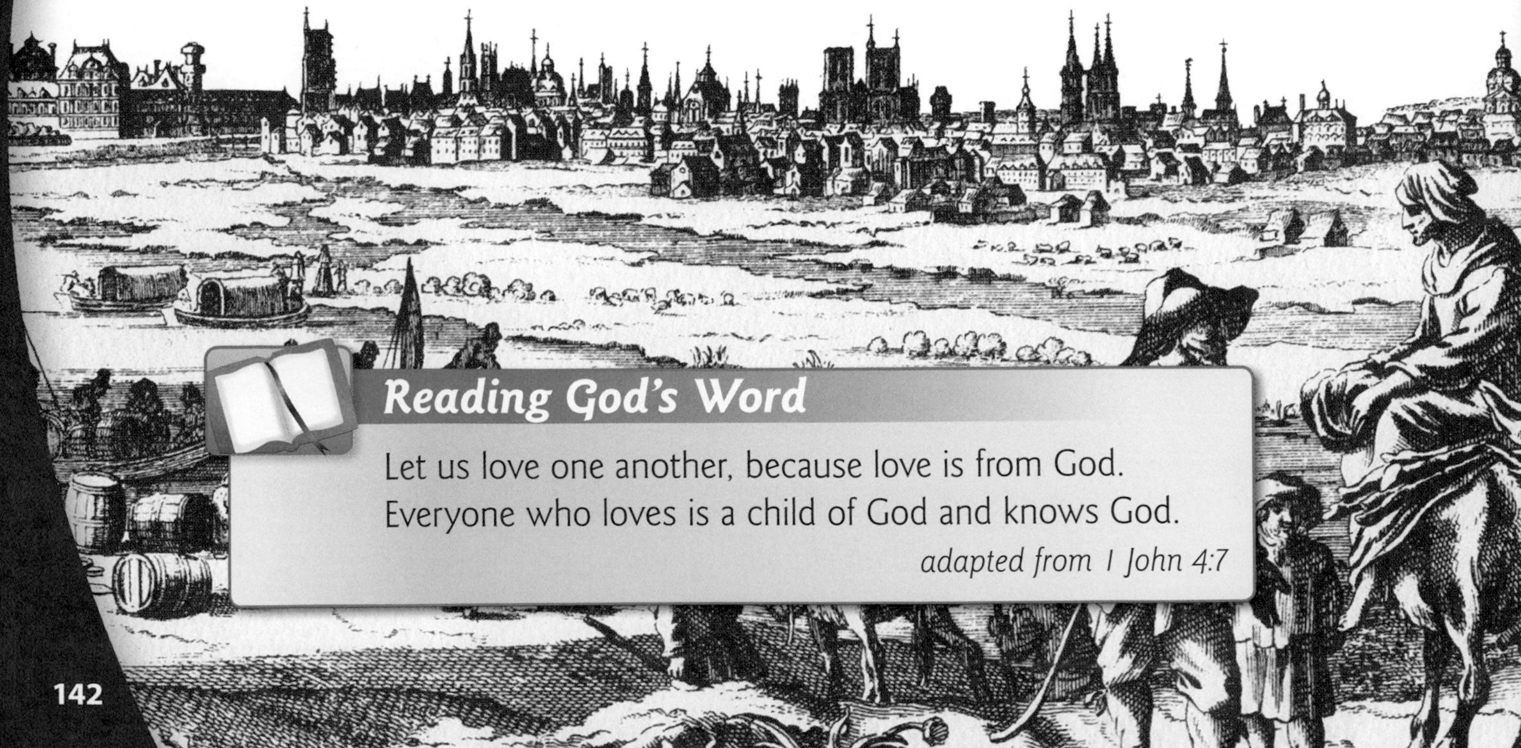

Reading God's Word

Let us love one another, because love is from God. Everyone who loves is a child of God and knows God.

adapted from 1 John 4:7

Treat Others with Respect

Frederic Ozanam knew that every person is special. He knew that all people are important members of the human family. God makes each person sacred from the first moment of life. Like Frederic we are to treat others with respect, no matter where they are from or what language they speak. God wants people and countries to live peacefully with one another.

Just as Frederic helped others, we are also reminded to go and serve others. With the words of the **Dismissal** at Mass, we are sent forth to glorify the Lord by our lives. We can glorify the Lord by serving others with respect.

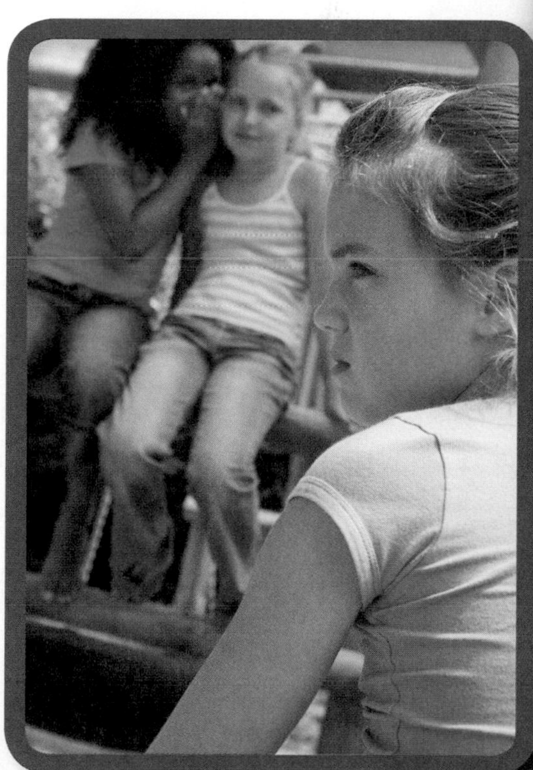

Make Choices That Show Respect

We can also show respect for others through the choices we make. God wants us to make choices that are good. Write the end to each sentence below, showing how you would make a good choice.

If I saw two people arguing over a game,

I would ______________________________

______________________________.

If someone made fun of another's clothes,

I would ______________________________

______________________________.

If a friend told me not to be friends with someone,

I would ______________________________

______________________________.

GO TO PAGE 250

Prayer

Thanking God for the School Year

Let us begin today's prayer by remembering what we have learned this year. Think of God the Father. Thank him for the wonderful world he has created for us.

Think of Jesus Christ. Thank him for teaching you about God's love and for showing you how to love God and others.

Think of the Holy Spirit. Thank him for guiding you through the year.

Sit quietly for a moment. Think about how much God loves you. He is with you always. Be still and know how special you are.

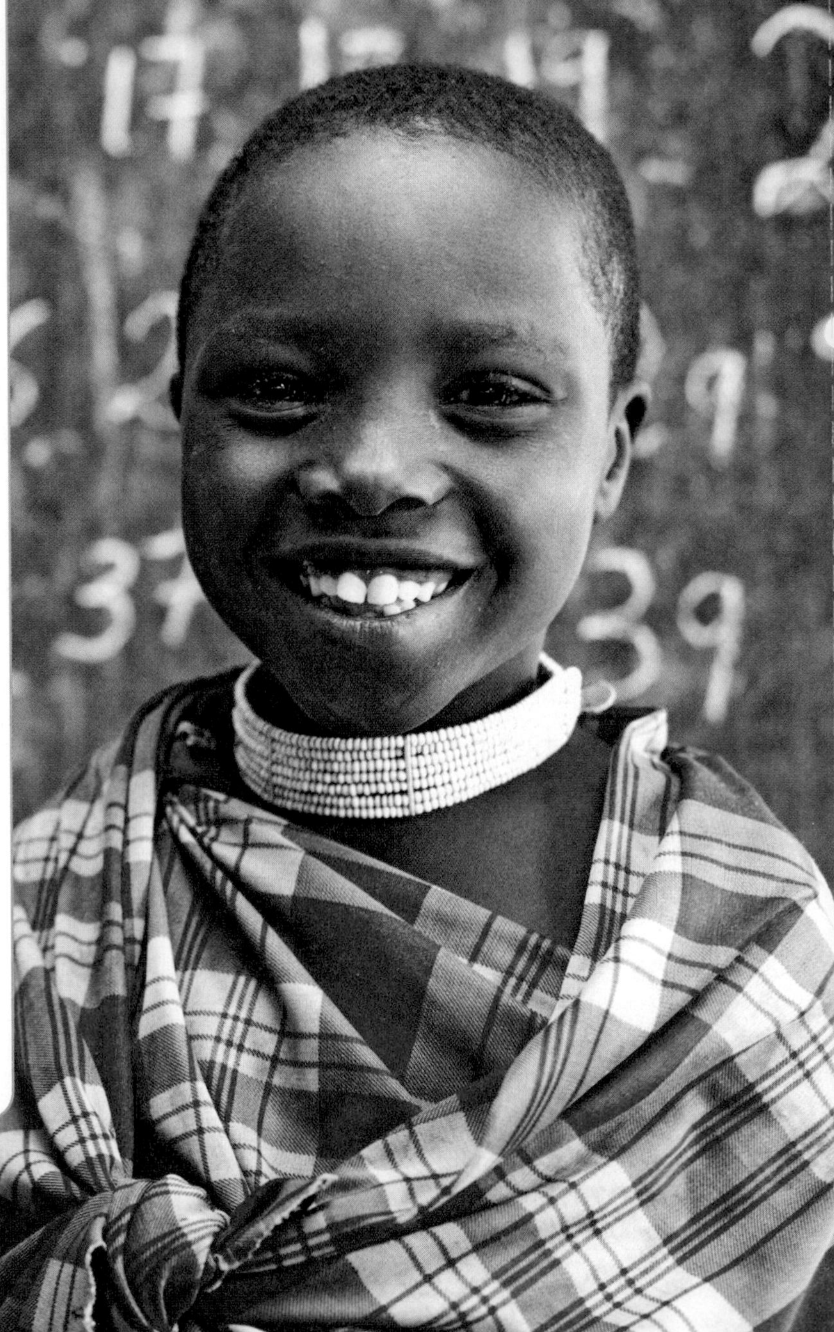

Praise for God's Creation

We are called to take care of all of God's creation. A bird, a river, and a friend are all part of God's creation.

> God has crowned us with glory and honor. He has asked us to care for his creation: sheep and oxen, the beasts of the field, the birds of the air, and the creatures in the sea.
>
> *adapted from Psalm 8:6–9*

Parts of Creation

Think of some parts of creation that begin with the letters below. Write the words on the lines. Use the pictures as hints or make up your own.

C R E A T I O N

C ________________

R ________________

E ________________

A ________________

T ________________

I ________________

O ________________

N ________________

RESPONDING

Living My Faith

Faith Summary

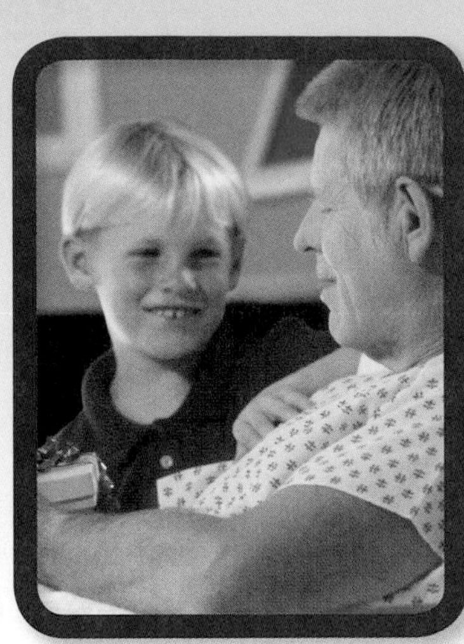

As Blessed Frederic Ozanam helped others through the Society of St. Vincent de Paul, we are called to treat every person as special. God calls us to take care of all he has created. At Mass the words of the Dismissal send us forth to glorify the Lord. We are called by God to care for his creation.

Word I Learned

Dismissal

Ways of Being Like Jesus

Jesus cared for sick people. *Brighten the day of someone who is sick. Do a simple activity with them or just sit and talk.*

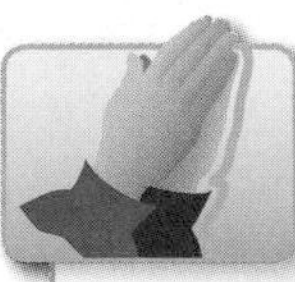

Prayer

Jesus, thank you for showing me how to respect people and the world. Help me always to live in peace with others.

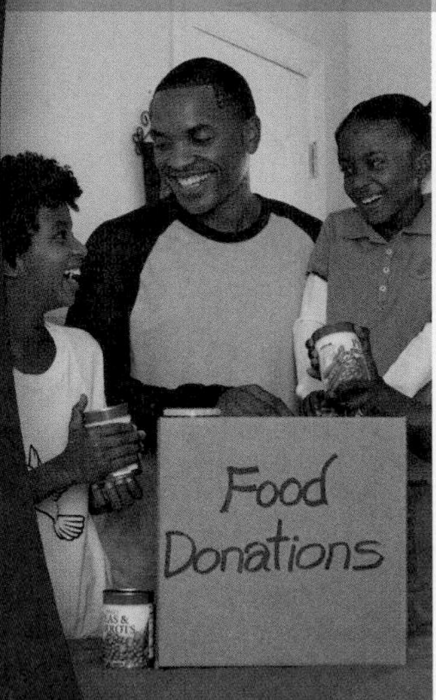

With My Family

Activity Look into opportunities for your family to serve at a local food pantry, soup kitchen, or clothing drive. Mark your calendar to do this.

Faith on the Go Ask one another: *If someone wrote a biography about you, what is a kind act you have done that he or she could describe?*

Family Prayer *Dear God, thank you for the world in which we live. Help us appreciate and care for this wonderful world. Amen.*

SESSION 25

Celebrating Easter

During the Easter season, we celebrate the Resurrection of Jesus. We are joyful that Jesus has risen from the dead. We pray "Alleluia! Alleluia!" and sing about welcoming the risen Christ into our lives and for God's merciful love.

Easter is the most important day of the Church year. It is celebrated on the first Sunday after the first full moon of spring. During this season we also celebrate the Feast of the Ascension, the day Jesus ascended into Heaven. The Easter season begins with the celebration of the Easter Vigil on Holy Saturday and continues for the next 50 days, ending on Pentecost Sunday.

Prayer

Dear Jesus, this Easter season help me to remember the mercy that you have given us and to show mercy to others.

Show Mercy During Easter

Easter is a time to reflect on God's merciful love. On the Second Sunday of Easter, we celebrate God's **mercy**—the mercy that Jesus showed to Thomas, the apostle, when he wanted a sign that Jesus had truly risen.

Thomas was not with the apostles when Jesus appeared. He wanted to see Jesus with his own eyes. The next time Jesus appeared, Thomas was present. He saw and believed. Jesus loved Thomas and showed him mercy.

We have not seen Jesus, but we are blessed by faith in him. We are called to show mercy to others and to treat others with love.

> Blessed are they who have not seen and have believed.
>
> *adapted from John 20:29*

Do I show compassion and forgiveness to others? How can I show mercy to my friends and my family?

The Mercy of Friendship

Write a prayer for a friend who needs your compassion and forgiveness.

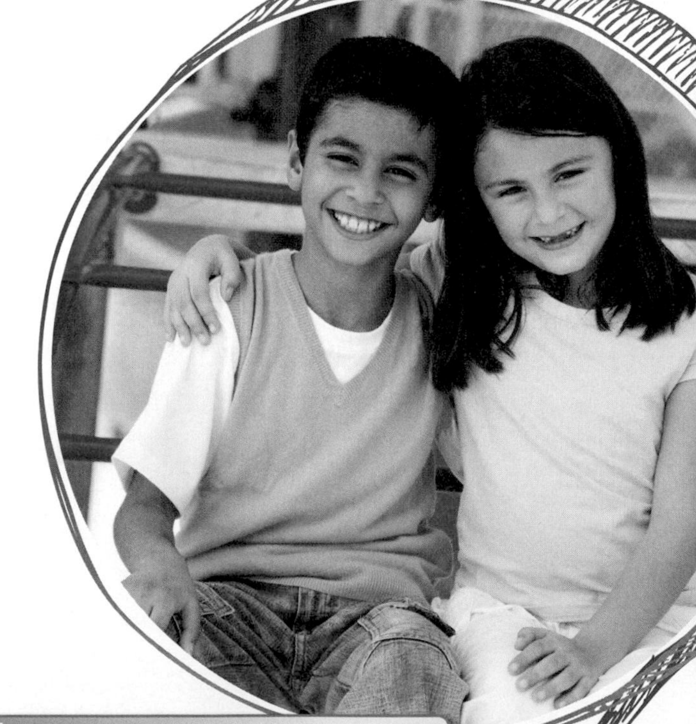

____

____

____

____

____

Reading God's Word

Do not doubt, but believe in me. *adapted from John 20:27*

Mass During Easter

When you go to Mass during Easter, pay special attention to praying the **Lamb of God** during the Breaking of the Bread. Before receiving Holy Communion, we call on Jesus, the Lamb of God, to have mercy on us. Jesus gave up his life for the Salvation of the world.

What We Experience

When you look around your church at Easter, you may see images of the Lamb of God. This reminds us of Jesus' great sacrifice. Joyful music is played because the parish rejoices that Jesus is with us always. White is the liturgical color of the season and represents the joy of Christ's Resurrection. The priest wears white or gold vestments, the altar cloth is white, and the white lilies symbolize our new life in the risen Christ.

What Lamb of God Means to You

Choose three of the words below to write a short paragraph to describe what the Lamb of God means to you.

Lamb	sacrifice	God	Easter
mercy	Jesus	church	communion

____

____

____

Did You Know?

The feast of the Ascension is celebrated 40 days after Easter Sunday.

GO TO PAGE 251

Faith Summary

Easter is a time to celebrate Jesus' Resurrection and how Jesus showed mercy to Thomas. It is also a time to reflect on God's merciful love. We pray to the Lamb of God to have mercy on us and to show others mercy.

Words I Learned

Lamb of God
mercy

Ways of Being Like Jesus

Jesus showed mercy to others. *Forgive others, even when it is difficult.*

Prayer

Dear Jesus, thank you for your love and mercy. Help me to love others and show mercy just as you did.

With My Family

Activity Decorate your home with signs of Easter. Place a potted lily on the table and play joyful music as a reminder of our new life in Christ.

Faith on the Go Ask one another: *How does Easter make us feel? How do we share how we feel with others?*

Family Prayer Use Easter to invite family members to grow in prayer by finding "quiet time" as a family. Close your eyes and invite God into your heart.

The Year in Our Church

Liturgical Calendar

The liturgical calendar shows us the feasts and seasons of the Church year.

Liturgical Year

Advent is the beginning of the Church year and a time of preparation for the birth of Jesus.

Christmas celebrates Jesus' birth. The **Epiphany** celebrates Jesus' coming for all people of the world.

Lent is the time for a change of heart, a turning toward God. It prepares us for Easter.

During **Holy Week** we recall the suffering and Death of Jesus.

On **Easter** Sunday we celebrate Jesus' being raised from the dead. It is a great feast of the Church, a time of hope and joy.

Pentecost celebrates the coming of the Holy Spirit to guide the Church. It ends the Easter season.

All Saints Day and All Souls Day celebrate all the holy people who now live with God in Heaven. On **All Souls Day,** we pray for those who have died but are still in purgatory.

The time set aside for everyday living of the Christian life is **Ordinary Time.**

Mary was a young woman who worked hard and prayed often. She loved God and wanted to serve him. An angel told Mary that she was to be the mother of Jesus. Because Mary said yes to God, we celebrate Jesus' birth. The Advent season is a time to prepare ourselves to celebrate Jesus' birth.

Prayer

Dear God, help me this Advent to prepare for Jesus with an open and welcoming heart.

The Angel Visits Mary

God sent the angel Gabriel to a town in Galilee called Nazareth. He was sent to a young woman named Mary, who was engaged to a man named Joseph. The angel said to her, "Hail, favored one! The Lord is with you." Mary was troubled by his words, but he told her not to be afraid. He said, "You will have a son and will name him Jesus. He will be great and will be called Son of the Most High." The angel told her that the child would be holy and that people would call him the Son of God.

adapted from Luke 1:26–35

Mary Said Yes to God

Mary trusted God. She said yes when God asked her to be the mother of his Son. She made possible our celebration of Jesus' birth.

As we prepare for Jesus' birth, let us ask Mary to pray for us so that we too will welcome Jesus into our hearts.

Celebrating Advent with Prayer

During Advent we prepare to welcome Jesus into our hearts. We pray daily as we count the days until Christmas.

My Daily Advent Prayer

Think of some ways you would like to follow Jesus during Advent. Then use your ideas to complete these prayer starters.

Jesus, help me to ______________________________.

Jesus, teach me to ______________________________.

Jesus, fill me with ______________________________.

Jesus, open my heart to ______________________________.

Completing Your Prayer

Now use all of your completed prayer starters to compose your own Advent prayer. Imagine sharing it in an e-mail to Jesus.

From: ______________________________

To: **Jesus**

Subject: **My Advent Prayer**

Send

____

____

____

____

____

Prayer Service

Leader: *During this holy season of Advent, we prepare, as Mary did, for the coming of Jesus. Let us listen to her words and ask her to pray for us.*

Reader: *A reading from the holy Gospel according to Luke.*

The angel Gabriel told Mary she would give birth to a child named Jesus, who would be the Son of God. Mary said, "I am the servant of the Lord. May it be done to me as you have said." Then the angel departed from her.

adapted from Luke 1:35,38

The Gospel of the Lord.

All: *Praise to you, Lord Jesus Christ.*

Leader: *We ask Mary to pray for us. Holy Mother of God,*

All: *Pray for us.*

Leader: *Most honored of women,*

All: *Pray for us.*

Leader: *Mary most prayerful,*

All: *Pray for us.*

Leader: *Let us close by praying the Hail Mary together.*

Christmas

On Christmas we celebrate the birth of Jesus. The shepherds heard the angels' message and went to welcome Jesus. As we welcome Jesus, we think about what Jesus' birth means to us.

Prayer

Jesus, as I celebrate your birth, help me to share in God's life by loving others and treating them fairly.

Good News

Mary and Joseph went to Bethlehem to be counted in the census. While they were there, Mary gave birth to Jesus. She put him in a manger because there was no room for them in the inn.

Some shepherds were in a field nearby watching their flock. An angel came to them and told them the good news: "Today in the city of David a savior has been born. He is Messiah and Lord." Then more angels came and said, "Glory to God in the highest."

The shepherds went to Bethlehem, where they found Mary, Joseph, and Jesus. They told Mary and Joseph the angels' message. Mary remembered all these things and kept them in her heart.

adapted from Luke 2:4–19

Like Mary we can keep the message of the angels in our hearts. What does the angels' message mean to you?

___

___

___

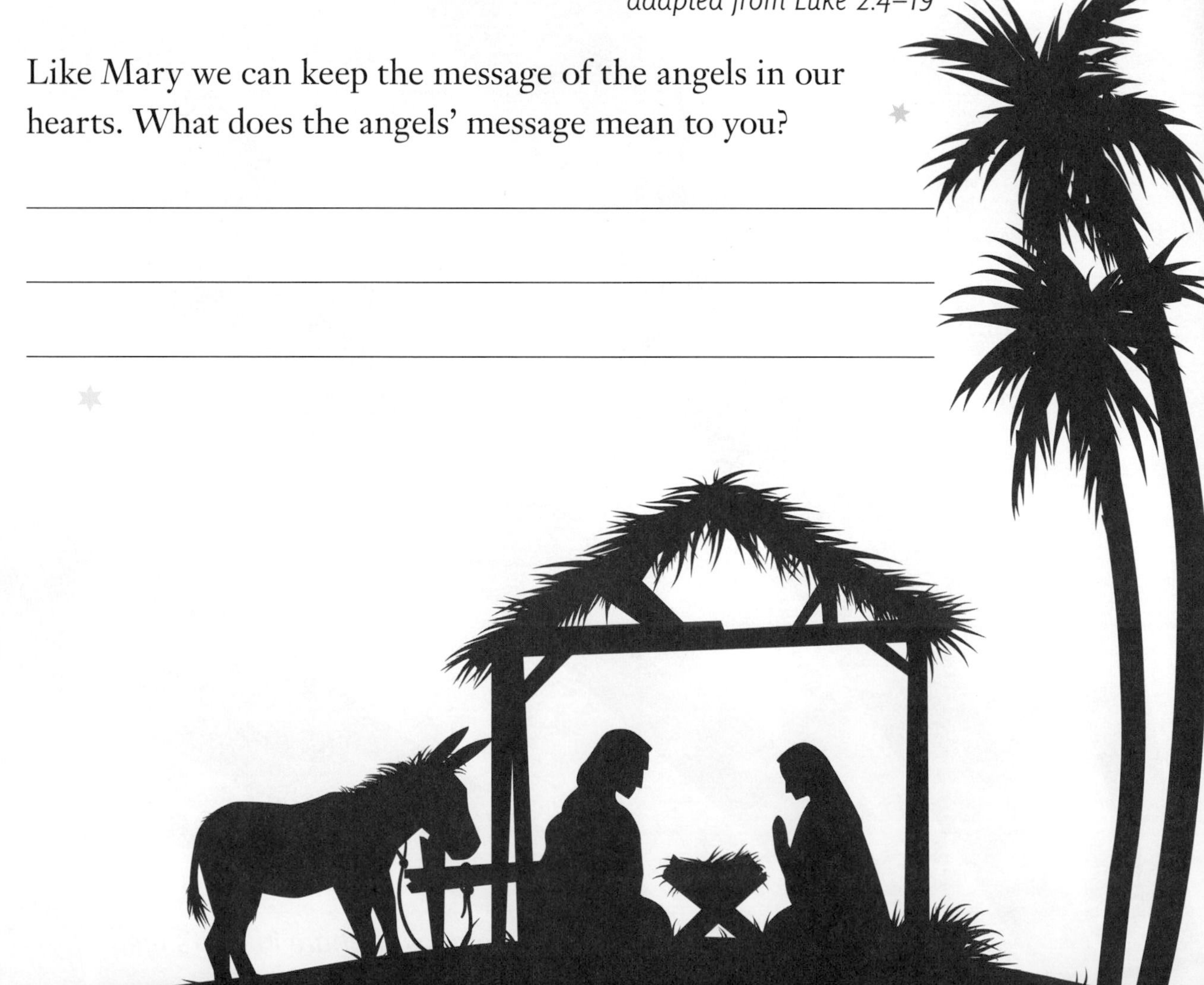

We Reflect

At Christmas we think about what Jesus' birth means to us. Jesus, the Son of God, became man to share God's life with us. We share in God's life when we love others and treat them fairly.

Symbols of Christmas

There are many symbols of Christmas. The trumpet is a sign of the angels' message to the shepherds. Christmas ornaments remind us of the beauty that Jesus brought into the world. The evergreen tree is a sign of everlasting life.

A Symbol for You

Think of a symbol for something you enjoy at Christmas. Write how it reminds you of Jesus' birth and then draw the symbol.

___

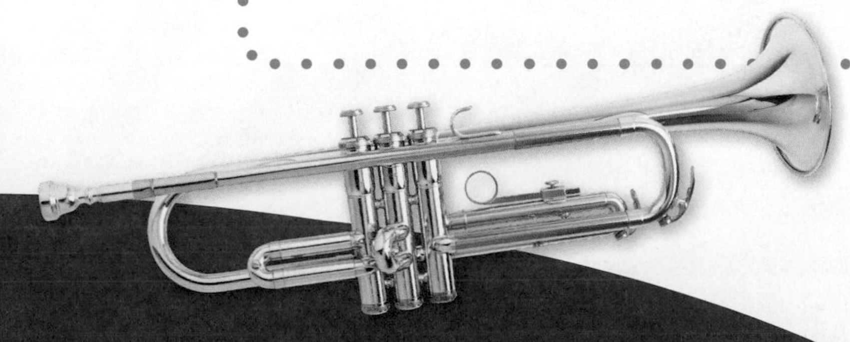

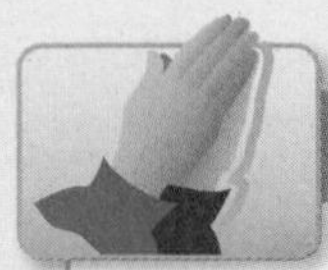

Prayer Service

Leader: *During this joyful Christmas season, let us praise God.*

Group A: Sing to the Lord a new song;

Group B: Sing to the Lord, all the earth.

Group A: Let all the trees of the forest rejoice before the Lord,

Group B: Who comes to rule the world.

Group A: He comes to rule the people

Group B: With justice and truth.

adapted from Psalm 96:1,12–13

Leader: *We thank God for the gift of his Son.*

All: *Glory to God in the highest.*

Leader: *We share the good news as the shepherds did.*

All: *Glory to God in the highest.*

Leader: *We share Jesus' love with the world.*

All: *Glory to God in the highest.*

Leader: *Let us praise God by praying the Glory Be to the Father.*

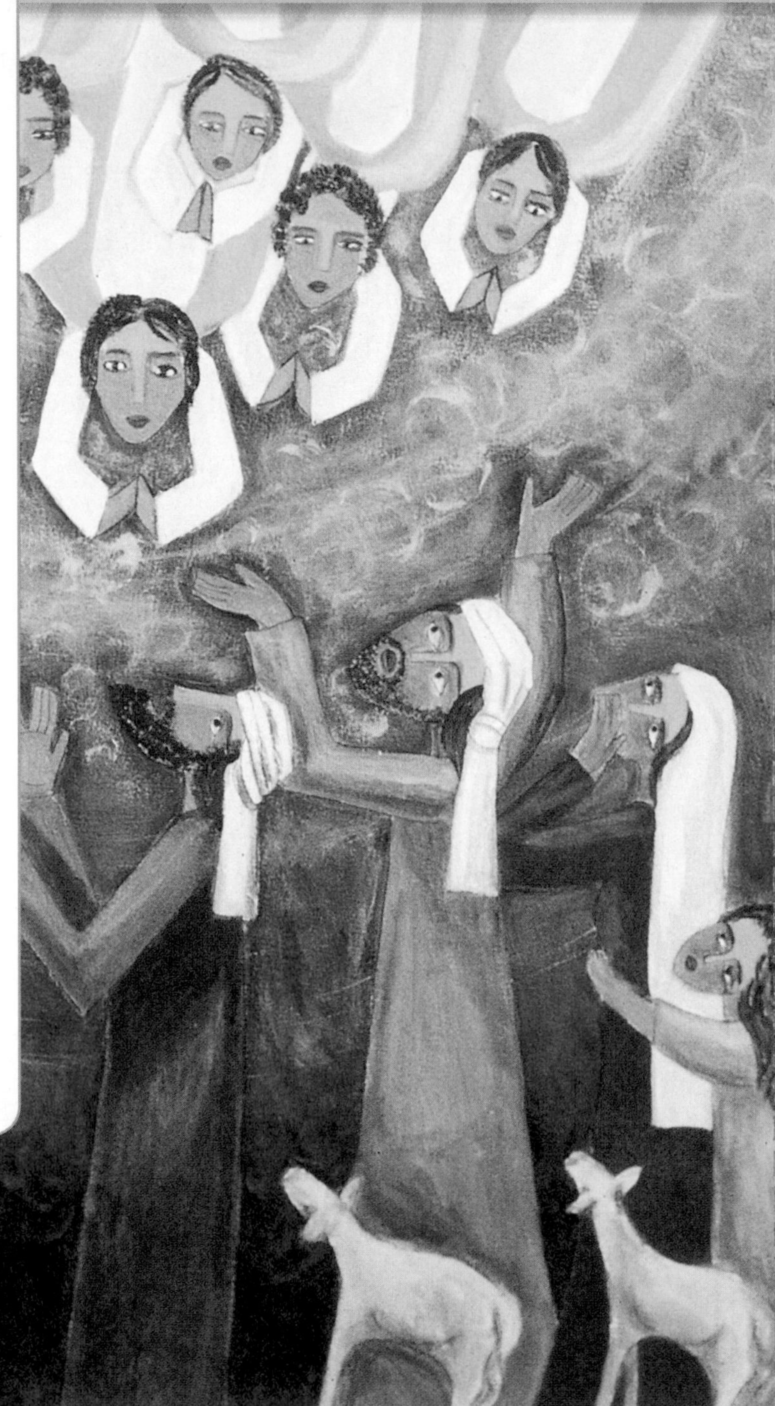

Lent

Before he began preaching, Jesus wanted to spend time with God. He went to the desert for 40 days to fast and to pray.

We follow Jesus' example during the 40 days of Lent. We begin the season of Lent on Ash Wednesday.

Jesus in the wilderness, William Hole, 1905, watercolor.

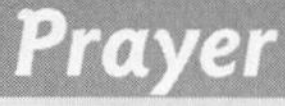

Prayer

Dear Jesus, help me to keep my Lenten promises. I want to follow your example so that I will be prepared to do what God wants me to do.

Jesus Shows Us the Way

The Holy Spirit led Jesus into the desert to fast and to pray. Jesus stayed there for 40 days. He was tempted by Satan but did not give up his fast. The angels took care of him.

adapted from Mark 1:12–13

The Season of Lent

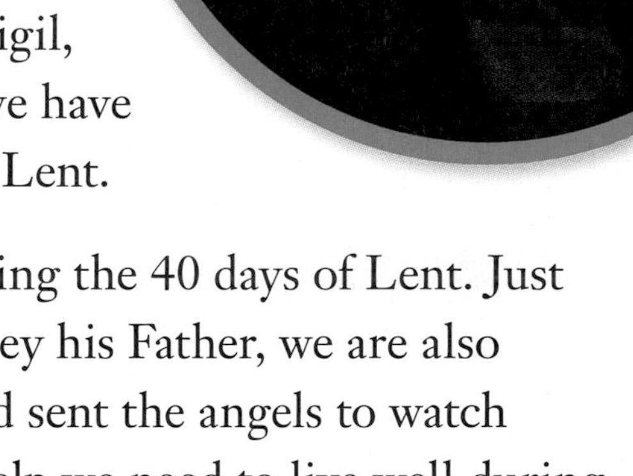

On Ash Wednesday we receive ashes on our foreheads as a sign of our need for God in our lives. The ashes we receive on Ash Wednesday are made from the palms blessed the year before on Palm Sunday. From Ash Wednesday until the Easter Vigil, we fast, pray, and share what we have with others. We call this time Lent.

The Holy Spirit guides us during the 40 days of Lent. Just as Jesus was tempted not to obey his Father, we are also tempted not to obey God. God sent the angels to watch over Jesus. God gives us the help we need to live well during the season of Lent.

Observing Lent

You can make these 40 days special. You can pray. You can be kind, unselfish, and helpful to others. The Holy Spirit will help you do these things every day.

Lenten Promises

During Lent we make promises to God. We can promise to give things up, such as a favorite food or a TV show. We can also promise to do special things, such as praying more often or volunteering at a food pantry. Reminders such as a Lenten calendar can help us keep our promises.

MY LENTEN CALENDAR

Sunday	Monday	Tuesday	Wednesday	Thursday	Friday	Saturday
1	2	3	4	5	6	7
8	9	10	11	12	13	14
15	16	17	18	19	20	21
22	23	24	25	26	27	28
29	30	31				

Do my homework right after school.
Be extra nice to my brother.
Do my chores cheerfully.
Read a book for 1/2 hour every day.

Keeping My Promise

Besides using a Lenten calendar, describe another way that could help you to keep your Lenten promise.

Keep a book by my bed so that I remember to read every day.

____

____

____

____

____

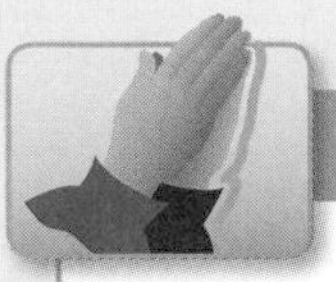

Prayer Service

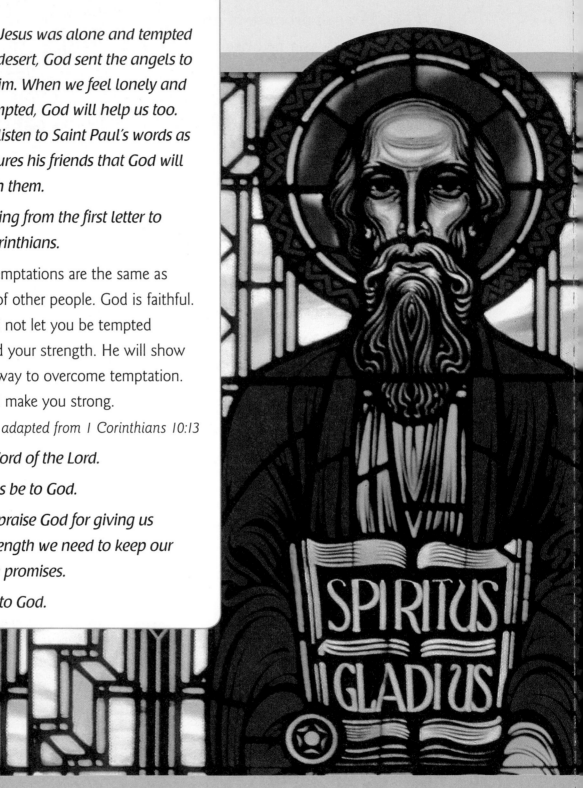

Leader: *When Jesus was alone and tempted in the desert, God sent the angels to help him. When we feel lonely and are tempted, God will help us too. Let us listen to Saint Paul's words as he assures his friends that God will be with them.*

Reader: *A reading from the first letter to the Corinthians.*

Your temptations are the same as those of other people. God is faithful. He will not let you be tempted beyond your strength. He will show you a way to overcome temptation. He will make you strong.

adapted from 1 Corinthians 10:13

The Word of the Lord.

All: *Thanks be to God.*

Leader: *Let us praise God for giving us the strength we need to keep our Lenten promises.*

All: *Praise to God.*

Holy Week

During Holy Week we remember that Jesus gave his life for us. The Stations of the Cross help us to remember his sacrifice for us.

Prayer

Jesus, my Savior, help me to remember your sacrifice for us. Thank you for all that you did and continue to do.

Taking Up the Cross

Trial, ceiling painting, Golgotha Chapel, Holy Sepulchre, Jerusalem.

After Jesus celebrated the Last Supper with the apostles, he was arrested and was brought to trial before Pontius Pilate, the Roman governor.

Pilate found him to be innocent. Pilate asked the people, "What evil has this man done? I don't think he should be put to death. I will have him whipped and released."

But the people kept shouting for Jesus to be crucified. Finally Pilate handed Jesus over to them to be put to death.

As they led Jesus away, they met a man named Simon of Cyrene. He was coming in from the country. They laid the cross on him and made him carry it behind Jesus.

adapted from Luke 23:22–26

Being Like Simon

Simon of Cyrene, a person who never met Jesus, helped him to carry the cross. We can help Jesus too. Like Simon we are called to do what is right in our lives, even if it is hard. We can comfort someone who is sad. We can help at home without complaining. Jesus said that when we do something to help someone else, we do it for him.

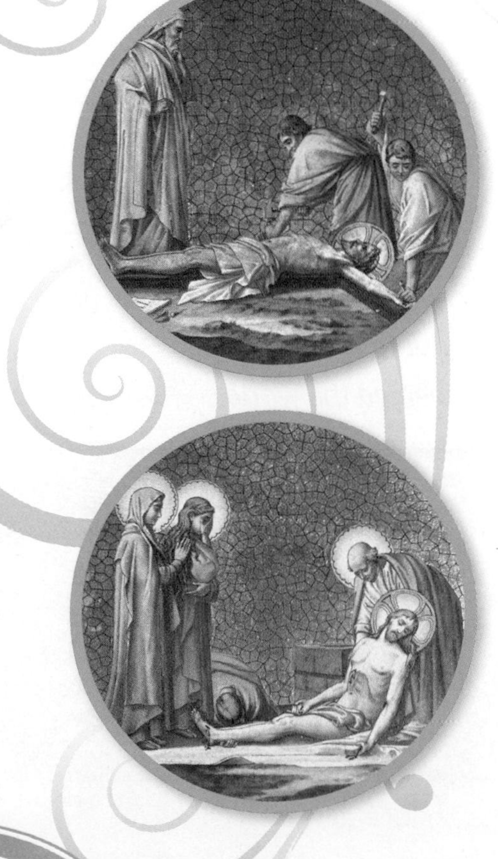

Stations of the Cross

After Jesus' Death and Resurrection, early Christians visited Jerusalem, the city where Jesus died, to walk in his footsteps. They stopped at different places along the way to remember what happened to Jesus. They marked the places where they stopped so that others could follow. These places became the Stations of the Cross.

Like the early Christians, we can pray the Stations of the Cross to remember all that Jesus did for us. At each station we stop, pray quietly, and thank Jesus for his great sacrifice.

A Message to Jesus

Imagine you are in the crowd as Jesus carries his cross. Write what you would say to Jesus.

Jesus, ______________________________

____

____

____

____

____

Prayer Service

Leader: *Just as Simon helped Jesus, we can help lighten the burdens of others. Let us listen to what Jesus tells us.*

Reader: *A reading from the holy Gospel according to Luke.*

Jesus said to all the people, "If any of you want to follow me, you must not think about yourself. You must take up your cross each day and follow me."

adapted from Luke 9:23

The Gospel of the Lord.

All: *Praise to you, Lord Jesus Christ.*

Leader: *We ask Jesus to help us take up our daily crosses. We ask him to give us the grace to help others bear their crosses.*

We adore you, O Lord Jesus Christ, and we bless your holy name.

All: *Because by your holy cross, you have redeemed the world.*

Easter

Jesus' friends were very sad. Their best friend had died. When they went to anoint his body one last time, they were surprised to find the tomb empty. Jesus had risen from the dead!

On Easter we remember this special day. We celebrate the Resurrection of Jesus. We share in the joy that Jesus' friends felt.

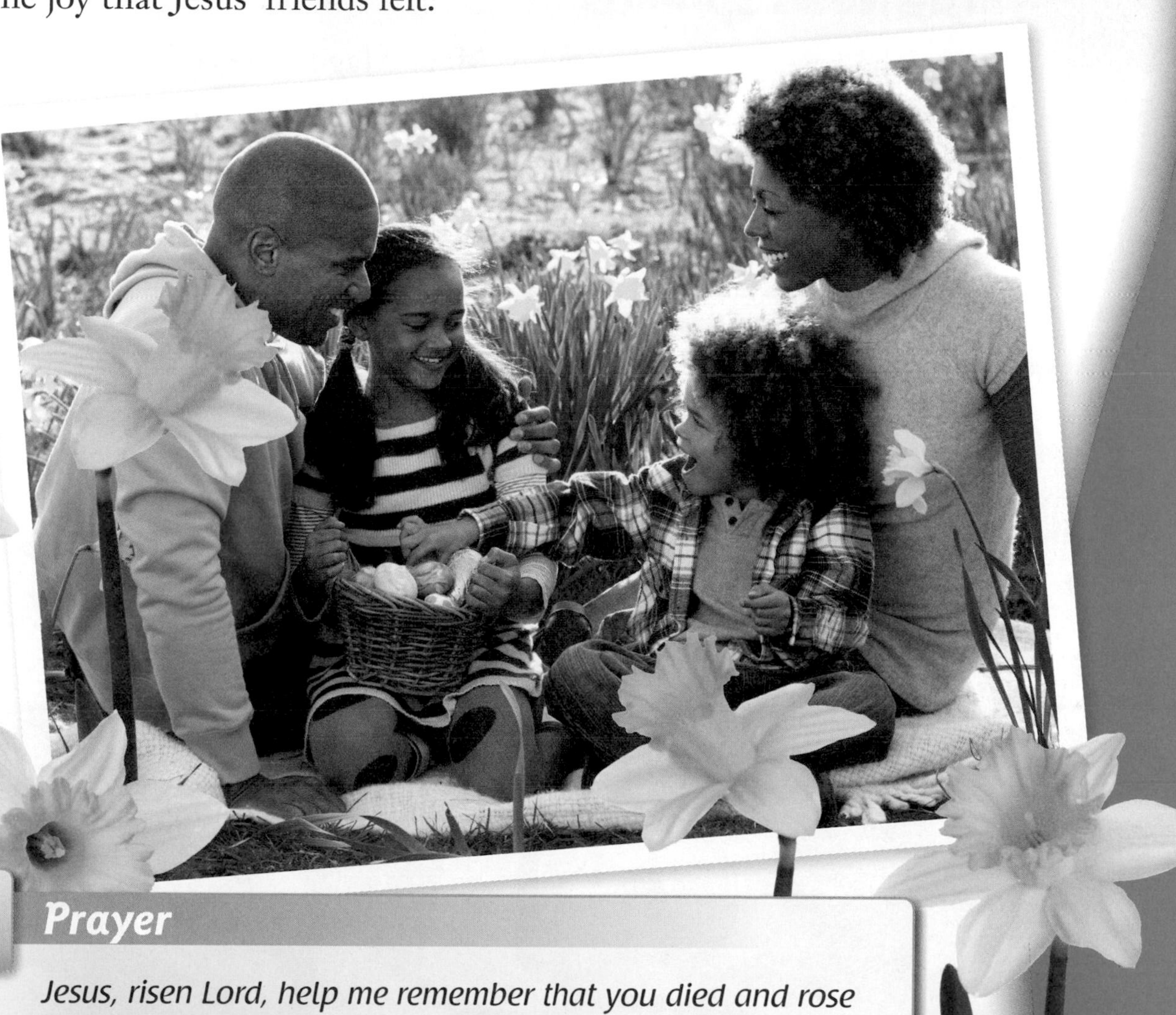

Prayer

Jesus, risen Lord, help me remember that you died and rose for me. I want to celebrate the miracle of your Resurrection by serving God and others.

Jesus Is Alive!

It was dawn on the first day of the week. Jesus' friend Mary Magdalene and several other women went to his tomb to serve him one last time. They brought spices to anoint his body. They found the tomb empty. Then two men in beautiful clothes came to them. The men said, "Why are you looking for Jesus among the dead? He is not here. He has been raised from the dead. Remember that Jesus told you he would rise on the third day." Upon hearing this, the women remembered Jesus' words. *adapted from Luke 24:1–8*

The News Spreads

After he rose, Jesus appeared to Mary Magdalene and the other women. He appeared to Peter, to the disciples, and to many more people. After some time Jesus returned to his Father, where he lives today. We will someday be happy with Jesus in Heaven.

The Lord's Day

On Sunday, the Lord's Day, we remember that Jesus was raised to new life. On this day we celebrate Jesus' living presence, especially in the Eucharist. Meeting Jesus in the Eucharist is important. The Church asks us to receive Jesus in Holy Communion often.

An Easter Message

After they found the tomb empty, Mary Magdalene and the other women told the disciples what they had seen and heard. We repeat their message on Easter.

Imagine you have a friend who does not understand why you celebrate Easter. In the spaces below, share the Easter message with your friend by answering his or her questions.

Friend: What happened on Easter?

You: ____

____

Friend: Why is Easter so important?

You: ____

____

Friend: What do you do to celebrate Easter?

You: ____

____

Prayer Service

Leader: *As believers in Jesus' Resurrection, we want to share the good news of Easter with others. Saint Paul wants his friends to share in the joy of Jesus' Resurrection. Let us listen to his words.*

Reader: *A reading from the first letter to the Corinthians.*

My friends, I want to remind you of the message I gave you that you believed. Through it, you are being saved. Jesus died for our sins. He was buried and was raised on the third day. All this was in keeping with the Scriptures.

adapted from 1 Corinthians 15:1–4

The Word of the Lord.

All: *Thanks be to God.*

Leader: *Let us close by proclaiming the mystery of our faith.*

All: *We proclaim your Death, O Lord,*
and profess your Resurrection
until you come again.

Alleluia, Alleluia.

Pentecost

On Pentecost we celebrate the gift of the Holy Spirit. The Church was born on this day because that is when the Holy Spirit came to the disciples. The Holy Spirit strengthens us to continue Jesus' mission. We can use God's special gifts to us, our special talents and abilities. The Holy Spirit calls us to share our gifts with the Church and community.

The word *Pentecost* comes from a Greek word that means "50." Pentecost is seven weeks, or 50 days, after Easter.

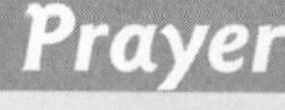

Prayer

Dear Jesus, help me to use my special gifts. I want to live as your disciple and continue your work.

One in the Spirit

Paul wanted his friends in Corinth to understand how the Holy Spirit works in each of us. He sent them this message.

Saint Paul, Manolis Grigoreas, 2001.

> There are different gifts, but one Spirit. The same God works in all of us. The Spirit gives each of us a different way to serve. If the Holy Spirit is in you, you will say, "Jesus is Lord."
>
> We are all different. We may be Jews or Greeks, enslaved or free persons. When we were baptized in one Spirit, we all became part of the one Body of Christ. The same Spirit helps us all.
>
> *adapted from 1 Corinthians 12:4–7,12–13*

Paul tells us that each of us has special gifts. The Holy Spirit helps us use these gifts. What are your gifts? How do you use them?

Finish the Story

In this story the gifts of many people help make the church play a success. Finish the story by filling in the gifts listed below.

kindness	singing	creativity
dance	joy	patience

The Big Night

Backstage the third graders were warming up for the church play. Marcos cleared his throat and practiced his ____________________. Maria put on her shoes and practiced her ____________________ steps. Everybody was filled with ____________________. Months of hard work were paying off. So much had gone into this play. It took the ____________________ of José and Brigitte to make the beautiful scenery. It took the ____________________ of the local store manager, who gave the cast beautiful costumes to wear. If it weren't for the ____________________ of their director, Mr. Joyce, the third graders might never have learned their lines. Thanks to the gifts they all shared, they knew the church play would be a success.

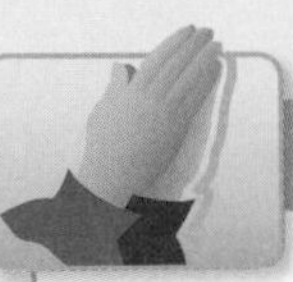

Prayer Service

Leader: *Praise be to God, who fills our lives with love and joy.*

All: *Amen.*

Leader: *Jesus kept his promise to send the Spirit to be with us. Let us pray that we will live according to the Spirit.*

All: *Amen.*

Reader: *A reading from the holy Gospel according to John.*

I will ask the Father to send you a helper. The Holy Spirit will come to you. He will stay with you always. I will not leave you orphans. I will come to you.

adapted from John 14:16–18

The Gospel of the Lord.

All: *Praise to you, Lord Jesus Christ.*

Leader: *Jesus, thank you for being with us.*

All: *Make us one with you and with one another. Amen.*

All Saints Day and All Souls Day

We celebrate All Saints Day on November 1 by remembering those who have died and are with God in Heaven. We can ask the saints to pray to God for us today and every day. Our prayer will help us to follow the good example of their lives.

We celebrate All Souls Day on November 2 by remembering those who have died but whose souls are being prepared in Purgatory to live with God forever.

Prayer

Jesus, help me to love and serve others as you did. I want to be united with you and with others.

Loving One Another

We become holy like the saints when we serve others as Jesus did. Jesus wants us to be kind to one another at school, at home, and wherever we are. Through the sacraments the Holy Spirit gives us the grace we need to love one another. In the New Testament, John tells us that God's love grows in us when we love one another.

> John says, "Friends, because God loves us so much, we also must love one another. If we love one another, God remains in us, and his love grows in us. This is how we know that we remain in him and he in us. God has given us his Spirit."
>
> *adapted from 1 John 4:11–13*

The Communion of Saints

We are not alone! We are united with all those who love God, both living and dead. This is called the Communion of Saints. We are to pray for one another and for those who have died.

Saints in Heaven and on Earth

When we celebrate All Saints Day and All Souls Day, we remember all who have died and are enjoying life with God in Heaven or who are awaiting Heaven in purgatory. We remember that as followers of Jesus on earth, we are united in Jesus Christ because we are part of the Communion of Saints.

A Saint in the Making

We are living like the saints when we help others. On the lines write what you can do to follow the example of the saints. Draw a picture of yourself in the frame below.

At home I can ______________________________.

At church I can ______________________________.

At school I can ______________________________.

In the neighborhood I can ______________________________.

Prayer Service

Leader: *Let us praise our loving God. Blessed be God forever.*

All: *Blessed be God forever.*

Leader: *Jesus is our example of God's love for us. We pray that in everything we do we will follow him and become holy.*

Reader: *A reading from the first letter to the Corinthians.*

A body is one, even though it has many parts. We were all baptized into the one body of Christ. We are one in the Spirit.

adapted from 1 Corinthians 12:12–13

The Word of the Lord.

All: *Thanks be to God.*

Leader: *We ask the saints in Heaven to pray to God for us. Let us close with our special prayer in which we ask Mary to pray for us.*

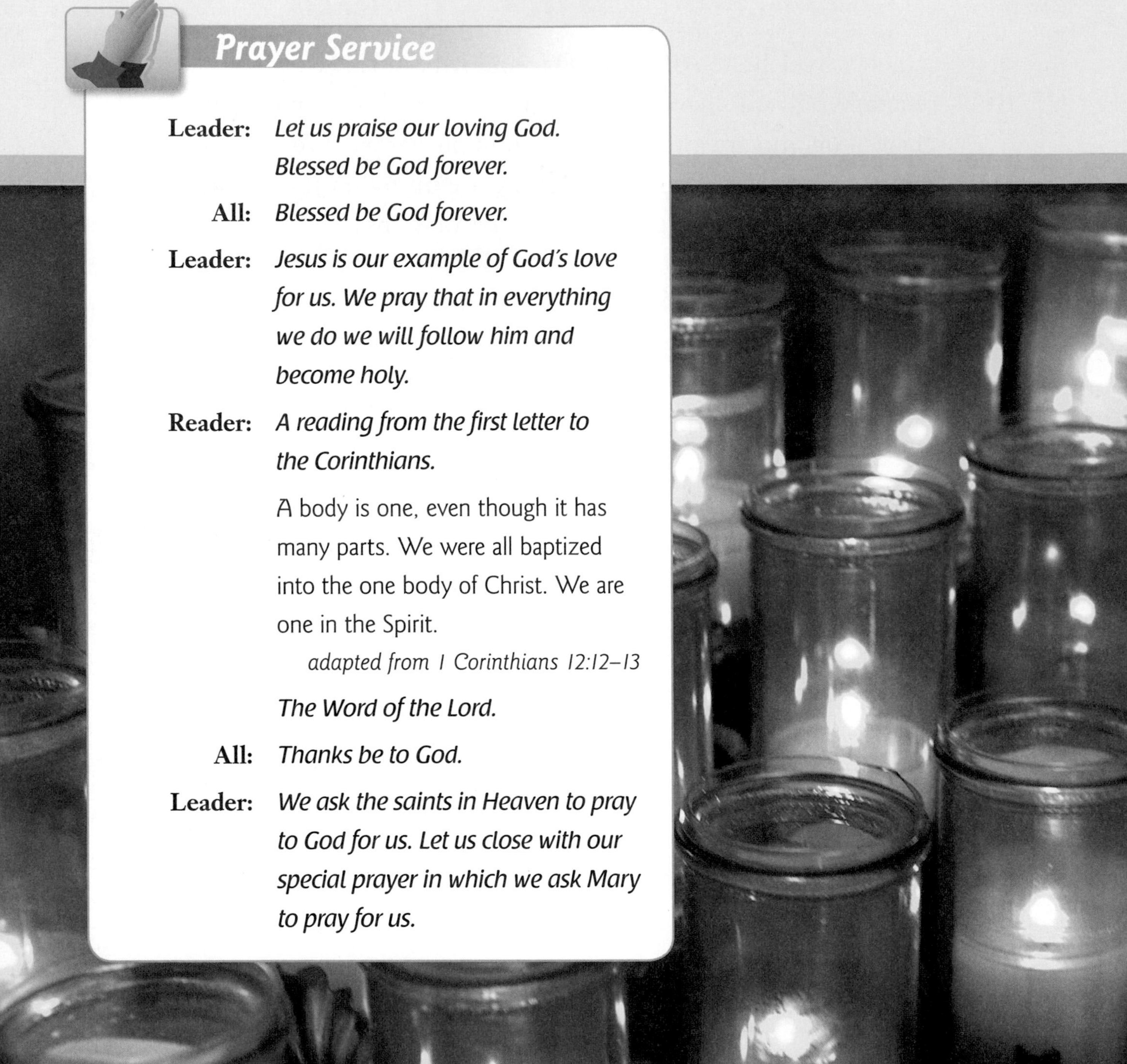

Prayers and Practices of Our Faith

Knowing and Praying Our Faith 184

The Bible and You 184

Prayer and How We Pray 185

Prayers to Take to Heart 186

- Sign of the Cross 186
- Lord's Prayer 186
- Hail Mary 187
- Glory Be to the Father 187
- Prayer Before Meals 188
- Prayer After Meals 188
- Act of Contrition 189
- Prayer to the Holy Spirit 190
- Morning Offering 190
- Apostles' Creed 191
- Hail, Holy Queen *(Salve Regina)* 192
- Prayer for Vocations 193

The Rosary 194

Stations of the Cross 198

Celebrating Our Faith 200

The Seven Sacraments 200
Celebrating the Lord's Day 204
The Order of Mass 204
Receiving Communion 207
Holy Days of Obligation 207
People and Things I See at Mass 208
An Examination of Conscience 210
How to Go to Confession 211

Living Our Faith 212

The Ten Commandments 212
The Great Commandment 213
The New Commandment 213
The Beatitudes 214
Making Good Choices 215
Fruits of the Holy Spirit 215
Showing Our Love for the World 216

Songs of Our Faith 218

Song of Love 218
Here I Am, God 219
All You Works of God 220
Come, O Holy Spirit / Wa Wa Wa Emimimo 222
Holy Is Your Name 223
I Say "Yes," Lord / Digo "Sí," Señor 224
Peace Walk 225
What Does It Mean to Follow Jesus? 226

Knowing and Praying Our Faith

The Bible and You

God speaks to us in many ways. One way is through the Bible. The Bible is the story of God's promise to care for us, especially through his Son, Jesus.

The Bible is made up of two parts. The Old Testament tells stories about the Jewish people before Jesus was born.

A beautiful part of the Old Testament is the Book of Psalms. A psalm is a prayer in the form of a poem. There are 150 psalms.

The New Testament tells stories about Jesus' life, Death, and Resurrection. In the New Testament, Jesus teaches us about the Father's love.

The Good Samaritan, Charles Delagrave, 19th century, Paris.

In the Gospels, Jesus taught, using parables. A parable is a simple story Jesus told to show us what God wants for the world. The story of the Good Samaritan is an example of a parable.

At Mass we hear stories from the Bible. We can also read the Bible on our own.

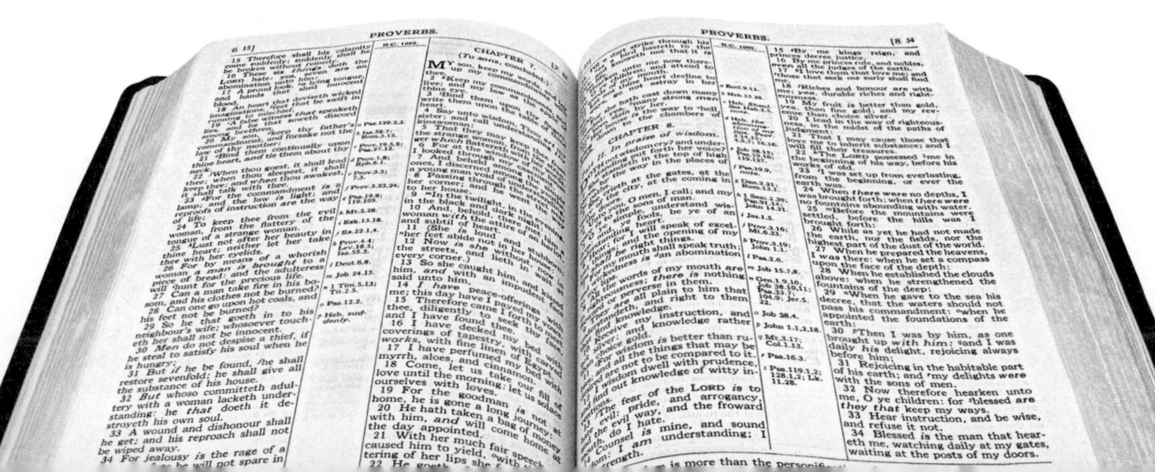

Prayer and How We Pray

Prayer is talking and listening to God. When we pray we raise our hearts and minds to God. We can talk to God in the special words of prayers or in our own words. We can pray aloud or quietly in our hearts.

We can pray to God often and in many different ways. We can praise God. We can thank God for what we have and ask him for what we need. We can pray for ourselves and for others.

Prayers to Take to Heart

It is good for us to know prayers by heart. To learn prayers by heart means that we not only learn, or memorize, the words but also understand and live them.

Sign of the Cross

In the name of the Father,
and of the Son,
and of the Holy Spirit.
Amen.

Lord's Prayer

Our Father, who art in heaven,
hallowed be thy name;
thy kingdom come,
thy will be done
on earth as it is in heaven.
Give us this day our daily bread,
and forgive us our trespasses,
as we forgive those who
trespass against us;
and lead us not into
temptation,
but deliver us from evil.
Amen.

Hail Mary

Hail Mary, full of grace,
the Lord is with you.
Blessed are you among women,
and blessed is the fruit of your womb, Jesus.
Holy Mary, Mother of God,
pray for us sinners,
now and at the hour of our death.
Amen.

Glory Be to the Father

Glory be to the Father,
and to the Son,
and to the Holy Spirit.
As it was in the beginning,
is now, and ever shall be,
world without end.
Amen.

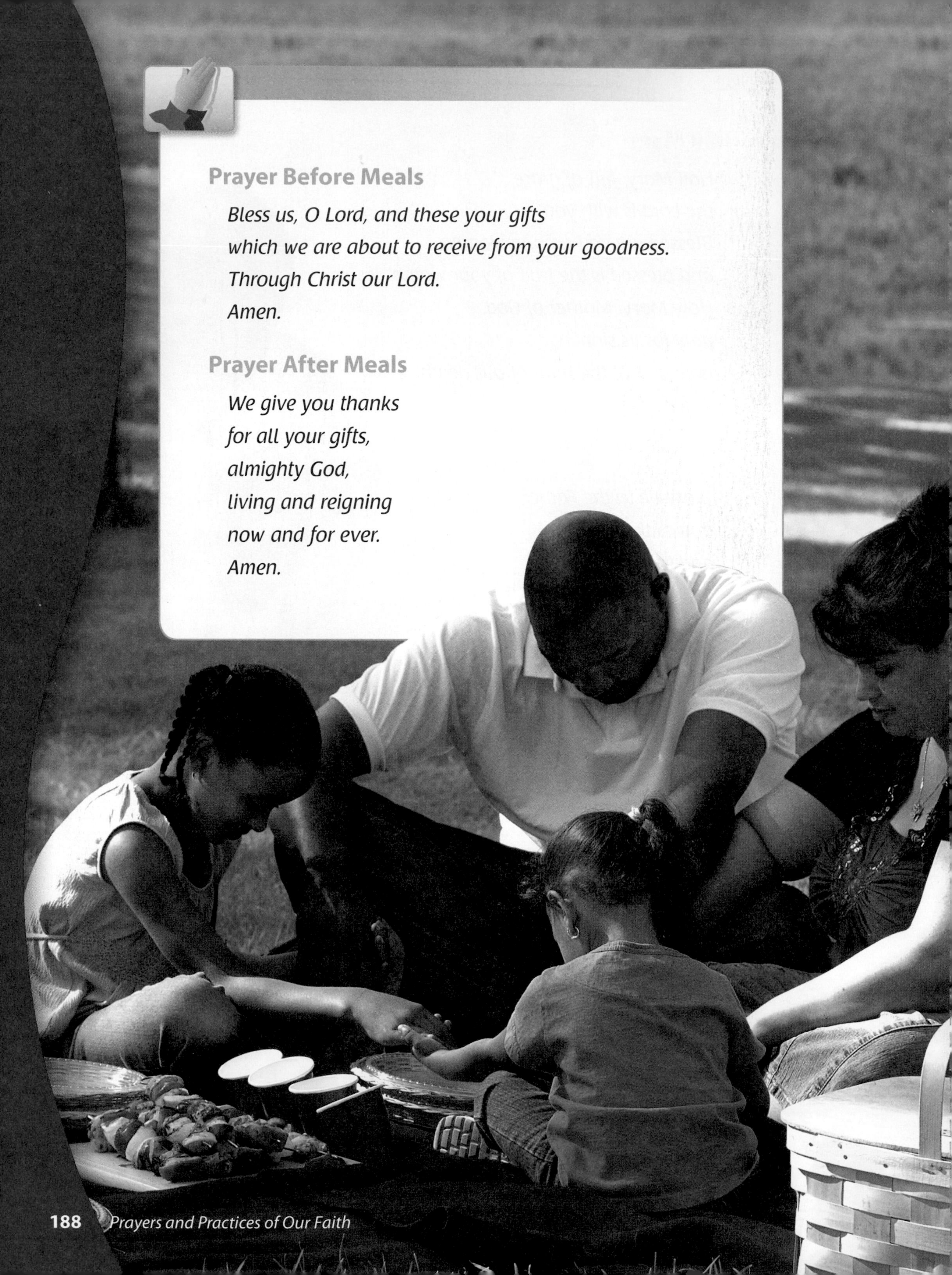

Prayer Before Meals

Bless us, O Lord, and these your gifts
which we are about to receive from your goodness.
Through Christ our Lord.
Amen.

Prayer After Meals

We give you thanks
for all your gifts,
almighty God,
living and reigning
now and for ever.
Amen.

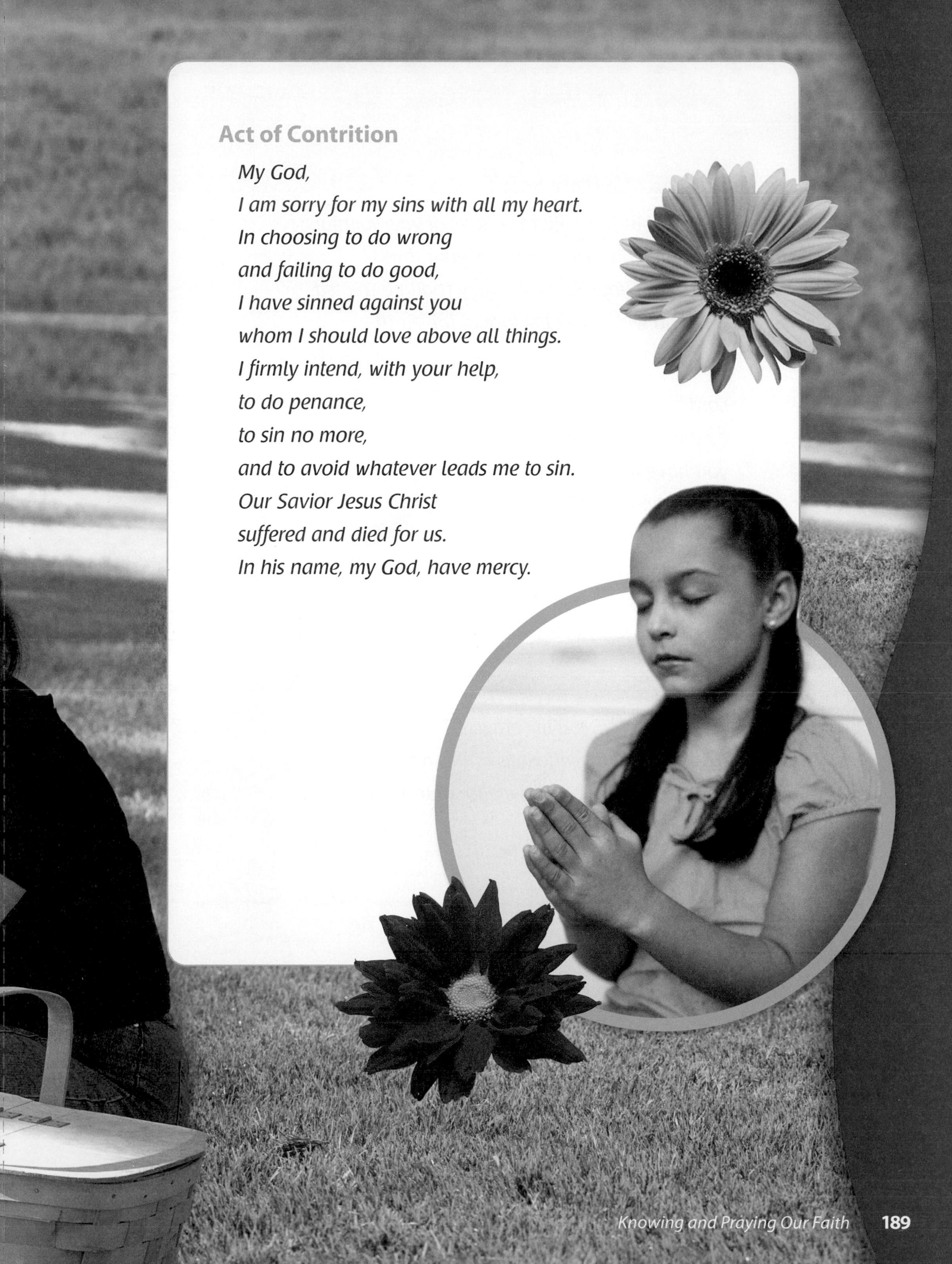

Act of Contrition

My God,
I am sorry for my sins with all my heart.
In choosing to do wrong
and failing to do good,
I have sinned against you
whom I should love above all things.
I firmly intend, with your help,
to do penance,
to sin no more,
and to avoid whatever leads me to sin.
Our Savior Jesus Christ
suffered and died for us.
In his name, my God, have mercy.

Prayer to the Holy Spirit

Come, Holy Spirit, fill the hearts of your faithful.
And kindle in them the fire of your love.
Send forth your Spirit and they shall be created.
And you will renew the face of the earth.
Let us pray.

Lord,
by the light of the Holy Spirit
you have taught the hearts of your faithful.
In the same Spirit
help us to relish what is right
and always rejoice in your consolation.
We ask this through Christ our Lord.
Amen.

Morning Offering

My God, I offer you my prayers,
works, joys, and sufferings of this day
in union with the holy sacrifice of the Mass
throughout the world.
I offer them for all the intentions
of your Son's Sacred Heart,
for the salvation of souls, reparation for sin,
and the reunion of Christians.
Amen.

Apostles' Creed

I believe in God,
the Father almighty,
Creator of heaven and earth,
and in Jesus Christ, his only Son, our Lord,
who was conceived by the Holy Spirit,
born of the Virgin Mary,
suffered under Pontius Pilate,
was crucified, died and was buried;
he descended into hell;
on the third day he rose again from the dead;
he ascended into heaven,
and is seated at the right hand of God the Father almighty;
from there he will come to judge the living and the dead.

I believe in the Holy Spirit,
the holy catholic Church,
the communion of saints,
the forgiveness of sins,
the resurrection of the body,
and life everlasting. Amen.

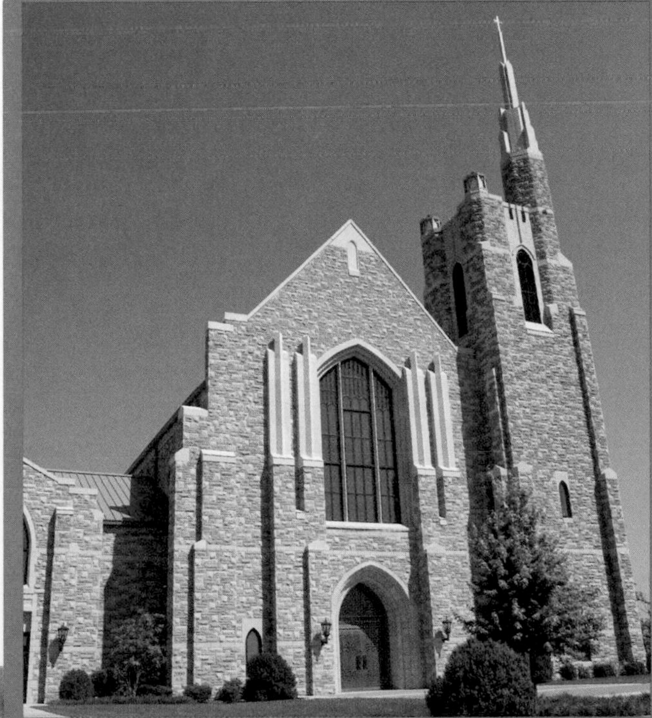

Hail, Holy Queen *(Salve Regina)*

Hail, holy Queen, Mother of mercy,
hail, our life, our sweetness, and our hope.
To you we cry, the children of Eve;
to you we send up our sighs,
mourning and weeping in this land of exile.
Turn, then, most gracious advocate,
your eyes of mercy toward us;
lead us home at last
and show us the blessed fruit of your womb, Jesus:
O clement, O loving, O sweet Virgin Mary.

Prayer for Vocations

God, thank you for loving me.
In Baptism you called me by name
to live as your child.
Help all your people to know their call in life.
For your greater glory, raise up generous leaders
to serve as priests, deacons, sisters, and brothers.
Amen.

The Rosary

The Rosary helps us to pray to Jesus through Mary. When we pray the Rosary, we think about the special events, or mysteries, in the lives of Jesus and Mary.

A rosary is made up of a string of beads and a crucifix. We hold the crucifix in our hands as we pray the Sign of the Cross. Then we pray the Apostles' Creed.

Next to the crucifix, there is a single bead, followed by a set of three beads and another single bead. We pray the Lord's Prayer as we hold the first single bead and a Hail Mary at each bead in the set of three that follows. Then we pray the Glory Be to the Father. On the next single bead, we think about the first mystery and pray the Lord's Prayer.

There are five sets of ten beads; each set is called a decade. We pray a Hail Mary on each bead of a decade as we reflect on a particular mystery in the lives of Jesus and Mary. The Glory Be to the Father is prayed at the end of each decade. Many people pray the Hail, Holy Queen after the last decade. Between decades is a single bead on which we think about one of the mysteries and pray the Lord's Prayer.

We end by holding the crucifix in our hands as we pray the Sign of the Cross.

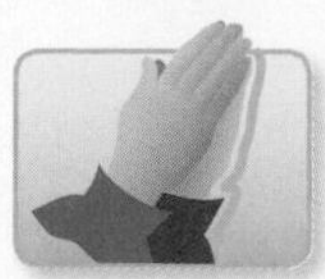

Praying the Rosary

1. Pray the Sign of the Cross and the Apostles' Creed.

2. Pray the Lord's Prayer.

3. Pray three Hail Marys and one Glory Be to the Father.

4. Think about the first mystery. Pray the Lord's Prayer.

5. Pray ten Hail Marys and one Glory Be to the Father.

6. Think about the second mystery. Pray the Lord's Prayer.

7. Pray ten Hail Marys and one Glory Be to the Father.

8. Think about the third mystery. Pray the Lord's Prayer.

9. Pray ten Hail Marys and one Glory Be to the Father.

10. Think about the fourth mystery. Pray the Lord's Prayer.

11. Pray ten Hail Marys and one Glory Be to the Father.

12. Think about the fifth mystery. Pray the Lord's Prayer.

13. Pray ten Hail Marys and one Glory Be to the Father.

Pray the Hail, Holy Queen.
Many people pray the Hail, Holy Queen after the last decade.

14. Pray the Sign of the Cross.

Mysteries of the Rosary

The Church has used three sets of mysteries for many years. In 2002 Pope John Paul II proposed a fourth set of mysteries—the Mysteries of Light, or Luminous Mysteries. According to his suggestion, the four sets of mysteries might be prayed on the following days: the Joyful Mysteries on Monday and Saturday, the Sorrowful Mysteries on Tuesday and Friday, the Glorious Mysteries on Wednesday and Sunday, and the Luminous Mysteries on Thursday.

The Annunciation

The Baptism of Jesus

The Wedding Feast at Cana

The Joyful Mysteries

1. **The Annunciation** Mary learns she has been chosen to be the mother of Jesus.
2. **The Visitation** Mary visits Elizabeth, who tells Mary that she will always be remembered.
3. **The Nativity** Jesus is born in a stable in Bethlehem.
4. **The Presentation** Mary and Joseph take the infant Jesus to the Temple to present him to God.
5. **The Finding of Jesus in the Temple** Jesus is found in the Temple, discussing his faith with the teachers.

The Mysteries of Light

1. **The Baptism of Jesus in the River Jordan** God proclaims Jesus is his beloved Son.
2. **The Wedding Feast at Cana** At Mary's request Jesus performs his first miracle.
3. **The Proclamation of the Kingdom of God** Jesus calls all to conversion and service to the Kingdom of God.
4. **The Transfiguration of Jesus** Jesus is revealed in glory to Peter, James, and John.
5. **The Institution of the Eucharist** Jesus offers his Body and Blood at the Last Supper.

The Sorrowful Mysteries

1. **The Agony in the Garden** Jesus prays in the Garden of Gethsemane on the night before he dies.
2. **The Scourging at the Pillar** Jesus is beaten with whips.
3. **The Crowning with Thorns** Jesus is mocked and crowned with thorns.
4. **The Carrying of the Cross** Jesus carries the cross on which he will be crucified.
5. **The Crucifixion** Jesus is nailed to the cross and dies.

The Agony in the Garden

The Glorious Mysteries

1. **The Resurrection** God the Father raises Jesus from the dead.
2. **The Ascension** Jesus returns to his Father in Heaven.
3. **The Coming of the Holy Spirit** The Holy Spirit comes to bring new life to the disciples.
4. **The Assumption of Mary** At the end of her life on earth, Mary is taken body and soul into Heaven.
5. **The Coronation of Mary** Mary is crowned as Queen of Heaven and Earth.

The Ascension

The Coronation of Mary

Stations of the Cross

The 14 Stations of the Cross represent events from Jesus' Passion and Death. At each station we use our senses and our imagination to reflect prayerfully on Jesus' suffering, Death, and Resurrection.

1

Jesus Is Condemned to Death.
Pontius Pilate condemns Jesus to death.

2

Jesus Takes Up the Cross.
Jesus willingly accepts and patiently bears the cross.

3

Jesus Falls the First Time.
Weakened by torments and loss of blood, Jesus falls beneath the cross.

4

Jesus Meets His Sorrowful Mother.
Jesus meets his mother, Mary, who is filled with grief.

5

Simon of Cyrene Helps Jesus Carry the Cross.
Soldiers force Simon of Cyrene to carry the cross.

6

Veronica Wipes the Face of Jesus.
Veronica steps through the crowd to wipe the face of Jesus.

7

Jesus Falls the Second Time.
Jesus falls beneath the weight of the cross a second time.

8

Jesus Meets the Women of Jerusalem.
Jesus tells the women not to weep for him but for themselves and for their children.

9

Jesus Falls the Third Time.
Weakened almost to the point of death, Jesus falls a third time.

10

Jesus Is Stripped of His Garments.
The soldiers strip Jesus of his garments, treating him as a common criminal.

11

Jesus Is Nailed to the Cross.
Jesus' hands and feet are nailed to the cross.

12

Jesus Dies on the Cross.
After suffering greatly on the cross, Jesus bows his head and dies.

13

Jesus Is Taken Down from the Cross.
The lifeless body of Jesus is tenderly placed in the arms of Mary, his mother.

14

Jesus Is Laid in the Tomb.
Jesus' disciples place his body in the tomb.

The closing prayer—sometimes included as a 15th station—reflects on the Resurrection of Jesus.

Celebrating Our Faith

The Seven Sacraments

The sacraments are signs of the grace we receive from God.

Sacraments show that God is part of our lives. They were given to the Church by Jesus. They help us to live the way God wants us to live. The sacraments are celebrated with us by priests.

Sacraments of Initiation

These sacraments lay the foundation for our lives as Catholics.

Baptism

Baptism is the first sacrament we receive. Through Baptism we become followers of Jesus and part of God's family, the Church. The pouring of water is the main sign of Baptism.

Confirmation

In this sacrament the Holy Spirit strengthens us to be witnesses to Jesus. Confirmation seals our life of faith in Jesus and helps us become better Christians.

The bishop places holy oil in the form of a cross on our foreheads. This is the main sign of Confirmation.

Eucharist

At Mass the Bread and Wine become the Body and Blood of Jesus Christ. This happens when the priest says the words of consecration that Jesus used at the Last Supper. The Eucharist is also called Holy Communion.

Sacraments of Healing

These sacraments celebrate the healing power of Jesus.

Penance and Reconciliation

We ask God to forgive our sins in the Sacrament of Penance and Reconciliation. The priest who celebrates this sacrament with us shares Jesus' gifts of peace and forgiveness.

The Holy Spirit helps us to be sorry for our sins. God always forgives us when we are sorry and do penance for our sins.

Anointing of the Sick

In this sacrament a sick person is anointed with holy oil and receives the spiritual—and sometimes even the physical—healing of Jesus.

Sacraments at the Service of Communion

These sacraments help members serve the community.

Holy Orders

Some men are called to be deacons, priests, or bishops. They receive the Sacrament of Holy Orders. Through Holy Orders the mission, or task, given by Jesus to his apostles continues in the Church.

Matrimony

Some men and women are called by the Holy Spirit to be married. They agree to live in faithful love in the Sacrament of Matrimony.

They make a solemn promise to be partners for life, both for their own good and for the good of the children they will raise.

Celebrating the Lord's Day

Sunday is the day on which we celebrate the Resurrection of Jesus. It is the Lord's Day. We gather for Mass and rest from work. People all over the world gather at God's eucharistic table as brothers and sisters.

The Order of Mass

The Mass is the most important sacramental celebration of the Church and it always follows a set order.

Introductory Rites—preparing to celebrate the Eucharist

We prepare to celebrate the Eucharist.

Entrance Chant

We gather as a community and praise God in song.

Greeting

We pray the Sign of the Cross. The priest welcomes us.

Penitential Act

We remember our sins and ask God for mercy.

Gloria

We praise God in song.

Collect Prayer

We ask God to hear our prayers.

Liturgy of the Word—hearing God's plan of Salvation

First Reading

We listen to God's Word, usually from the Old Testament.

Responsorial Psalm

We respond to God's Word in song.

Second Reading

We listen to God's Word from the New Testament.

Gospel Acclamation

We sing "Alleluia!" During Lent we use a different acclamation to praise God for his Word.

Gospel Reading

We stand and listen to the Gospel of the Lord.

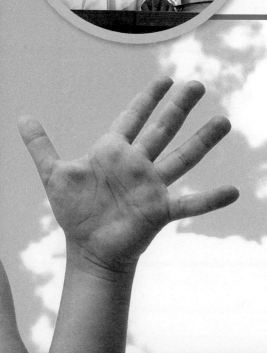

Homily

The priest or the deacon explains God's Word.

Profession of Faith

We proclaim our faith through the Creed.

Prayer of the Faithful

We pray for our needs and the needs of others.

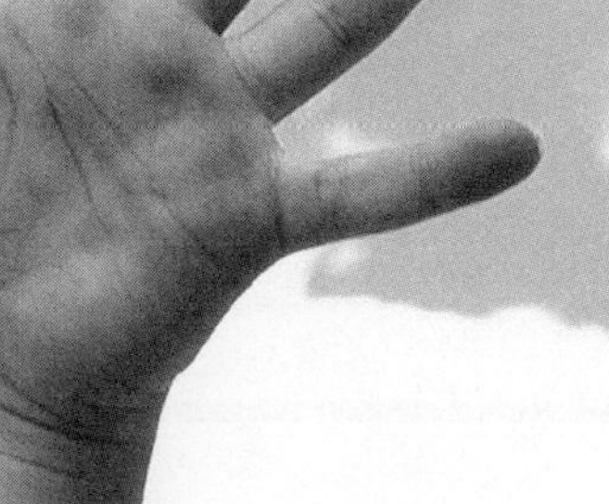

Liturgy of the Eucharist—celebrating Christ's presence in the Eucharist

Presentation and Preparation of the Gifts

We bring gifts of bread and wine to the altar.

Prayer over the Offerings

The priest prays that God will accept our sacrifice.

Eucharistic Prayer

This prayer of thanksgiving is the center and high point of the entire celebration. During this prayer the bread and wine are consecrated and truly become Jesus' Body and Blood.

- **Preface**—We give thanks and praise to God.
- **Holy, Holy, Holy**—We sing an acclamation of praise.
- **The Mystery of Faith**—We proclaim Jesus' Death and Resurrection.

Communion Rite—receiving the Body and Blood of Jesus Christ

The Lord's Prayer

We pray the Lord's Prayer.

Sign of Peace

We offer one another Christ's peace.

Lamb of God

We pray for forgiveness, mercy, and peace.

Communion

We receive the Body and Blood of Jesus Christ.

Prayer after Communion

We pray that the Eucharist will strengthen us to live as Jesus did.

Concluding Rites—going forth to glorify the Lord by our lives

Final Blessing

We receive God's blessing.

Dismissal

We go in peace to glorify the Lord by our lives.

Receiving Communion

When we go to communion, we receive the Body of Christ—in the form of bread—in our hands or on our tongues. The priest or the extraordinary minister of Holy Communion says, "The Body of Christ." We reply, "Amen."

We can also receive the Blood of Christ in the form of wine. The priest or the extraordinary minister of Holy Communion offers us the chalice and says, "The Blood of Christ." We reply, "Amen." We take the chalice in our hands and drink from it; we then hand it back to the priest or the extraordinary minister of Holy Communion.

Holy Days of Obligation

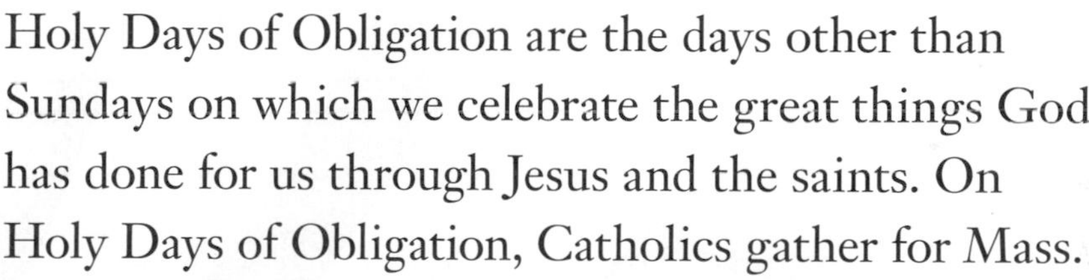

Holy Days of Obligation are the days other than Sundays on which we celebrate the great things God has done for us through Jesus and the saints. On Holy Days of Obligation, Catholics gather for Mass.

Six Holy Days of Obligation are celebrated in the United States.

January 1—Mary, Mother of God
40 days after Easter—Ascension
August 15—Assumption of the Blessed Virgin Mary
November 1—All Saints Day
December 8—Immaculate Conception
December 25—Nativity of Our Lord Jesus Christ

People and Things I See at Mass

sanctuary lamp

processional cross

Paschal Candle

tabernacle

ambo

extraordinary minister of Holy Communion

altar servers

stole
chasuble
deacon
priest
lector
INRI
cantor
altar
chalice
paten

An Examination of Conscience

An examination of conscience is the act of reflecting on how we have hurt our relationships with God and with others. Questions such as the following will help us in our examination of conscience.

My Relationship with God

Do I use God's name with love and reverence?

What steps am I taking to grow closer to God and to others?

Do I actively participate at Mass on Sundays and holy days?

Do I pray?

Am I willing to turn to God often, especially when I am tempted?

My Relationships with Family, Friends, and Neighbors

Have I set a bad example by my words or actions? Do I treat others fairly? Do I spread stories that hurt other people?

Am I loving to those in my family? Am I respectful of my neighbors, my friends, and those in authority?

Do I show respect for my body and for the bodies of others?

Have I taken or damaged anything that did not belong to me? Have I cheated, copied homework, or lied?

Do I quarrel or fight with others? Do I try to hurt people who I think have hurt me?

How to Go to Confession

An examination of conscience is an important part of preparing for the Sacrament of Penance and Reconciliation. The Sacrament of Reconciliation includes the following steps:

1. The priest greets us, and we pray the Sign of the Cross. He invites us to trust in God. He may read God's Word with us.
2. We confess our sins. The priest may help and counsel us.
3. The priest gives us a penance to perform. Penance can be an act of kindness or prayers to pray, or both.
4. The priest asks us to express our sorrow, usually by praying the Act of Contrition.
5. We receive absolution. The priest says, "I absolve you from your sins in the name of the Father, and of the Son, and of the Holy Spirit." We respond, "Amen."
6. The priest dismisses us by saying, "Go in peace." We go forth to perform the act of penance he has given us.

Living Our Faith

The Ten Commandments

God gave us the Ten Commandments. They teach us how to live for God and for others. They help us follow the moral law to do good and avoid evil.

1. I am your God; love nothing more than me.
2. Use God's name with respect.
3. Keep the Lord's Day holy.
4. Honor and obey your parents.
5. Treat all human life with respect.
6. Respect married life.
7. Respect what belongs to others.
8. Tell the truth.
9. Respect your neighbors and your friends.
10. Be happy with what you have.

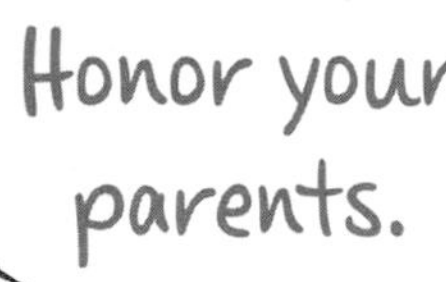

The Great Commandment

People asked Jesus, "What is the most important commandment?"
Jesus said, "First, love God. Love him with your heart, soul, and mind.
The second is like it: Love your neighbor as much as you love yourself."

adapted from Matthew 22:37–39

We call this the Great Commandment.

The New Commandment

Before his death on the cross, Jesus gave his disciples a new commandment:
"Love one another. As I have loved you, so you also should love one another."

adapted from John 13:34

The Beatitudes

Jesus gave us the Beatitudes in the Sermon on the Mount. They show us the way to true happiness.

Blessed are those who need God.
They will live in heaven one day.

Blessed are those who are sad.
They will be comforted.

Blessed are those who have little.
They will be given many things.

Blessed are those who have mercy on others.
They will be shown mercy.

Blessed are those who make peace.
They are the children of God.

adapted from Matthew 5:3–10

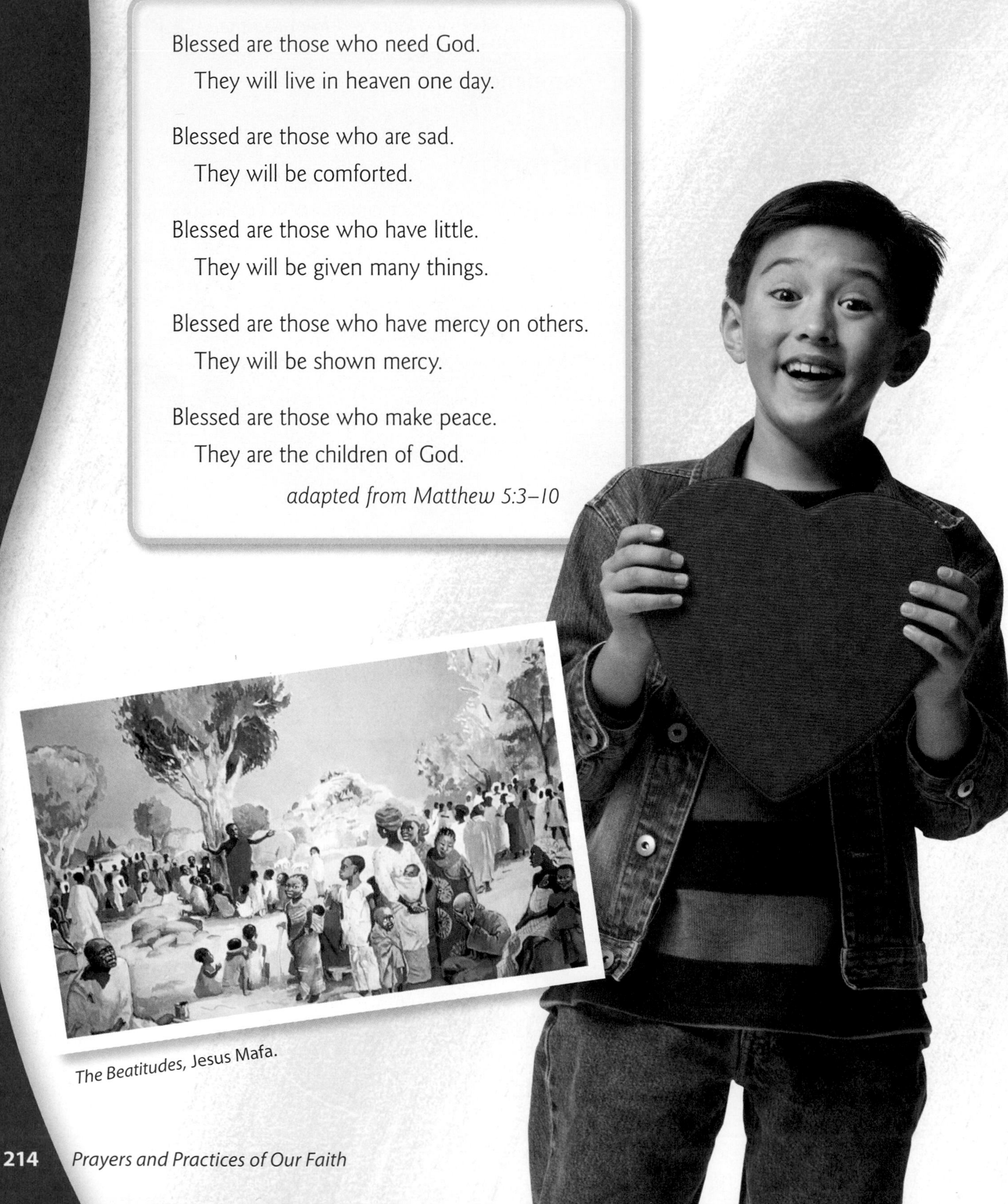

The Beatitudes, Jesus Mafa.

Making Good Choices

The Holy Spirit helps us to make good choices. We get help from the Ten Commandments, the grace of the sacraments, and the teachings of the Church. We also get help from the example of saints and fellow Christians. To make good choices, we ask the following questions:

1. Is the thing I'm choosing to do a good thing?
2. Am I choosing to do it for the right reasons?
3. Am I choosing to do it at the right time and place?

Fruits of the Holy Spirit

When we realize that the Holy Spirit lives within us, we live the way God wants us to. The Fruits of the Holy Spirit are signs of the Holy Spirit's action in our lives.

love	joy	peace
patience	kindness	generosity
faithfulness	gentleness	self-control

Church Tradition also includes goodness, modesty, and chastity as Fruits of the Holy Spirit.

Showing Our Love for the World

Jesus taught us to care for those in need. The social teachings of the Church call for us to follow Jesus' example in each of the following areas.

Life and Dignity

God wants us to care for everyone. We are all made in his image.

Family and Community

Jesus wants us to be loving helpers in our families and communities.

Rights and Responsibilities

All people should have what they need to live good lives.

The Poor and Vulnerable

Jesus calls us to do what we can to help people in need.

Work and Workers

The work that we do gives glory to God.

Solidarity

Since God is our Father, we are called to treat everyone in the world as a brother or a sister.

God's Creation

We show our love for God's world by taking care of it.

Songs of Our Faith

Song of Love

Chorus

Thank you, Jesus, for helping me to see.
Thank you, God, for the heart you've given me.
Thank you, Spirit, for coming to me,
and for showing me how to sing your song of love.

Verse 1

I saw someone lonely by the road,
someone my age sadly all alone.
I shared my friendship, and we talked a while.
I gave my hand. Jesus gave back a smile.

(Sing Chorus)

Verse 2

I saw Jesus inside my heart,
making me God's own work of art.
If I spread my joy in life each day,
I can show my love for God's
world in every way.

Verse 3

I saw Jesus in friends and family
by my side, sharing and supporting me.
I found my heart had room for everyone.
Thank you, Spirit, for what you have begun.

(Sing Chorus)

Lyrics by E. Strauss. Music by Neilson Hubbard.

Here I Am, God

Refrain

Here I am, God. I am coming.
My delight is to do your will!
Here I am, God. I am coming.
My delight is to do your will!

Verse 1

Pull me out of the muddy mire,
set my feet upon solid ground.
In my heart you have put new laws,
on my lips you have put new songs.

(Sing Refrain)

Verse 2

When my trouble and sins surround me,
and my eyes cannot see the way,
may your love and your kindness save me.
God, my rescuer, don't delay.

(Sing Refrain)

Verse 3

Of your love I cannot be silent;
I will shout of your wondrous plans.
You have given me ears to hear you.
Now I answer you, here I am!

(Sing Refrain)

All You Works of God

Refrain

All you works of God,
every mountain, star and tree,
bless the One who shapes your beauty,
who has caused you all to be
one great song of love and grace,
ever ancient, ever new.
Raise your voices, all you works of God!

Verse 1

Sun and moon: Bless your Maker!
Stars of heaven: Chant your praise!
Showers and dew: Raise up your joyful song!

(Sing Refrain)

Verse 2

Winds of God: Bless your Maker!
Cold and winter: Chant your praise!
Snowstorms and ice: Raise up your joyful song!

(Sing Refrain)

Verse 3

Wells and springs: Bless your Maker!
Seas and rivers: Chant your praise!
Whales in the deep: Raise up your joyful song!

(Sing Refrain)

Verse 4

Flying birds: Bless your Maker!
Beasts and cattle: Chant your praise!
Children at play: Raise up your joyful song!

(Sing Refrain)

"All You Works of God" by Marty Haugen.

Come, O Holy Spirit/Wa Wa Wa Emimimo

Verse 1

Come, O Holy Spirit, come.
Come, Almighty Spirit, come.
Come, come, come.

Verse 2

Come, O Holy Spirit, come.
Come, Almighty Spirit, come.
Come, come, come.

Verse 3

Wa wa wa Emimimo.
Wa wa wa Alagbara.
Wao, wao, wao.

Verse 4

Wa wa wa Emimimo.
Wa wa wa Alagbara.
Wao, wao, wao.

"Come, O Holy Spirit/Wa Wa Wa Emimimo" from traditional Nigerian text. English transcription and paraphrase © 1990 I-to-Loh (World Council of Churches).

Holy Is Your Name

Refrain

And holy is your name through all generations!
Everlasting is your mercy to the people you have chosen,
and holy is your name.

Verse 1

My soul is filled with joy
as I sing to God my savior:
you have looked upon your servant,
you have visited your people,
and holy is your name.

(Sing Refrain)

Verse 2

I am lowly as a child,
but I know from this day forward
that my name will be remembered,
for all will call me blessed,
and holy is your name.

(Sing Refrain)

Verse 3

In your love you now fulfill
what you promised to your people.
I will praise you, Lord, my Savior,
everlasting is your mercy,
and holy is your name.

(Sing Refrain)

"Holy Is Your Name" by David Haas.

I Say "Yes," Lord / Digo "Sí," Señor

Verse 1

I say "Yes," my Lord,
in all good times, through all the bad times,
I say "Yes," my Lord,
to every word you speak.

Verse 2

Digo "Sí," Señor,
en tiempos malos, en tiempos buenos,
Digo "Sí," Señor,
a todo lo que hablas.

"I Say 'Yes,' Lord/Digo 'Sí,' Señor" by Donna Peña.

Peace Walk

Refrain

Come, let us walk in the way of our God,
let us walk in the way of our God.
Come, let us walk in the way of our God,
let us walk in the way of our God.

Verse 1

Pray for God's gentle peace within.
May the pilgrimage now begin.
Peace abide within our hearts.
All who love God, walk in peace.

(Sing Refrain)

Verse 2

Pray for peace in our families.
May all bitterness be released.
Peace abide within our homes.
All who love God, walk in peace.

(Sing Refrain)

Verse 3

Pray for peace and the end of war.
May the suffering be no more.
Peace abide within our world.
All who love God, walk in peace.

(Sing Refrain)

What Does It Mean to Follow Jesus?

Refrain

What does it mean to follow Jesus?
What does it mean to go his way?
What does it mean to do what he wants me to,
every day?

Verse 1

I can love my neighbor, just as Jesus said.
I can help my brother, see that he is fed.
I can show my sister kindness and care.
I can show my friends that I know how to share.

(Sing Refrain)

Verse 2

I can say I'm sorry when I've done some wrong.
I can sing his praises in both words and song.
I'll be friends with others who aren't like me.
They belong to Jesus: we all do, you see.

(Sing Refrain)

*"What Does It Mean to Follow Jesus?"
by Lois Brokering.*

Name ________________________ Date ____________

Art Print 1 shows a lush garden filled with flowers, beautiful leaves, and birds. What beautiful gifts from God do you see around you?

God's Wonders

God created the earth and all the beauty in it.

> After God created light, God brought different kinds of plants and trees to the world. He wanted to give us delicious fruit. Later he created all kinds of animals, including wild ones, cattle, and creeping animals.
>
> *adapted from Genesis 1:3–25*

Through prayer and taking care of his creation, we can give glory to God for all his wonderful gifts.

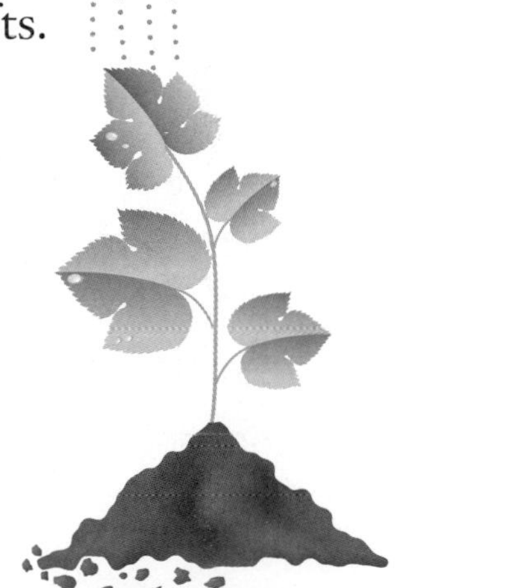

Small Wonders

God created many wonderful things with amazing details. These details are small wonders. The dots on a ladybug, the eyelashes on a calf, and the shades of the colors on flowers are all created by God. These are all beautiful gifts that God has given us.

I Spy a Small Natural Wonder

Look around you and choose something that interests you, such as a plant or a feather. Examine it closely, noticing the details. Draw a picture of your small wonder.

Name ______________________________ Date ______________

Art Print 2 shows Saint Elizabeth spinning wool for people who were poor. How are you an instrument of God's love?

Sharing God's Love

Though her family was wealthy, Saint Elizabeth of Hungary lived a simple life. She devoted her life to feeding and clothing those who were poor. She started a hospital and cared for people who were sick. Elizabeth pleased God by sharing his love and by being kind to those in need.

All love comes from God.
God loves us so much that he sent his Son, Jesus, to give us life. We bring God's love to life in our world by loving one another.

adapted from 1 John 4:7–11

Showing Your Love

In the space below, write one way that you could show your love for a friend.

____

____

____

____

____

Name ________________________________ Date ______________

Art Print 3 shows two children making peace with each other. Have you ever had to say you were sorry to someone or forgive someone for hurting you?

Caring Friends

God wants us to care for others. There are many ways you can be a caring friend to those who need you. You can do this by thinking of their feelings. Listening to people can help you understand how they feel. Another way to care for people is to forgive them. God wants us to forgive others, just as he forgives us. In the Lord's Prayer, we ask God to forgive us as we forgive others. It takes love and strength to be able to forgive someone. That is why we are like Jesus when we forgive others.

What Would You Do?

Sometimes people do things that hurt us. Circle how you could show forgiveness in these situations.

1. Your little brother rode your new bike and fell. The chain on the bike came off.
   - **a.** You tell him that he can never ride your bike again.
   - **b.** You ask him if he is hurt and suggest you fix the bike together.
2. Your good friend went to the park with another friend and did not invite you. Later she told you she was sorry she did not include you.
   - **a.** You tell her it is OK, and you invite both of them to play.
   - **b.** You do not invite your friend the next time you do something special.

EXPLORE ART PRINT 4

Name ______________________ Date ____________

Art Print 4 shows the names of different angels. What names are important to you? When you hear them, how do they make you feel?

A Name Is Special

Sometimes names can tell us about a person. We have many special names for Jesus. Each name tells us something different about him. *Jesus* means "God saves" us. Joseph knew that Jesus would also be called *Emmanuel*, which means "God is with us." The first disciples used *Christ*, which means "the anointed one."

Names of Jesus' Followers

Jesus' followers had special names too. Peter's name means "rock." That name fits him well because Peter was strong in his faith. John's name means "God is gracious." Matthew's name means "gift of God."

Our Names

Our names are special too. Some of us may be named after a saint or a family member. Do you know what your name means? Write about how your name was chosen and what it means.

____

____

____

____

____

Jesus

Sean

Joshua

Hannah

Katherine

Jacob

Elizabeth

Natalia

Santiago

Miguel

Andrew

Sarah

Ethan Rachel Isabella

Name ______________________ Date ____________

Art Print 5 shows the presence of God in the Celebration of the Eucharist. Where do you see the presence of God in your life during Ordinary Time?

Rejoice and Be Glad

We know that God's love is present in our lives every day. We see God's gifts all around us and are thankful for our blessings. When we receive the Eucharist on the Lord's Day, we gather with other parish members together as a Church community.

"This is the day the LORD has made;
let us rejoice in it and be glad."

Psalms 118:24

During Ordinary Time we celebrate the gift of our Church community. After Mass we show our care for our community by being more like Christ. We can help those in need in many ways. We also notice how our Church community helps us and others with the gift of caring.

Give Thanks for Your Gifts

Write a short prayer giving thanks for how your Church community helps you or someone else.

____

____

____

____

____

EXPLORE ART PRINT 6

Name ______________________________ Date ______________

Art Print 6 shows Saint Benedict and his sister Saint Scholastica, both of whom served God's kingdom. How do you serve God's kingdom?

Saints Serve the Kingdom

Benedict founded a **monastery** in Monte Cassino, Italy. This monastery was a home for a group of men called monks who wanted to work and pray together. Some of Benedict's monks went on to start other monasteries. With her twin brother's guidance, Scholastica founded a convent five miles away. Benedict's work was like planting a mustard seed. The small seed of his monastery sprouted many branches.

The monks worked the land, prayed, and copied the Bible by hand. Benedict's motto was "pray and work." This motto was the beginning of several of Benedict's rules for the monastery. Benedict wrote rules for how the monks should live. Here are some of the monastery's rules:

- Seek Jesus' love above all else.
- Do not speak evil of others.
- Let a wise man stand at the gates of the monastery to greet visitors.
- A brother's clothing should be suited to the weather where he lives.

What's Your Motto?

Think of what your motto could be and write it here.

____

Did You Know?

The name *Benedict* means "blessed." A benediction is a blessing. The name *Scholastica* means "learned woman."

EXPLORE ART PRINT 7

Name ______________________ Date ____________

Art Print 7 shows a girl quietly praying outside. When do you make time to pray and speak with God?

Showing Our Love

Praying often is one way to become closer to God. When we show love to others, we show our love of God and our neighbor. God gave Moses the Ten Commandments to teach us how to love God and one another. Through the commandments we can become closer to God. We should also keep an open heart and always be ready to help our neighbor.

Paying Attention

Consider the following situations. Circle the letter of the action that helps you become closer to God.

1. You are playing baseball with your friends. A girl you do not know comes up to the group and asks if she can play. You should

   a. ignore her and keep playing.

   b. tell her that she can take your turn.

   c. say, "Maybe next time."

2. At school it is finally lunchtime. You notice that a boy at the next table is sitting quietly with no food. You should

   a. tease him about forgetting his lunch.

   b. tell your friends, "He must have the worst parents in the world!"

   c. offer him some of your lunch.

Reading God's Word

For where your treasure is, there also will your heart be.

Matthew 6:21

Name ______________________ Date ______________

Art Print 8 shows the apostles and the disciples spreading God's Word. What is one way that you serve Jesus?

Proclaiming the Kingdom

Jesus knew he needed help spreading God's Word. He chose Peter, the other apostles, and the followers called disciples to help with his work. Jesus' apostles and disciples accepted the **mission** that Jesus gave them to proclaim God's kingdom.

Jesus depended on his friends to help him do the job God gave him. We can work together with our friends to help answer Jesus' call.

Lean on Me

Think of jobs you have at school or home. Describe a time when you depended on a friend for help.

____

____

____

Describe a time when you depended on Jesus for help.

____

____

____

Did You Know?

Jesus chose 12 apostles to lead the Church. The pope and bishops of the Catholic Church continue the apostles' mission today.

Name ____________________ Date ____________

Art Print 9 shows Saint Paul with his letters that helped spread God's Word. How do you spread God's Word to others?

Remember My Message

Saint Paul wrote a letter to his friends in Corinth. He was worried that they had forgotten what he had told them about Jesus' Death and Resurrection. This is what Paul wrote, so that the people in Corinth would believe and be saved.

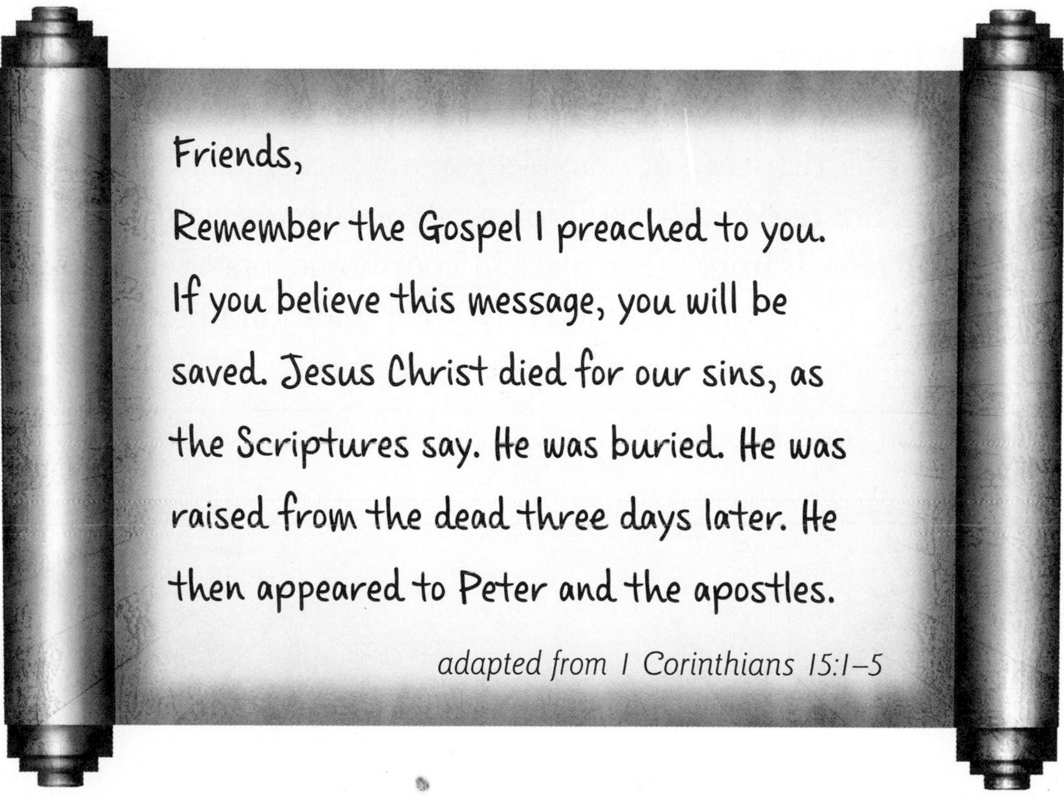
Friends,

Remember the Gospel I preached to you. If you believe this message, you will be saved. Jesus Christ died for our sins, as the Scriptures say. He was buried. He was raised from the dead three days later. He then appeared to Peter and the apostles.

adapted from 1 Corinthians 15:1–5

God sent Jesus to teach his people how to follow him. Jesus died to show how much God loves us. He would do anything to help us know and love God.

What Would You Say?

Imagine you were Saint Paul. What would you want the people in Corinth to know about Jesus? Write one idea on the lines.

____

____

EXPLORE ART PRINT 10

Name ______________________________ Date ______________

Art Print 10 shows a family preparing for the celebration of Jesus' birth. What is something you do to prepare during Advent?

Celebrating Advent

Advent begins four weeks before Christmas. During the season we prepare to celebrate the anniversary of Jesus' birth. In the season of Advent, we thoughtfully await Christmas. We pray that Jesus' love will grow in us in a more complete way.

Family Traditions

During Advent your family might have special traditions to prepare for Christmas. For example, you may decorate a Christmas tree. Think of one family tradition that you like to celebrate during Advent. It might take place in your home, outside, in your community, or in your church. Draw your tradition in the box. Then complete the sentence below the picture.

One Advent tradition that helps my family prepare for the birth of Jesus is ______________________________

______________________________.

Name ______________________ Date ____________

Art Print 11 shows doves, which represent the presence of the Holy Spirit. How do you feel the Holy Spirit's presence in your life?

The Holy Spirit Is with Us

Jesus sent the Holy Spirit to be with us and to guide us. The Holy Spirit helps us live prayerful lives and guides us on the journey to Heaven.

Finish the sentence to show how you can be a witness to Jesus Christ.

I can be a witness to Jesus Christ when I ______________________

______________________________________.

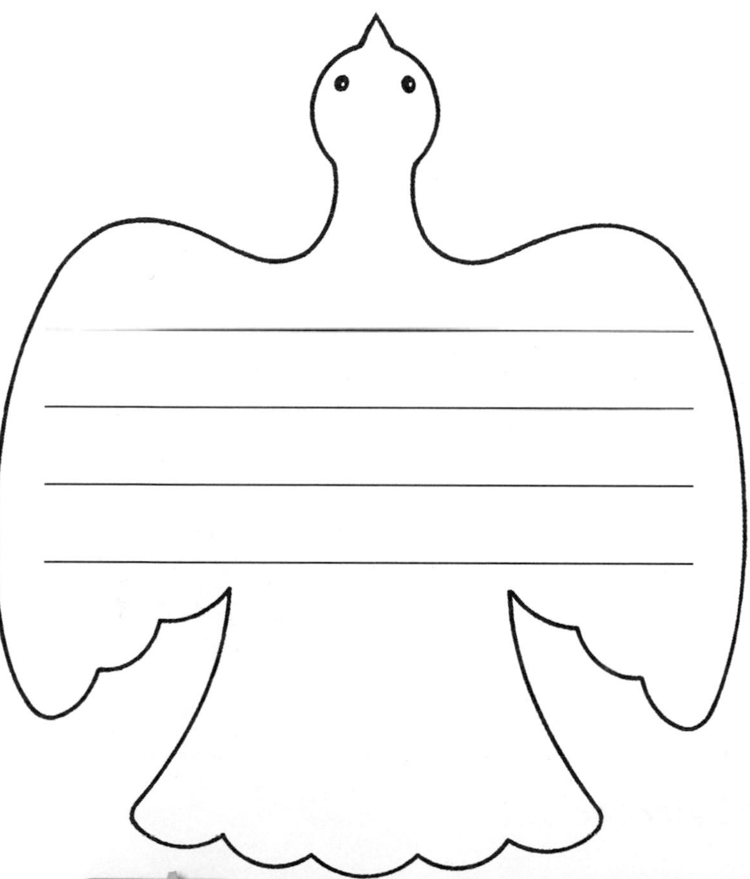

Doves

The dove has been a religious symbol in art for more than 1,000 years. Its appearance can indicate peace, hope, forgiveness, inspiration, and the presence of the Holy Spirit. On the lines in the dove, write about a time in your life when you needed the Holy Spirit.

Sacred Site

Katharine Drexel was inspired by the Holy Spirit to dedicate her life to Jesus. She gave her fortune to help others. She is remembered at the Shrine of Saint Katharine Drexel in Bensalem, Pennsylvania. It is also the motherhouse of the Sisters of the Blessed Sacrament, the order that she began.

Name ______________________________ Date ______________

Art Print 12 shows Saint Peter, the apostle whom Jesus chose to lead the Church. What qualities do you look for in a leader?

Peter and the Church

Peter became the first pope of the Catholic Church.

> Peter said he believed Jesus was the Messiah. Jesus replied, "Peter, you are the rock upon which I will build my Church. Even death will not destroy it. I will give you the keys to the Kingdom of Heaven."
>
> *adapted from Matthew 16:18–19*

Symbols of Peter

Rocks and keys are symbols of Peter. What do you think of when you see a rock? What do keys make you think of? Write your ideas on the lines. Then write about why these things are symbols of Peter.

A rock makes me think of ______________________

____

____.

Keys make me think of ______________________

____

____.

Rocks and keys are symbols of Peter because

____

____.

Did You Know?

Peter's name means "rock." Jesus named him this because he knew Peter would be a strong foundation for the Church.

Name ______________________________ Date ______________

Art Print 13 shows Jesus healing a servant through an officer's faith. How do you care for others?

Jesus and the Roman Officer

Before we receive Holy Communion, we pray special words. Read about when these words were first spoken.

Jesus went to the town of Capernaum. A Roman officer there had a servant who was very sick. When the officer heard about Jesus, he sent men to ask Jesus to save the servant's life. They urged Jesus, "Please do this for him. This man loves our nation, and he has helped us." Jesus went with them.

As they neared the house, the officer sent his friends to tell Jesus, "Lord, do not trouble yourself. I am not worthy to have you enter my home. Just say the word and let my servant be healed."

The officer knew that he could order his soldiers to do something far away. In the same way, he believed Jesus could send his power to heal someone far away. Jesus was amazed when he heard this. He said, "I have never found such faith, even in Israel." The officer's friends returned to find the servant healthy.

adapted from Luke 7:1–10

The officer had never met Jesus, but he had faith in Jesus. Jesus showed that his mission was to all people. On a separate sheet of paper, write how you can show you care for all people as Jesus does.

Link to Liturgy

Before we receive Holy Communion at Mass, we pray "Lord, I am not worthy that you should enter under my roof, but only say the word and my soul shall be healed."

EXPLORE ART PRINT 14

Name ______________________________ Date ______________

Art Print 14 shows Mary receiving good news from an angel about God's blessing. What gifts make you feel blessed by God?

Mary, Full of Grace

The angel Gabriel appeared to Mary and said, "Hail Mary, full of grace, the Lord is with you!" When Mary learned that God would give her a child, she knew that she had been blessed. Mary was so excited that she had to share the news with her family. She visited Elizabeth, her cousin. Elizabeth said to Mary, "Blessed are you among women, and blessed is the fruit of your womb." These words are part of the Hail Mary.

Mary as Our Mother

When God called Mary to be the mother of his Son, God also called her to be the Mother of the Church and of all God's children. We are God's children, so Mary is our mother too! We know Mary had to be special to be the mother of Jesus. She always tried to love and serve God, and she became very holy. Mary was filled with God's love.

I am blessed to have Mary as my mother because she

____

____

____.

Reading God's Word

Blessed are you who believed and trusted that what the Lord told you would really happen.

adapted from Luke 1:45

EXPLORE ART PRINT 15

Name ____________________ Date __________

Art Print 15 shows the moment when Jesus was born to us. How do you share your happiness that Jesus is with you?

Celebrating Christmas

An important feast during the Christmas season is the Feast of the Epiphany, when Jesus was revealed to the whole world. The Magi, or the Wise Men, believed that someday a star would announce the birth of the Son of God. They studied charts of the stars and waited for the special star to appear in the sky. When it finally appeared, the Wise Men packed their camels and traveled a long time to reach him. When they saw the baby Jesus, they honored him with gifts.

The Gift of Jesus

Although the celebration of Christmas comes with lights, presents, and parties, God's gift of Jesus to the world teaches us how to show our love to others. Christmas reminds us how much God loves us, and that is what we celebrate.

". . . God is love, and whoever remains in love remains in God and God in him." *1 John 4:16*

A Gift for Baby Jesus

Imagine you were traveling with the Wise Men. Draw a picture of a gift you would bring to Jesus.

EXPLORE ART PRINT 16

Name ______________________________ Date ______________

Art Print 16 shows Philip welcoming an official to the Church through Baptism. In what ways have you been welcomed to the Church?

Philip and the Court Official

Many disciples traveled long distances to continue Jesus' mission.

Philip was called to make one of these journeys. Philip was traveling a desert road from Jerusalem to Gaza. He met a court official from Ethiopia. The official was returning home from Jerusalem. He was in his carriage, reading the Scriptures.

The Holy Spirit told Philip to join the official. Philip ran up to him and asked, "Do you understand what you are reading?" The official said, "How can I, unless someone teaches me?" He invited Philip to sit with him and teach him.

The man was reading about someone being silent as he was led to be killed. He read about a man being denied justice. He wondered who the man was.

Philip told the official that the man he read about was Jesus. As they traveled, Philip told the official all about Jesus.

Then they came to a stream. The official said, "Look, there is water. Why can't I be baptized?" They walked to the water, and Philip baptized him. The official went joyfully on his way. Philip continued on his journey, spreading Jesus' message in each town he visited. *adapted from Acts of the Apostles 8:26–40*

Welcome to the Church

Imagine that the official is a new member of your parish. On a separate sheet of paper, write what you would say to make him feel welcome.

Name ______________________________ Date ______________

Art Print 17 shows two women happy to greet each other. They accept each other. How do you show acceptance to someone who asks for forgiveness?

A Peaceful Ending

Although we try, it might be hard to get along with everyone all the time. Sometimes we do things that hurt one another or God.

When we sin, we can ask God for forgiveness in the Sacrament of Reconciliation. We confess our sins to a priest and receive absolution. Then we can be at peace with others and with God. When someone asks us for our forgiveness, we share reconciliation by forgiving that person.

Forgiveness

Write about a time you hurt someone and asked for forgiveness.

____

____

____

____

____

Reading God's Word

I will listen for the Word of God. The Lord will give peace to his people, to those who have faith and trust in him.

adapted from Psalm 85:9

Name ______________________ Date ____________

Art Print 18 shows a girl receiving the Sacrament of the Eucharist. How did you feel the day you first received Holy Communion?

The Mass Makes Us One Family

No matter who we are or where we come from, participating in Mass together makes us one family. When we celebrate Mass, we gather with other members of our parish to pray together in thanksgiving and to ask God for his blessing. In some parishes Mass is celebrated in different languages. Even if we do not understand all the words, we can still know what is happening. The same Mass is celebrated all over the world.

When the time for Holy Communion comes during Mass, we process to the front of the church with other parishioners. When we receive Jesus' Body and Blood, we feel one with the Church community. No matter what language we pray in, we are all one family in Jesus Christ.

Your Special Day

On the lines below, write three special things you remember from your First Holy Communion.

____

____

____

Name ________________________ Date ____________

Art Print 19 shows a brother and sister helping prepare for their meal. How do you use your gifts to help others?

Many Gifts, One Spirit

Saint Paul wrote this letter to his friends, explaining how they can use their gifts to help others. We can learn from his letter too.

> There are many different kinds of spiritual gifts. They all come from the same Holy Spirit. There are different ways to serve the same God. We each do different work, but the same God helps us. The Holy Spirit works in each of us to help us do things for the good of others.
>
> Some of us can speak with knowledge and teach others. Some can heal sick people. The Holy Spirit decides which gifts to give us and calls us to use them.
>
> *adapted from 1 Corinthians 12:4–11*

Working Together

Think of ways in which you have used your gifts to help someone in your life. Choose four people and write something you can do to serve them.

mother ________________________

father ________________________

sister/brother ________________________

teacher ________________________

neighbor ________________________

friend ________________________

Link to Liturgy

At the Dismissal of the Mass, the priest or deacon sends us forth to glorify the Lord by our lives.

Name ______________________ Date __________

Art Print 20 shows how Jesus sacrificed his life for us. How do you make your heart ready during Lent in remembrance of his sacrifice?

Jesus in the Desert

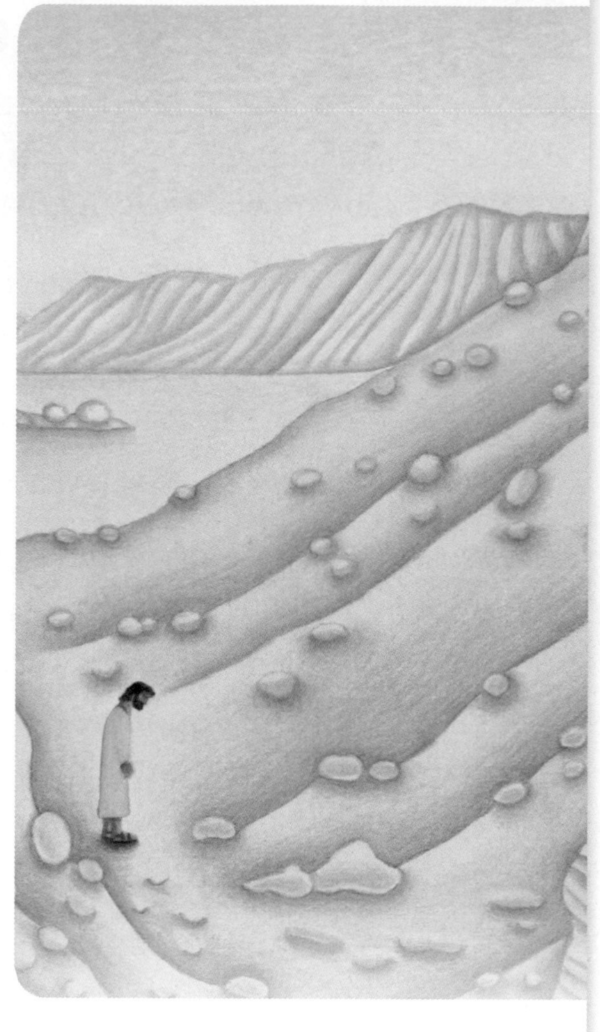

During Lent we remember how Jesus suffered and died before his Resurrection. To prepare for his sacrifice, he spent 40 days in the desert. During those 40 days, Jesus fasted and resisted temptation by the devil. By caring for those in need and resisting temptation, we can make our hearts ready for Easter. Catholics abstain from meat on Fridays. Some Christians fast during Lent by choosing a food or an activity to give up. Others choose to do something to remind them of Jesus, such as pray every morning before school.

Jesus once said this in a parable.

> And the king will say to them in reply,
> "Amen, I say to you, whatever you did
> for one of these least brothers of mine,
> you did for me." *Matthew 25:40*

When you help others, you show you care for Jesus too.

A Lenten Promise

Write an idea for a Lenten promise. Choose something that would remind you daily of Christ's strength to resist temptation and his ultimate sacrifice—his Crucifixion.

____

____

____

Name ______________________________ Date ______________

Art Print 21 shows Jesus and his heart, which is the symbol for the virtue of charity. Which virtue did you show someone today?

Symbols of the Virtues

Symbols stand for something else or remind us of something. Butterflies are used as symbols of Jesus' Resurrection, doves symbolize the Holy Spirit, and water symbolizes Baptism. The cross is a symbol of our faith. It reminds us that Jesus died for our sins. An anchor is a symbol of hope. Just as an anchor holds a ship, so does hope help us hold on to Jesus. When we think of charity, or love, a heart comes to mind because the heart is a symbol of love.

Matching Virtues

Label each symbol and each sentence using *faith*, *hope*, or *charity*.

____

____

____

1. Martha trusts that God will always guide her. ______________________
2. Anton shows his love by visiting a sick classmate. ______________________
3. Ethan believes that Jesus lived and died for us. ______________________

Name ______________________________ Date ______________

Art Print 22 shows Jesus alone in the desert, praying for the strength to follow God's plan for him. What helps you make good moral choices?

Jesus Is Tempted

The Holy Spirit led Jesus into the desert. Jesus didn't eat for 40 days and 40 nights. He was very hungry. The devil came and said to him, "If you are the Son of God, turn these stones into loaves of bread." Jesus said, "The Scriptures say that people do not live only on bread, but on every word that God speaks."

Then the devil took Jesus to the top of the Temple. He said to Jesus, "If you are the Son of God, throw yourself down. The Scriptures say that God will tell the angels to protect you." Jesus answered, "The Scriptures also say you shall not put God to the test."

The devil took Jesus to a high mountain and showed him all the kingdoms of the world. The devil said, "All these I shall give you if you worship me." Jesus said, "Go away, Satan! The Scriptures say that you shall worship God alone, and you shall serve only him." Then the devil left Jesus, and angels came and cared for him.

adapted from Matthew 4:1–11

A Prayer of Petition

Write a prayer of petition, asking God for help in making good moral choices.

____

____

____

Did You Know?

After Jesus was tempted in the desert, he went out into the world to begin teaching others.

Name ______________________ Date ______________

Art Print 23 shows Saint Paul in bright, happy colors. Paul was happy that people were growing in their faith. How do you feel when you think of God's love?

Saint Paul's Joy

We are joyful when our family is happy and peaceful. Saint Paul was excited when he heard how some of his friends were growing in their faith. He knew that the more they grew in the love of Jesus Christ, the more they would serve others. He wrote his friends a letter telling them how much he loved them.

I give thanks to God every time I think of you. I pray for you with joy as you help spread the Gospel. I hold you in my heart. I long to see all of you, and pray that your love and understanding will keep growing. May you continue to make good choices so that you will be pure and blameless when Jesus Christ returns.

adapted from Philippians 1:3–11

Would you like to receive a letter like this? Which words would make you happy? ______________________________

____

Link to Liturgy

We hear many of Paul's writings in the Second Reading at Sunday Mass.

Name ____________________ Date ____________

Art Print 24 shows people sharing God's creation and helping one another. When have you worked with others on a project or task?

Small Acts Make a Big Difference

Taking care of our planet is our job. God expects us to care for all the people, plants, and animals living on earth. This sounds like a very big job! It may feel overwhelming to consider how we could accomplish such a task. However, every big accomplishment begins with one small step. We can work together with our faith community to care for one another and all of God's creation. Working together makes the job feel smaller and more fun.

Small Steps and Teamwork

Draw a picture of yourself taking a small step toward caring for the earth or one another, or draw yourself and a few friends working together to care for God's creation. Describe the scene on the line below.

____

Name ____________________ Date ____________

Art Print 25 shows many Christian symbols. What symbols are used in your home to celebrate the joyful time of Easter?

Celebrate Easter

Easter is the celebration of life. Jesus was born and lived to teach us how to be closer to God his Father. Jesus died so that our sins could be forgiven and our souls could be joined forever with God. God sent his Son, Jesus, to show us his mercy and love.

The Resurrection

After his death Jesus' friends came to his tomb and found it empty. His friends were afraid. Jesus appeared to Mary Magdalene and told her not to be sad. He also appeared many times to comfort and encourage the apostles. On one occasion he appeared to Peter and said, "Tend my sheep." The sheep he spoke of were his people. As disciples we are called to do the same as Peter. We celebrate Easter by committing ourselves to the service of others.

In Celebration of Easter

Jesus showed us how to treat others with compassion, respect, and mercy. In celebration of Easter, draw a picture of yourself doing one of those things.

Glossary

A

Abba an informal name for *Father* in the language Jesus spoke. Jesus called God the Father "Abba." [Abba]

absolution the forgiveness God offers us in the Sacrament of Penance and Reconciliation. After we say that we are sorry for our sins, we receive God's absolution from the priest. [absolución]

Advent the four weeks before Christmas. It is a time of joyful preparation for the celebration of Jesus' birth as our Savior. [Adviento]

Alleluia a prayer of praise to God. It is usually sung as the Gospel Acclamation before the Gospel Reading at Mass except during Lent. [Aleluya]

All Saints Day November 1, the day on which the Church honors all who have died and now live with God as saints in Heaven. This group includes those who have been declared saints by the Church and many others known only to God. [Día de Todos los Santos]

All Souls Day November 2, the day on which the Church remembers all who have died as friends of God. We pray that they may rest in peace. [Día de los Fieles Difuntos]

almsgiving the practice of giving money to those in need as an act of love [limosna, dar]

altar the table in the church on which the priest celebrates Mass, during which the sacrifice of Christ on the cross is made present in the Sacrament of the Eucharist. The altar represents two aspects of the mystery of the Eucharist. First, it is where Jesus Christ offers himself for our sins. Second, it is where he gives us himself as our food for eternal life. [altar]

ambo a raised stand from which a person reads the Word of God during Mass [ambón]

Amen the final word in any prayer. *Amen* means "This is true." When we pray "Amen," it shows that we really mean what we have just said. [Amén]

angel a spiritual creature who brings a message from God [ángel]

Angelus a Catholic devotion recited three times a day—morning, noon, and evening. The devotion recalls the mystery of the Incarnation beginning with the coming of the angel to Mary, her acceptance of the invitation to be Jesus' mother, and on the Word made flesh. [Ángelus]

Annunciation the announcement to Mary by the angel Gabriel that God had chosen her to be the mother of Jesus [Anunciación]

Anointing of the Sick one of the seven sacraments. In this sacrament a sick person is anointed with holy oil and receives the strength, peace, and courage to overcome the difficulties that come with illness. [Unción de los enfermos]

apostle one of twelve chosen men who accompanied Jesus in his ministry and were witnesses to the Resurrection [apóstol]

Apostles' Creed a statement of Christian belief. The Apostles' Creed, developed out of a creed used during Baptism in Rome, lists simple statements of belief in God the Father, Jesus Christ the Son, and the Holy Spirit. The profession of faith used in Baptism today is based on the Apostles' Creed. [Credo de los Apóstoles]

apostolic one of the four Marks of the Church. The Church is apostolic because it hands on the teachings of the apostles through their successors, the bishops. [apostólica]

Ascension the return of Jesus to Heaven. In the Acts of the Apostles, it is written that Jesus, after his Resurrection, spent 40 days on earth, instructing his followers. He then returned to his Father in Heaven. [Ascensión]

Ash Wednesday the first day of Lent, on which we receive ashes on our foreheads. The ashes remind us to prepare for Easter by showing sorrow for the choices we make that offend God and hurt our relationships with others. [Miércoles de Ceniza]

B

Baptism one of the three Sacraments of Initiation. Baptism frees us from Original Sin and gives us new life in Jesus Christ through the Holy Spirit. [Bautismo]

Beatitudes the eight ways we can behave to live a blessed life. Jesus teaches us that if we live according to the Beatitudes, we will live a happy Christian life. [Bienaventuranzas]

Bible the history of God's promise to care for us and his call for us to be faithful to him. God asked that people be faithful first through the beliefs of the Jewish people and then through belief in the life, Death, and Resurrection of Jesus Christ. [Biblia]

bishop a man who has received the fullness of Holy Orders. He has inherited his duties from the original apostles. He cares for the Church today and is a principal teacher in the Church. [obispo]

Blessed Sacrament the Eucharist that has been consecrated by the priest at Mass. It is kept in the tabernacle to adore and to be taken to those who are sick. [Santísimo Sacramento]

blessing a prayer that calls for God's power and care upon some person, place, thing, or special activity [bendición]

Body and Blood of Christ the Bread and Wine that has been consecrated by the priest at Mass. It still looks like bread and wine, but it is actually the Body and Blood of Jesus Christ. [Cuerpo y Sangre de Cristo]

Bread of Life a title for Jesus that tells us that he is the Bread that is food for the faithful [pan de vida]

C

capital sins those sins that can lead us to more serious sin. The seven capital sins are pride, covetousness, envy, anger, gluttony, lust, and sloth. [pecados capitales]

cast lots to throw down small stones or pebbles called lots to help determine a decision needing divine guidance. Lots were cast to choose the disciple to replace Judas in Acts of the Apostles 1:23–26. Roman soldiers also cast lots to divide Jesus' clothing among them as in John 19:24. [echar a suertes]

catholic one of the four Marks of the Church. The Church is catholic because Jesus is fully present in it and because Jesus has given the Church to the whole world. [católico]

celebrant a bishop or priest who leads the people in praying the Mass. A deacon who baptizes or witnesses a marriage is also a celebrant. [celebrante]

celebrate worshiping and praising God with prayers and songs, especially in the celebration of the Eucharist [celebrar]

charity a virtue given to us by God. Charity helps us love God above all things and our neighbor as ourselves. [caridad]

chasuble the visible liturgical vestment worn by the bishop or priest at Mass. A newly ordained priest receives a chasuble as part of the ordination ritual. [casulla]

Christ a title that means "anointed with oil." It is from a Greek word that means the same thing as the Hebrew word *Messiah*, or "anointed." It is the name given to Jesus after the Resurrection. [Cristo]

Christian the name given to all those who have been anointed through the gift of the Holy Spirit in Baptism and have become followers of Jesus Christ [cristiano]

Christmas the day on which we celebrate the birth of Jesus (December 25) [Navidad]

Church the name given to all of Christ's followers throughout the world. It is also the name of the building where we gather to pray to God and the name of our community as we gather to praise God. [Iglesia]

commandment a standard, or rule, for living as God wants us to live. Jesus summarized all the commandments into two: love God and love your neighbor. [mandamiento]

Communion of Saints the union of all who have been saved in Jesus Christ, both those who are alive and those who have died [Comunión de los Santos]

community Christians who are gathered in the name of Jesus Christ to receive his grace and live according to his values [comunidad]

compassion God's fundamental attitude toward his people. This is best seen in Jesus' reaching out to care for those in need. Acting with compassion and mercy toward those in need identifies a person as belonging to God. [compasión]

confession the act of telling our sins to a priest in the Sacrament of Penance and Reconciliation. The sacrament itself is sometimes referred to as confession. [confesión]

Confirmation the sacrament that completes the grace we receive in Baptism. Confirmation seals, or confirms, this grace through the seven Gifts of the Holy Spirit that we receive as part of Confirmation. This sacrament also unites us more closely in Jesus Christ. [confirmación]

conscience the inner voice that helps each of us to know the law that God has placed in our hearts. It guides us to do good and avoid evil. [conciencia]

consecration the making of a thing or person to be special to God through a prayer or blessing. At Mass the words of the priest are a consecration of the bread and wine that become the Body and Blood of Christ. People or objects set apart for God in a special way are also consecrated. For example, churches and altars are consecrated for use in liturgy. In the same way, bishops are consecrated as they receive the fullness of the Sacrament of Holy Orders. [consagración]

contrition the sorrow we feel when we know that we have sinned, followed by the decision not to sin again. Contrition is the most important part of our celebration of the Sacrament of Penance and Reconciliation. [contrición]

conversion the change of heart that directs each person away from sin and toward God [conversión]

Corporal Works of Mercy kind acts by which we help our neighbors with their everyday material needs. Corporal Works of Mercy include feeding the hungry, finding a home for the homeless, clothing the naked, visiting the sick and those in prison, giving alms to the poor, and burying the dead. [obras corporales de misericordia]

Covenant a solemn agreement between people or between people and God. God made covenants with humanity through agreements with Noah, Abraham, and Moses. These covenants offered Salvation. God's new and final covenant was established through Jesus' life, Death, Resurrection, and Ascension. [alianza]

covet the excessive desire to possess something of value belonging to another person to the point of letting envy destroy the relationship [codiciar]

creation God's act of making everything that exists outside himself. Creation is everything that exists. God said that all of reation is good. [creación]

Creator God, who made everything that is and whom we can come to know through everything he created [Creador]

creed a brief summary of what people believe. The Apostles' Creed is a summary of Christian beliefs. [credo]

crosier the staff carried by a bishop. This staff shows that the bishop cares for us in the same way that a shepherd cares for his sheep. It also reminds us that he represents Jesus, the Good Shepherd. [báculo]

D

deacon a man ordained through the Sacrament of Holy Orders to help the bishop and priests in the work of the Church [diácono]

diocese the members of the Church in a particular area, gathered under the leadership of a bishop [diócesis]

disciple a person who has accepted Jesus' message and tries to live as Jesus did [discípulo]

discipleship for Christians, the willingness to answer the call to follow Jesus. The call is received in Baptism, nourished in the Eucharist, and practiced in service to the world. [discipulado]

Dismissal the part of the Mass in which the people are sent forth by the priest or deacon to do good works and praise and bless God [despedida]

Divine Praises a series of praises beginning with "Blessed be God," traditionally prayed at the end of the worship of the Blessed Sacrament in benediction [alabanzas de desagravio]

E

Easter the celebration of the bodily raising of Jesus Christ from the dead. Easter is the most important Christian feast. [Pascua]

Emmanuel a name from the Old Testament that means "God with us." Because Jesus is always with us, we often call him by the name *Emmanuel*. [Emanuel]

envy a feeling of resentment or sadness because someone has a quality, a talent, or a possession that we want. Envy is one of the seven capital sins, and it is contrary to the Tenth Commandment. [envidia]

Epiphany the day on which we celebrate the visit of the Magi to Jesus after his birth. This is the day that Jesus was revealed as the Savior of the whole world. [Epifanía]

epistle a letter written by Saint Paul or another leader to a group of Christians in the early Church. Twenty-one of the 27 books of the New Testament are epistles. [epístola]

eternal life living happily with God in Heaven when we die in grace and friendship with him [vida eterna]

Eucharist the sacrament in which we give thanks to God for the consecrated Bread and Wine that is the Body and Blood of Jesus Christ. This sacrament brings us into union with Jesus Christ and his saving Death and Resurrection. [Eucaristía]

Evangelists the four men credited with writing the Gospels of Matthew, Mark, Luke, and John [evangelista]

examination of conscience the act of prayerfully thinking about what we have said or done that may have hurt our relationship with God or with others. An examination of conscience is an important part of preparing to celebrate the Sacrament of Penance and Reconciliation. [examen de conciencia]

F

faith a gift of God that helps us to believe in him and live as he wants us to live. We express our faith in the words of the Apostles' Creed. [fe]

fasting limiting the amount we eat for a period of time to express sorrow for sin and to make ourselves more aware of God's action in our lives [ayuno]

forgiveness the willingness to be kind to people who have hurt us but have then said that they are sorry. Because God always forgives us when we say that we are sorry, we forgive others in the same way. [perdón]

fortitude the strength to do the right thing even when that is difficult. Fortitude is one of the four central human virtues, called the cardinal virtues, by which we guide our Christian life. It is also one of the Gifts of the Holy Spirit. [fortaleza]

free will our ability to choose to do good because God has made us like him [libre albedrío]

Fruits of the Holy Spirit the ways in which we act because God is alive in us [frutos del Espíritu Santo]

G

genuflect to show respect in church by touching a knee to the ground, especially when we are before the Blessed Sacrament in the tabernacle [genuflexión, hacer la]

gestures the movements we make, such as the Sign of the Cross or bowing, to show our reverence during prayer [gestos]

gift of peace the peace that Jesus gives to us that flows from his relationship with his Father. This is the peace that the world cannot give, for it is the gift of Salvation that only Jesus can give. [don de la paz]

God the Father, Son, and Holy Spirit: one God in three distinct Persons. God created us, saves us, and lives in us. [Dios]

godparent a witness to Baptism who helps the baptized person follow the path of Christian life [padrino/madrina de Bautismo]

Gospel the good news of God's mercy and love. We experience this news in the story of Jesus' life, Death, Resurrection, and Ascension. The story is presented to us in four books in the New Testament: the Gospels of Matthew, Mark, Luke, and John. [Evangelio]

grace the gift from God given to us without our deserving it. Sanctifying grace fills us with God's life and enables us always to be his friends. Grace also helps us to live as God wants us to live. [gracia]

Great Commandment Jesus' essential teaching that we are to love both God and our neighbor as we love ourselves [Mandamiento Mayor, el]

guardian angel the angel who has been appointed to pray for and help the person live a holy life [ángel de la guarda]

H

Heaven the life with God that is full of happiness and never ends [cielo]

holy one of the four Marks of the Church. It is the kind of life we live when we share in the life of God, who is all holiness. The Church is holy because of her union with Jesus Christ. [santa]

Holy Communion the consecrated Bread and Wine that we receive at Mass, which is truly the Body and Blood of Jesus Christ. It brings us into union with Jesus Christ and his saving Death and Resurrection. [Sagrada Comunión]

Holy Days of Obligation the principal feast days, other than Sundays, of the Church. On Holy Days of Obligation, we celebrate the great things that God has done for us through Jesus Christ and the saints. [días de precepto]

Holy Family the family made up of Jesus; his mother, Mary; and his foster father, Joseph [Sagrada Familia]

Holy Orders the sacrament through which the mission, or task, given by Jesus to his apostles continues in the Church. Holy Orders has three degrees: deacon, priest, and bishop. [sacramento del Orden]

Holy Spirit the third Person of the Trinity, who is sent to us as our helper, and, through Baptism and Confirmation, fills us with God's life [Espíritu Santo]

Holy Thursday the Thursday of Holy Week on which the Mass of the Lord's Supper is celebrated, commemorating the institution of the Eucharist. The season of Lent ends with the celebration of the Mass of the Lord's Supper. [Jueves Santo]

holy water the water that has been blessed and is used as a sacramental to remind us of our Baptism [agua bendita]

Holy Week the celebration of the events surrounding Jesus' establishment of the Eucharist, his suffering, Death, and Resurrection. Holy Week commemorates Jesus' triumphal entry into Jerusalem on Palm Sunday, the gift of himself in the Eucharist on Holy Thursday, his Death on Good Friday, and his Resurrection at the Easter Vigil on Holy Saturday. [Semana Santa]

Homily an explanation of God's Word. The Homily explains the Word of God that we hear in the Bible readings at church. [homilía]

honor giving God or a person the respect that they are owed. God is given this respect as our Creator and Redeemer. All people are worthy of respect as children of God. [honrar]

hope the trust that God will always be with us. We also trust that he will make us happy now and help us to live in a way that keeps us with him forever. [esperanza]

I

idolatry in the Bible, the false, pagan worship of physical images given adoration as gods. For Christians today idolatry occurs whenever someone honors and reveres something in place of God. This can mean giving honor to power, pleasure, race, ancestors, money, or the state rather than giving God the honor owed to him. [idolatría]

J

Jesus the Son of God, who was born of the Virgin Mary and who died, was raised from the dead, and ascended into Heaven so that we can live with God forever. *Jesus* means "God saves." [Jesús]

Joseph the foster father of Jesus, who was engaged to Mary when the angel announced that Mary would have a child through the power of the Holy Spirit [José]

justice the strong, firm desire to give to God and others what is due them. Justice is one of the four central human virtues, called the cardinal virtues, by which we guide our Christian life. [justicia]

K

Kingdom of God God's rule over us. We experience the Kingdom of God in part now, and we will experience it fully in Heaven. The Kingdom of God was announced in the Gospel and is present in the Eucharist. [reino de Dios]

L

Lamb of God the title for Jesus that emphasizes his willingness to give up his life for the Salvation of the world. Jesus is the Lamb without blemish or sin who delivers us through his sacrificial Death. [cordero de Dios]

Last Supper the last meal Jesus ate with his disciples on the night before he died. At the Last Supper, Jesus took bread and wine, blessed them, and said that they were his Body and Blood. Every Mass is a remembrance of this last meal. [Última Cena]

Lectionary for Mass the book that contains all the Bible stories we read at Mass [Leccionario]

Lent six weeks during which we prepare to celebrate, with special prayers and action, the rising of Jesus from the dead at Easter. Jesus rose from the dead to save us. [Cuaresma]

Light of the World a name that helps us to see that Jesus is the light that leads us to the Father. Jesus lights up our minds and hearts with knowledge of God. [luz del mundo]

liturgical year the calendar that tells us when to celebrate the feasts of Jesus' birth, life, Death, Resurrection, and Ascension [año litúrgico]

liturgy the public prayer of the Church that celebrates the wonderful things God has done for us in Jesus Christ [liturgia]

Liturgy of the Eucharist a main part of the Mass in which the bread and wine are consecrated and truly become the Body and Blood of Jesus Christ. We then receive the Body and Blood of Jesus Christ in Holy Communion. [Liturgia de la Eucaristía]

Liturgy of the Word a main part of the Mass in which we listen to God's Word from the Bible and consider what it means for us today [Liturgia de la Palabra]

M

Magnificat Mary's song of praise to God for the great things he has done for her and for his plans for us through Jesus [Magníficat]

Marks of the Church the four most important characteristics of the Church. The Church is one, holy, catholic, and apostolic. [atributos de la Iglesia]

Mary the mother of Jesus. She is called blessed and "full of grace" because God chose her to be the mother of the Son of God. [María]

Mass the most important sacramental celebration of the Church. The celebration of the Mass was established by Jesus at the Last Supper as a remembrance of his Death and Resurrection. At Mass we listen to God's Word from the Bible and receive Jesus Christ in the consecrated Bread and Wine that are his Body and Blood. [misa]

Matrimony a solemn agreement between a woman and a man to be partners for life, both for their own good and for raising children. Marriage is a sacrament when the agreement is properly made between baptized Christians. [Matrimonio]

mercy the gift to be able to respond to those in need with care and compassion. The gift of mercy is a grace given to us by Jesus Christ. [misericordia]

Messiah a title that means "anointed with oil." It is from a Hebrew word that means the same thing as the Greek word *Christ*, the name given to Jesus after the Resurrection. [Mesías]

ministry service or work done for others. Ministry is also done by bishops, priests, and deacons in the celebration of the sacraments. All those baptized are called to different kinds of ministry in the liturgy and in service to the needs of others. [ministerio]

miracle the healing of a person, or an occasion when nature is controlled that can only be recognized as God's action [milagro]

mission the work of Jesus Christ that is continued in the Church through the Holy Spirit. The mission of the Church is to proclaim Salvation through Jesus' life, Death, Resurrection, and Ascension. [misión]

monastery a place where men or women live out their solemn promises of poverty, chastity, and obedience. They live a stable, or firm, community life; they spend their days in public prayer, work, and meditation. [monasterio]

moral choice a choice to do what is right. We make moral choices because they help us grow closer to God. We make them also because we have the freedom to choose what is right and to avoid what is wrong. [opción moral]

moral law a rule for living that has been established by God and people in authority who are concerned about the good of all people. Moral laws are based on God's direction to us to do what is right and avoid what is wrong. [ley moral]

mortal sin a decision to turn away from God by doing something that we know is seriously wrong and so cuts us off from God's life [pecado mortal]

Mystical Body of Christ the members of the Church formed into a spiritual body and bound together by the life communicated by Jesus Christ through the sacraments. Christ is the center of this body and the source of its life. In it we are all united. Each member of this body receives from Christ gifts fitting for him or her. [Cuerpo Místico de Cristo]

N

Nativity scene a picture or crèche that shows Jesus, Mary, and Joseph in the stable after the birth of Jesus as described in the Gospels of Matthew and Luke [escena de la Natividad del Señor]

neighbor according to Jesus, every person, as each person is made in God's image. We are meant to form mutually supportive relationships with our neighbors. [prójimo]

New Testament the 27 books of the second part of the Bible, which tell of the teaching, ministry, and saving events of the life of Jesus. The four Gospels present Jesus' life, Death, and Resurrection. The Acts of the Apostles tells the story of Jesus' Ascension into Heaven. It also shows how Jesus' message of Salvation spread through the growth of the Church. Various letters instruct us in how to live as followers of Jesus Christ. The Book of Revelation offers encouragement to Christians living through persecution. [Nuevo Testamento]

O

obedience the act of willingly following what God asks us to do for our Salvation. The Fourth Commandment requires children to obey their parents, and all people are required to obey civil authority when it acts for the good of all. [obediencia]

obey follow the teachings or directions given by God or by someone who has authority over us [obedecer]

oil of the sick the oil blessed by the bishop during Holy Week and used in the Sacrament of the Anointing of the Sick, which brings spiritual and, if it is God's will, physical healing [óleo de los enfermos]

Old Testament the first 46 books of the Bible, which tell of God's Covenant with the people of Israel and his plan for the Salvation of all people. The first five books are known as the Torah. The Old Testament is fulfilled in the New Testament, but God's Covenant presented in the Old Testament has permanent value and has never been revoked or set aside. [Antiguo Testamento]

one one of the four Marks of the Church. The Church is one because of its source in the one God and because of its founder, Jesus Christ. Jesus, through his Death on the cross, united all to God in one body. Within the unity of the Church, there is great diversity because of the variety of the gifts given to its members. [una]

ordained those men who have received the Sacrament of Holy Orders so that they may preside at the celebration of the Eucharist and serve as leaders and teachers of the Church [ordenado]

Ordinary Time the longest liturgical season of the Church year. It is divided into two periods—the first after the Christmas season and the second after Pentecost. The first period focuses on Jesus' childhood and public ministry. The second period focuses on Christ's reign as King of Kings. [Tiempo Ordinario]

Original Sin the result of the sin by which the first human beings disobeyed God and chose to follow their own will rather than God's will. Because of this act, all human beings lost the original blessing that God had intended, and they became subject to sin and death. In Baptism we are restored to life with God through Jesus Christ. [pecado original]

P

Palm Sunday the celebration of Jesus' triumphant entry into Jerusalem on the Sunday before Easter. It begins a week-long commemoration of the saving events of Holy Week. [Domingo de Ramos]

parable one of the stories that Jesus told to show us what the Kingdom of God is like. Parables present images, or scenes, drawn from everyday life. These images show us the radical, or serious, choice we make when we respond to the invitation to enter the Kingdom of God. [parábola]

parish a community of believers in Jesus Christ who meet regularly in a specific area to worship God under the leadership of a pastor [parroquia]

Paschal Mystery the work of Salvation accomplished by Jesus Christ through his Passion, Death, Resurrection, and Ascension. The Paschal Mystery is celebrated in the liturgy of the Church. We experience its saving effects in the sacraments. [Misterio Pascual]

pastor a priest who is responsible for the spiritual care of the members of a parish community [pastor]

peacemaker a person who teaches us to be respectful in our words and actions toward one another [paz, los que trabajar por la]

penance the turning away from sin with a desire to change our life and more closely live the way God wants us to live. We express our penance externally by praying, fasting, and helping those who are poor. This is also the name of the action that the priest asks us to take or the prayers that he asks us to pray after he absolves us in the Sacrament of Penance and Reconciliation. (*See* Sacrament of Penance and Reconciliation.) [penitencia]

Pentecost the 50th day after Jesus was raised from the dead. On this day the Holy Spirit was sent from Heaven, and the Church was born. [Pentecostés]

People of God another name for the Church. In the same way that the people of Israel were God's people through the Covenant he made with them, the Church is a priestly, prophetic, and royal people through the new and eternal covenant in Jesus Christ. [pueblo de Dios]

personal sin a sin we choose to commit, whether serious (mortal) or less serious (venial). Although the result of Original Sin is to leave us with a tendency to sin, God's grace, especially through the sacraments, helps us to choose good over sin. [pecado personal]

petition a request of God, asking him to fulfill a need. When we share in God's saving love, we understand that every need is one that we can ask God to help us with through petition. [petición]

plague a natural calamity or disease that is seen as being inflicted by God as a remedial event to make people more conscious of their duties toward God and one another. (Numbers 14:37) In Exodus 7:14—12:30, the plagues inflicted on the Egyptians are seen as the means by which God convinced the Egyptians to free the Hebrew people from slavery. [plaga]

pope the bishop of Rome, successor of Saint Peter, and leader of the Roman Catholic Church. Because he has the authority to act in the name of Christ, the pope is called the Vicar of Christ. The pope and all of the bishops together make up the living, teaching office of the Church, the Magisterium. [Papa]

praise the expression of our response to God, not only for what he does, but simply because he is. In the Eucharist the whole Church joins with Jesus Christ in expressing praise and thanksgiving to the Father. [alabanza]

prayer the raising of our hearts and minds to God. We are able to speak to and listen to God in prayer because he teaches us how to do so. [oración]

Precepts of the Church those positive requirements that the pastoral authority of the Church has determined as necessary. These requirements describe the minimum effort we must make in prayer and the moral life. The Precepts of the Church ensure that all Catholics move beyond the minimum by growing in love of God and love of neighbor. [preceptos de la Iglesia]

pride a false image of ourselves that goes beyond what we deserve as God's creation. Pride puts us in competition with God. It is one of the seven capital sins. [soberbia]

priest a man who has accepted God's special call to serve the Church by guiding it and building it up through the celebration of the sacraments [sacerdote]

prudence the virtue that directs us toward the good. It also helps us to choose the correct means to achieve that good. Prudence is one of the cardinal virtues that guide our conscience and influence us to live according to the law of Christ. [prudencia]

psalm a prayer in the form of a poem. Psalms were written to be sung in public worship. Each psalm expresses an aspect, or feature, of the depth of human prayer. Over several centuries 150 psalms were gathered to form the Book of Psalms, used in worship in the Old Testament. [salmo]

R

reconciliation the renewal of friendship after that friendship has been broken by some action or lack of action. In the Sacrament of Penance and Reconciliation, through God's mercy and forgiveness, we are reconciled with God, the Church, and others. [reconciliación]

Redeemer Jesus Christ, whose life, Death on the cross, Resurrection from the dead, and Ascension into Heaven set us free from sin and brings us redemption [Redentor]

redemption our being set free from sin through the life, Death on the cross, Resurrection from the dead, and Ascension into Heaven of Jesus Christ [redención]

repentance our turning away from sin with a desire to change our lives and live more closely as God wants us to live. We express our penance externally by prayer, fasting, and helping those who are poor. [arrepentimiento]

Resurrection the bodily raising of Jesus Christ from the dead on the third day after his Death on the cross. The Resurrection is the crowning truth of our faith. [Resurrección]

Revelation God's communication of himself to us through the words and deeds he has used throughout history. Revelation shows us the mystery of his plan for our Salvation in his Son, Jesus Christ. [revelación]

rite one of the many forms followed in celebrating liturgy in the Church. A rite may differ according to the culture or country where it is celebrated. *Rite* also means "the special form for celebrating each sacrament." [rito]

Rosary a prayer in honor of the Blessed Virgin Mary. When we pray the Rosary, we meditate on the mysteries of Jesus Christ's life while praying the Hail Mary on five sets of ten beads and the Lord's Prayer on the beads in between. [Rosario]

S

sacrament one of seven ways through which God's life enters our lives through the work of the Holy Spirit. Jesus gave us three sacraments that bring us into the Church: Baptism, Confirmation, and the Eucharist. He gave us two sacraments that bring us healing: Penance and Reconciliation and Anointing of the Sick. He also gave us two sacraments that help members serve the community: Matrimony and Holy Orders. [sacramento]

sacramental an object, a prayer, or a blessing given by the Church to help us grow in our spiritual life [sacramental]

Sacrament of Penance and Reconciliation the sacrament in which we celebrate God's forgiveness of our sins and our reconciliation with God and the Church. Penance includes sorrow for the sins we have committed, confession of sins, absolution by the priest, and doing the penance that shows our sorrow. [sacramento de la Penitencia y de la Reconciliación]

Sacraments of Initiation the sacraments that are the foundation of our Christian life. We are born anew in Baptism, strengthened by Confirmation, and receive in the Eucharist the food of eternal life. [sacramentos de iniciación]

Sacrifice of the Mass the sacrifice of Jesus on the cross, which is remembered and made present in the Eucharist [Sacrificio de la Misa]

saint a holy person who has died united with God. The Church has said that this person is now with God forever in Heaven. [santo]

Salvation the gift of forgiveness of sin and the restoration of friendship with God. God alone can give us Salvation. [salvación]

Savior Jesus, the Son of God, who became man to forgive our sins and restore our friendship with God. *Jesus* means "God saves." [Salvador]

Scriptures the holy writings of Jews and Christians collected in the Old and New Testaments of the Bible [Sagrada Escritura]

seal of confession the obligation on the part of the priest not to reveal what he has heard in the Sacrament of Penance and Reconciliation under any circumstances [sigilo sacramental]

Sermon on the Mount the words of Jesus, written in Chapters 5 through 7 of the Gospel of Matthew, in which Jesus reveals how he has fulfilled God's Law given to Moses. The Sermon on the Mount begins with the eight Beatitudes and includes the Lord's Prayer. [Sermón de la montaña]

Sign of Peace the part of the Mass in which we offer a gesture of peace to one another as we prepare to receive Holy Communion [rito de la paz]

Sign of the Cross the gesture that we make that signifies our belief in God the Father, the Son, and the Holy Spirit [señal de la cruz]

sin a choice we make that offends God and hurts our relationships with others. Some sin is mortal and needs to be confessed in the Sacrament of Penance and Reconciliation. Other sin is venial, or less serious. [pecado]

sloth a carelessness of heart that leads a person to ignore his or her development as a person, especially spiritual development and a relationship with God. Sloth is one of the seven capital sins, and it is contrary to the First Commandment. [pereza]

solidarity the principle that all people exist in equal dignity as children of God. Therefore, individuals are called to commit themselves to working for the common good in sharing material and spiritual goods. [solidaridad]

Son of God the title revealed by Jesus that indicates his unique relationship to God the Father [Hijo de Dios]

soul the part of us that makes us human and an image of God. Body and soul together form one unique human nature. The soul is responsible for our consciousness and for our freedom. [alma]

Spiritual Works of Mercy the kind acts through which we help our neighbors meet needs that are more than material. The Spiritual Works of Mercy include instructing, advising, consoling, comforting, forgiving, and bearing wrongs with patience. [obras esprituales de misericordia]

T

tabernacle a container in which the Blessed Sacrament is kept so that Holy Communion can be taken to those who are sick and dying [sagrario]

temperance the cardinal virtue that helps us to control our attraction to pleasure so that our natural desires are kept within proper limits. This moral virtue helps us choose to use created goods in moderation. [templanza]

Temple the Temple in Jerusalem, the most important place where the Jewish people came to pray. They believed that this was the place where they could be closest to God. Jesus often came to pray in the Temple. [Templo, judío]

temptation an attraction, from outside us or from inside us, that can lead us to not follow God's commands [tentación]

Ten Commandments the ten rules that God gave to Moses on Mount Sinai that sum up God's Law and show us what is required to love God and our neighbor [Diez Mandamientos]

Theological Virtues those virtues given to us by God, not by human effort. They are faith, hope, and charity. [virtudes teologales]

Torah the Hebrew word for "instruction" or "law." It is also the name of the first five books of the Old Testament: Genesis, Exodus, Leviticus, Numbers, and Deuteronomy. [Torá]

transubstantiation when the bread and wine become the Body and Blood of Jesus Christ. When the priest speaks the words of consecration, the substance of the bread and wine is changed into the substance of Christ's Body and Blood. [transubstanciación]

trespasses unlawful acts committed against the property or rights of another person, or acts that physically harm a person [ofensas]

Trinity the mystery of one God existing in three Persons: the Father, the Son, and the Holy Spirit [Trinidad]

U

universal Church the entire Church as it exists throughout the world. The people of every diocese, along with their bishops and the pope, make up the universal Church. [Iglesia universal]

V

venial sin a choice we make that weakens our relationship with God or with others. It wounds and diminishes the divine life in us. [pecado venial]

Vicar of Christ the title given to the pope who, as the successor of Saint Peter, has the authority to act in Christ's place. A vicar is someone who stands in for and acts for another. [Vicario de Cristo]

virtue an attitude or a way of acting that helps us do good [virtud]

Visitation Mary's visit to Elizabeth to share the good news that Mary is to be the mother of Jesus. Elizabeth's greeting of Mary forms part of the Hail Mary. During this visit Mary sings the Magnificat, her praise of God. [Visitación]

vocation the call each of us has in life to be the person God wants us to be. Our vocation is also the way we serve the Church and the Kingdom of God. Each of us can live out his or her vocation as a layperson, as a member of a religious community, or as a member of the clergy. [vocación]

W

witness the passing on to others, by our words and by our actions, the faith that we have been given. Every Christian has the duty to give witness to the good news about Jesus Christ that he or she has come to know. [testimonio]

worship the adoration and honor given to God in public prayer [culto]

Index

A

Abba, 16, 253
absolution, 211, 253
Act of Contrition, 102, 189
Acts of the Apostles, 92, 255, 262
Advent, 57–60, 152, 153–56, 236, 253. *See also* Christmas
Agony in the Garden, 197
All Saints Day, 152, 177–80, 253
All Souls Day, 152, 177–80, 253
"All You Works of God" (song), 220–21
Alleluia, 253
almsgiving, 118, 253
altar, 209, 253
altar server, 208
ambo, 208, 253
Amen, 253
Andrew Kim Taegon, Saint, 113
angel, 154, 157, 158, 240, 253, 258
Angelus, 253
Annunciation, 83, 84, 196, 253
Anointing of the Sick, Sacrament of the, 202, 253, 262
apostle, 4, 49, 52, 92, 148, 253. *See also* specific apostles
  chosen, 46–47, 238
  mission of, 234
Apostles' Creed, 4, 6, 24, 53, 54, 72, 83, 191, 194, 254
apostolic, 71, 254
Ascension, 147, 149, 197, 254
Ash Wednesday, 117, 161, 162, 254
Assumption of Mary, 197
Augustine, Saint, 121, 122, 125

B

Baptism, Sacrament of, 77, 94, 95, 101, 200, 242, 254
  of Jesus in River Jordan, 196
  of the Lord, 87
  of Paul, 92
  symbol of, 247
Beatitudes, 214, 254, 266
belonging, 94
Benedict, Saint, 31, 32, 232
Bethlehem, 88, 158
Bible, 184, 254. *See also* New Testament
  Gospels, 46
bishop, 71, 254
Blessed Sacrament, 254, 267
blessing, 231, 244, 254
Body and Blood of Christ, 95, 108, 201, 207, 254, 267. *See also* Eucharist, Sacrament of the
bread and wine, 95, 106, 107, 254
Bread of Life, 90, 254
Breaking of the Bread, 149

C

cantor, 209
capital sin, 254, 257. *See also* sin
cardinal virtues, temperance as, 267
caring for others, 136, 137, 142, 229. *See also* charity; moral choice
Carrying of the Cross, 197
cast lots, 255
catholic, 71, 255
Catholic Church, 69–74
celebrant, 255
celebrate, 255
chalice, 209
charity, 125, 126, 247, 255
chasuble, 209, 255
Christ, 22, 28, 255. *See also* Jesus
Christian, 255
Christmas, 57, 87–90, 152, 157–60, 241, 255. *See also* Advent
  meaning, 88
  symbols of, 159
Church, the, 255
  apostolic, 71
  built through Holy Spirit, 65
  Catholic Church, 69–74
  leaders of, 70, 238
  Marks of, 71
  Mother of, 82
  as People of God, 94
  Precepts of, 264
  universal, 267
Collect Prayer, 204
"Come, O Holy Spirit/Wa Wa Wa Emimimo" (song), 222
commandment, 133, 255. *See also* Ten Commandments
  Great Commandment, 213, 258
  new commandment, 213
Communion, 17, 149. *See also* Eucharist, Sacrament of the; Holy Communion
  First Holy, 76
  receiving, 207
  Rite, 206
Communion of Saints, 82, 178, 179, 255
community, 28, 231, 255
  loving, 216
compassion, 255
confession, 101, 211, 256. *See also* Penance and Reconciliation, Sacrament of
  seal of, 266

Confirmation, Sacrament of, 95, 201, 256
conscience, 210, 256
examination of, 257
consecration, 256
contrition, 102, 256
convent, 232
conversion, 41, 256
Corinth, 235
Coronation of Mary, 197
Corporal Works of Mercy, 256
Covenant, 256, 262
covet, 256
creation, 227, 256
beauty of, 141
caring for, 142
caring for our planet, 250
goodness of, 3–8
loving, 7, 217
praise for, 145
praising God for, 5
Creator, 256. *See also* God
creed, 4, 256. *See also* Apostles' Creed
crosier, 256
cross, 77
carrying of the, 197
processional, 208
Sign of the Cross, 10, 12, 83, 186
Stations of the Cross, 165, 167, 198–99
as symbol, 247
taking up, 166
Crowning with Thorns, 197
crucifix, 77, 83, 194
Crucifixion, 166, 197, 246

D

deacon, 209, 257
devil, 130, 248
dignity, 216
diocese, 257
disciple, 234, 251, 257
gathering, 45–50
Holy Spirit, strengthened by, 64, 100
Jesus' gifts to, 100
spread God's love, 234
discipleship, 257
Dismissal, 143, 245, 257
Divine Praises, 257
doves, as religious symbol, 237, 247

E

earth, taking care of, 250
Easter, 65, 94, 117, 147–50, 152, 169–72, 246, 251, 257
Easter Vigil, 147, 162
Elizabeth, 83, 84, 240
Elizabeth of Hungary, Saint, 228
Emmanuel, 22, 257. *See also* Jesus
Entrance Chant, 204
envy, 257
Ephesians, Letter to the, 96
Epiphany, Feast of the, 87, 152, 241, 257
epistle, 106, 257
eternal life, 257
Eucharist, Sacrament of the, 95, 201, 244, 257
celebrating, 82, 105–10
Institution of the, 196
Jesus Christ's presence in, 171
Last Supper, 107
Liturgy of the, 206, 260
Paul's epistle, 106
Eucharistic Prayer, 107
Evangelist, 257
examination of conscience, 210, 257. *See also* Penance and Reconciliation, Sacrament of
extraordinary minister of Holy Communion, 208

F

40, as symbolic number, 119
fables, 33
faith, 124, 125, 126, 258
celebrating, 200–203
Profession of, 205
symbol of, 247
Faithful, Prayer of the, 205
family
loving, 216
peaceful, 139
praying for, 138
relationship with, 210
fasting, 161, 246, 258
feast days, 27, 82. *See also* specific saints
Feast of the Baptism of the Lord, 87
Finding of Jesus in the Temple, 83, 84, 196
First Holy Communion, 76. *See also* Eucharist, Sacrament of the
forgiveness, 17, 19, 20, 100, 101, 102, 103, 229, 243, 258
fortitude, 258
Frederic Ozanam, Blessed, 142, 143
free will, 258
friendship, 229, 234
mercy of, 148
Fruits of the Holy Spirit, 67, 215, 258. *See also* Holy Spirit

G

Gabriel, 84, 154, 240
Galilee, 154
genuflect, 258
gestures, 258
gift of peace, 258
gifts from God, 79, 88, 112–13, 114, 174, 227, 231, 241, 245
Gloria, 204

Glorious Mysteries, 197
Glory Be to the Father, 11, 83, 187, 194
God, 258. *See also* Holy Spirit; Jesus
- choosing, 41
- Creator, 227, 250
- Father of all, 15–20
- gifts from, 79, 88, 112–13
- Kingdom of, 34, 35, 79, 196, 232, 234, 260
- knowing, 7
- Lamb of, 149, 206, 260
- Lord, 52
- love for us, 26, 178, 228, 231
- obeying, 131
- praising, 5
- praying to, 185, 233
- relationship with, 210
- serving, 111
- signs of, 75
- Son of, 241
- speaks through Bible, 184
- trusting, 22
- Word of, 234, 243

godparent, 258
good choices, 215
Good Friday, 117
Gospel, 46, 156, 184, 205, 235, 257, 258, 262
grace, 77, 94, 258
Greeting, 204
guardian angel, 258

H

Hail, Holy Queen, 192, 194
Hail Mary, 83, 187, 194, 240
Healing, Sacraments of, 202
Heaven, 170, 179, 258
"Here I Am, God" (song), 219
holy, 178, 259
Holy Communion, 17, 76, 109, 171, 201, 239, 244, 259. *See also* Eucharist, Sacrament of the
- extraordinary minister of, 208

Holy Days of Obligation, 109, 207, 259
Holy Family, 259
"Holy Is Your Name" (song), 223
Holy Orders, Sacrament of, 112, 203, 259, 263
Holy Saturday, 117, 147
Holy Spirit, 237, 259. *See also* God; Jesus
- Church, builds, 65
- Coming of the, 197
- Fruits of the, 67, 215
- gifts of, 95, 112, 115
- guides us, 162, 237
- helps us, 174
- Jesus sends, 63–68
- living with others, 136
- Prayer to the, 66
- presence at Pentecost, 152, 173
- present in sacraments, 76
- symbols of, 237, 247

Holy Thursday, 117, 259
holy water, 77, 259
Holy Week, 117–20, 152, 165–68, 259
Homily, 205, 259
honor, 259
hope, 124, 126, 259

I

"I Say 'Yes,' Lord/Digo 'Si,' Señor" (song), 224
idolatry, 259
Ignatius of Loyola, Saint, 1, 2
Initiation, Sacraments of, 93–98, 200, 254, 266
Institution of the Eucharist, 196
Introductory Rites, 204

J

Jeanne Jugan, Saint, 127
Jerusalem, 167, 242
Jesus, 260. *See also* Resurrection
- birth, 57, 84, 87–90, 153, 154, 157, 236, 241
- Bread of Life, 90
- Death and Resurrection, 51–56, 117, 251
- events in life, 84
- examples for living, 25
- following, 39–44, 48, 49
- gathering disciples, 45–50
- God's love, revelation of, 16
- imitation of, 107
- love for all, 13, 35
- Mary, love for, 82
- mission of, 65
- name, meaning of, 22, 230
- presence at Mass, 76, 107
- rich young man, encounter with, 40
- Roman officer and, 239
- sacraments, presence in, 76
- Savior, 22
- serving others and, 178
- Son of God, 26
- teaches us to pray, 17
- in the Temple, 84
- temptation in the desert, 248
- thanking for the sacraments, 78, 108
- Transfiguration, 196
- in the wilderness, 246
- wind from heaven and, 64
- with us, 21–26, 52

John, Gospel of, 178, 230
John Paul II, Pope, 196
Joseph, Saint, 22, 158, 260
Joyful Mysteries, 196
joyfulness, 249
Judas, 255
justice, 136, 260

K

Katharine Drexel, Saint, 61, 62, 237
kindness, 13, 34, 35

Kingdom of God, 34, 35, 79, 232, 260
Proclamation of the, 196, 234

L

Lamb of God, 149, 206, 260
Last Supper, 107, 201, 260. *See also* Eucharist, Sacrament of the
Lectionary for Mass, 260
lector, 209
Lent, 117–20, 152, 161–64, 246, 260
Lenten calendar, 163
Leo XIII, Pope, 62
Light of the World, 260
listening, 23
Little Sisters of the Poor, 127
liturgical calendar, 82, 151
liturgical year, 27, 57, 152, 260
liturgy, 260
Liturgy of the Eucharist, 206, 260
Liturgy of the Word, 205, 260
Lord, 52. *See also* Jesus
Lord's Day, 109, 171, 204–5, 231
Lord's Prayer, 18, 83, 186, 194, 206, 229, 266
lots, casting, 255
Louise de Marillac, Saint, 137
love, 247
demonstrating toward others, 35, 107, 131, 178, 233
sharing God's, 228, 231
Luke, Gospel of, 46, 156, 248
Luminous Mysteries, 196

M

Magi, 87, 241
Magisterium, 264
Magnificat, 85, 260
Marks of the Church, 71, 254, 261, 262. *See also* Church, the
marriage. *See* Matrimony, Sacrament of
Mary, 81–86, 261. *See also* Magnificat; Visitation
Assumption of, 197
blessed by God, 240
celebrating, 83
Coronation of, 197
at Crucifixion, 198
events in life, 84
Jesus' birth, 22, 153, 154, 158
mother of Jesus, 240
mother to all, 82
song of praise, 85
Mary Magdalene, 170, 171, 251
Mass, 71, 208–9, 244, 261
Advent, 59
Bible readings during, 184
Christmas, 87, 88, 89
Dismissal, 143, 245
Easter, 94, 149
importance of, 261
Jesus Christ's presence at, 76, 107
Lent and Holy Week, 119
Order of, The, 204
in Ordinary Time, 29
sign of peace, 41
Sign of the Cross, 10
Matrimony, Sacrament of, 113, 203, 261
Matthew, 230
medals, 77
mercy, 148, 261
Messiah, 158, 238, 261. *See also* Jesus
ministry, 261
miracle, 261
mission, 50, 65, 234, 239, 261
missionaries, 62
monastery, 32, 38, 232, 261
Monica, Saint, 121, 122, 124
monks, 232
Monserrat, 2
moral choices, 129–34, 143, 261
moral law, 131, 261
Morning Offering, 132, 190
mortal sin, 101, 261. *See also* sin
Moses, 233
Mother of God, 82, 240, 261. *See also* Mary
Mother of the Church, 82, 240. *See also* Mary
Mysteries of Light, 196
Mysteries of the Rosary, 83, 194, 196–97. *See also* Rosary
Mystical Body of Christ, 71, 262. *See also* Church, the

N

Nativity, 83, 84, 196
Nativity scene, 262
Nazareth, 35, 154
need, 43
neighbor, 262
loving, 131
relationship with, 210
New Testament, 178, 184, 262

O

obedience, 131, 262
obey, 262
oil of the sick, 262
Old Testament, 184, 262
one, 71, 262
ordained, 263
Ordinary Time, 27–30, 152, 231, 263
Original Sin, 94, 95, 101, 263
Our Father. *See* Lord's Prayer

P

Palm Sunday, 162, 263
parable, 34, 184, 263
  as Jesus' puzzles, 36
  mustard seed, 36, 37
  yeast, 37
parish, 29, 231, 244, 263
Paschal Candle, 208
Paschal Mystery, 52, 53, 263
pastor, 70, 263
paten, 209
Paul, Saint, 91, 92, 106, 124, 235, 245, 249
peace
  family, 139
  forgiveness and, 103
peace, sign of, 41, 206, 266
"Peace Walk" (song), 225
peacemaker, 263
penance, 263. *See also* Penance and Reconciliation, Sacrament of
Penance and Reconciliation, Sacrament of, 100, 101, 103, 202, 211, 256, 265
  peace received through, 211
Penitential Act, 204
Pentecost, 64, 65, 147, 152, 173–76, 263
People of God, 94, 263. *See also* Church, the
personal sin, 101, 264. *See also* sin
Peter, Saint
  chosen, 46, 47
  Jesus' mission and, 234
  keys to the Kingdom of Heaven, 238
  leader of Church, 238
  rock of the Church, 230, 238
petition, 264
Philip, Saint, 242
Pilate, Pontius, 166, 198
plague, 264
poor, remembering those who are, 118, 217
pope, 71, 238, 264. *See also* specific popes
  Vicar of Christ, 70, 264
praise, 5, 145, 264
  song of, 85
prayer, 10, 75–80, 185, 233, 264. *See also* specific prayers
  Advent, 155
  beliefs, 72
  Eucharistic, 107
  for family, 138
  gifts and talents, 114
  how we pray, 185
  Jesus teaches us how, 17
  learning by heart, 186–93
  Lent, 161
  over the offerings, 206
  Rosary, 77, 83, 194–97
  to Trinity, 10, 11
Prayer After Meals, 188
Prayer Before Meals, 188
Prayer for Vocations, 193
Prayer of the Faithful, 205
prayer service, 156, 160, 164, 168, 172, 176, 180
Prayer to the Holy Spirit, 66, 190
Praying the Rosary, 195
Precepts of the Church, 264
Presentation, 83, 84, 196
pride, 264
priest, 209, 264
processional cross, 208
Proclamation of the Kingdom of God, 196
Profession of Faith, 205
prudence, 264
psalm, 184, 264
Psalms, Book of, 184
Purgatory, 179

R

reconciliation, 99–104, 265. *See also* Penance and Reconciliation, Sacrament of
Reconciliation, Sacrament of. *See* Penance and Reconciliation, Sacrament of
Redeemer, 265
redemption, 265
repentance, 265
respect, 143
Resurrection, 51–56, 100, 109, 117, 147, 149, 169–71, 197, 199, 246, 247, 251, 265
Revelation, 265
  Book of, 262
rights and responsibilities, 216
rite, 265
Roman officer, Jesus and, 239
Rosary, 77, 83, 194–97, 265
  Mysteries of the, 196–97
Rules of Benedict, 232

S

sacrament, 71, 97, 200–203, 265
  Anointing of the Sick, 202, 253, 262
  Baptism, 77, 95, 200, 254
  Confirmation, 95, 201, 256
  Eucharist, 76, 82, 95, 105–10, 201, 244, 257
  Healing, 202
  Holy Orders, 112, 203, 259, 263
  Initiation, 93–98, 200, 266
  Jesus Christ's presence in, 76
  Matrimony, 113, 203, 261
  Penance and Reconciliation, 100, 101, 103, 202, 211, 265
  Service of Communion, 203
  thanking Jesus for, 78

sacramental, 77, 97, 265
sacredness of life, 141–46
Sacrifice of the Mass, 149, 266. *See also* Mass
saint, 82, 266. *See also* All Saints Day; specific saints
  Communion of, 178, 179
  in heaven and on earth, 179
  serve Kingdom of God, 232
Salvation, 149, 205, 266
sanctuary lamp, 208
Satan, 162, 248
Savior, 22, 158, 266. *See also* Jesus
Scholastica, Saint, 31, 32, 232
Scourging at the Pillar, 197
Scriptures, 23, 76, 266
seal of confession, 266
Sermon on the Mount, 214, 266
Service of Communion, Sacraments at the, 203
shepherds, 158
Sign of Peace, 41, 206, 266
Sign of the Cross, 10, 12, 83, 186, 194, 266
Simon of Cyrene, 166, 198
sin, 266
  capital, 254
  confession of, 211
  conversion, 41
  forgiving, 100, 103, 243, 251
  mortal, 101, 261
  Original, 94, 95, 101, 263
  personal, 101, 264
  redemption from, 265
  sloth, 266
  venial, 101, 267
Sisters of Charity, 137
Sisters of the Blessed Sacrament, 237
sloth, 266
small wonders, 227
Society of St. Vincent de Paul, 142
solidarity, 217, 266
Son of God, 26, 241, 266. *See also* Jesus
"Song of Love" (song), 218
song of praise, 85
Sorrowful Mysteries, 196, 197
soul, 266
Spiritual Exercises, 2
Spiritual Works of Mercy, 267
Stations of the Cross, 165, 167, 198–99
Stephen, Saint, 92
stole, 209
Sunday, 109, 171
symbolic number, 40 as, 119
symbols
  of Easter, 251
  of Holy Spirit, 237, 247
  of Peter, 238
  of virtues, 247

T

tabernacle, 208, 267
teamwork, 250
temperance, 267
Temple, 267.
temptation, 130, 248, 267
Ten Commandments, 41, 43, 131, 212, 233, 267
Theological Virtues, 267
Thomas, 148
Torah, 262, 267
Tradition, Church, 215
Transfiguration of Jesus, 196
transubstantiation, 267
trespasses, 267
Trinity, 259, 267
  prayer to, 10, 11
  Sign of the Cross, 12
trusting, 22, 23, 39

U

universal Church, 267

V

venial sin, 101, 267. *See also* sin
Veronica, 198
vestments, Christmas, 89
Vicar of Christ, 70, 264, 267. *See also* pope
Vincent de Paul, Saint, 137, 142
virtue, 247, 268
  temperance as cardinal, 267
Visitation, 83, 84, 196, 268
vocation, 112, 268

W

want, and need, 43
Way of the Cross. *See* Stations of the Cross
Wedding Feast, at Cana, 196
"What Does It Mean to Follow Jesus?" (song), 226
Wise Men, 87, 241
witness, 65, 268
Word of God, 234, 243
work and workers, 217
Works of Mercy
  Corporal, 256
  Spiritual, 267
worship, 107, 268. *See also* prayer

Y

yeast, parable, 37

Acknowledgments

Excerpts from the *New American Bible with Revised New Testament and Psalms.* Copyright © 1991, 1986, 1970 Confraternity of Christian Doctrine, Inc., Washington, DC. Used with permission. All rights reserved. No part of the *New American Bible* may be reprinted without permission in writing from the copyright holder.

The English translation of the Act of Contrition from *Rite of Penance* © 1974, International Commission on English in the Liturgy Corporation (ICEL); the English translation of the *Salve, Regina* from *A Book of Prayers* © 1982, ICEL; the English translation of Prayer Before Meals and Prayer After Meals from *Book of Blessings* © 1988; the English translation of the Apostles' Creed from *The Roman Missal* © 2010, ICEL. All rights reserved.

For more information related to the English translation of the *Roman Missal, Third Edition,* see www.loyolapress.com/romanmissal.

Loyola Press has made every effort to locate the copyright holders for the cited works used in this publication and to make full acknowledgment for their use. In the case of any omissions, the publisher will be pleased to make suitable acknowledgments in future editions.

Art and Photography

When there is more than one picture on a page, positions are abbreviated as follows: (t) top, (c) center, (b) bottom, (l) left, (r) right, (bg) background, (bd) border.

Photos and illustrations not acknowledged are either owned by Loyola Press or from royalty-free sources including but not limited to Alamy, Corbis/Veer, Getty Images, Jupiterimages, PunchStock, Thinkstock, and Wikipedia Commons. Loyola Press has made every effort to locate the copyright holders for the cited works used in this publication and to make full acknowledgment for their use. In the case of any omissions, the publisher will be pleased to make suitable acknowledgments in future editions.

Frontmatter: **i** Rafael Lopez. **ii** Christina Balit. **iii**(tl) ©iStockphoto.com/huronphoto. **iii**(tr) Christina Balit. **iii**(bl) Christina Balit. **iii**(br) Hill Street Studios/Blend Images/ Getty Images. **iv**(tl) OJO Images Ltd/Alamy. **iv**(tr) ©iStockphoto.com/ gabycontrreras. **iv**(br) ©iStockphoto.com/RainforestAustralia. **iv**(bl) Royalty-free image.

©iStockphoto.com: **1**(t) dawnn. **6**(t) gbh007. **7**(bg) Yougen. **7**(t) aloha_17. **7**(b) aloha_17. **14**(t) lisafx. **17**(b) DorianGray. **18** STEVECOLEccs. **24**(c) MariaPavlova. **25**(cl) perkmeup. **25**(cr) iofoto. **26**(br) ozgurdonmaz. **31**(t) fotoVoyager. **35**(bg) mitza. **36** mandygodbehear. **37**(t) kemalbas. **38**(c) carlosalvarez. **38**(b) Meggj. **40**(t) LPETTET. **42**(c) busypix. **43**(tl) SharonDay. **43**(cl) MightyIsland. **43**(c) stocksnapper. **49**(bg) kentarcajuan. **50**(c) Royalty-free image. **50**(b) sonyae. **55**(t, cb, br) enjoynz. **55**(ct) Vladimirovic. **55**(bl) paulaphoto. **58**(t) huronphoto. **58**(c) HelpingHandPhotos. **58–59**(b) billberryphotography. **60**(t) sjlocke. **60**(c) busypix. **60**(br) redmal. **64**(tr) lumpynoodles. **65**(t) HKPNC. **66** caracterdesign. **67** lumpynoodles. **68**(t) ArtisticCaptures. **68**(c) Gerville. **71**(t) KathrynSK. **71**(b) epicurean. **79** mart_m. **80**(t) ManoAfrica. **85**(b) sonyae. **86**(b) THEPALMER. **88–89**(b) ultra_generic **92**(bg) Bastar. **91**(t) PTB-images. **102** ImagineGolf. **102–103**(doves) ussr. **104**(t) MaszaS. **104**(bl) kirin_ photo. **107**(b) kryczka. **109**(b) MiquelMunill. **110**(bl) cglade. **115**(l) Anterovium. **115**(r) ktaylorg. **116**(t) ALEAIMAGE. **118**(t) Maica. **120**(t) iofoto. **120**(b) mm88. **124**(t) DNY59. **125**(t) Funwithfood. **125**(c) Kativ. **130**(t) RusN. **130**(b) DarleneSanguenza. **130**(c) sextoacto. **134**(b) gradyreese. **136**(l) whitemay. **136**(r) bonniej. **138** Clockwise from upper left, (a) MentalArt. **138**(b) monkeybusinessimages. **138**(c) Goldmund. **138**(d) Tsuji. **138**(e) LisaValder. **138**(f) phildate. **139** STEEX. **142**(b) horstklinker. **143**(b) monkeybusinessimages. **144** ranplett. (g) macroworld. **148**(t, bl) Faye78. **148**(bd) blue67. **150**(b) nicolesy. **152** Clockwise from top, (a) cotesebastien. **152**(b) art-4-art. **152**(d) RainforestAustralia. **152**(e) kulicki. **158** ultra_generic. **159**(t) Lezh. **161**(b) rest. **163**(tl, cr, bl) RainforestAustralia. **166**(b) yalayama. **169**(b) Liliboas. **173**(bg) lumpynoodles. **174**(cl) duncan1890. **174**(cr) DGM007. **174**(bl) ktaylorg. **174**(br) aleksandarvelasevic. **175** princessdlaf. **178–179**(t) gabycontrreras. **178**(tr) shironosov. **182**(t) Tjanze. **182**(b) monkeybusinessimages. **183**(b) kryczka. **184**(b) duckycards. **185**(t, c) aloha_17. **185**(bl) aloha_17. **188–189** McIninch. **190–191** gbh007. **191**(br) Stratol. **207**(b) kryczka. **210**(t) juanestey. **210**(b) Kativ. **214**(bg) Yougen. **215** Maica. **216**(t) sjlocke. **218**(bd) aloha_17. **218**(b) yalayama. **219**(bd) aloha_17. **219**(t) STEEX. **219**(b) skynesher. **220–221**(b) antb. **224** Photo_Concepts. **226**(b) nicolesy. **227**(t) 13spoon. **244** Illustrious. **249** DNY59. **250** art12321.

Thinkstock: **4**(cl) Jupiterimages/Polka Dot. **30**(b) Stockbyte. **59**(t) George Doyle/Valueline. **69** Jupiterimages/Polka Dot. **108**(t) Jupiterimages/Creatas. **140**(b) Jupiterimages/Comstock. **146**(t) Thinkstock Images/Comstock. **146**(c) Jupiterimages/Brand X Pictures. **189**(c) George Doyle/Valueline. **197**(b) iStockphoto.

Unit 1: **1**(b) From The Spiritual Journey of St. Ignatius Loyola by Dora Nikolova Bittau. Photo by Ken Wagner @ 1998 Seattle University. **2**(t) From The Spiritual Journey of St. Ignatius Loyola by Dora Nikolova Bittau. Photo by Ken Wagner @ 1998 Seattle University. **2**(b) Nik Wheeler/Corbis. **3** Blend Images/Veer. **4**(t) Royalty-free image. **4**(cr) Royalty-free image. **4**(bl) Blend Images Photography/Veer. **4**(br) Stockbyte/Getty Images. **5**(bg) David De Lossy/Photodisc/Getty Images. **5**(t) Royalty-free image. **5**(b) Jupiterimages. **6**(b) alpha_zara/ Flickr. **8**(t) GK Hart/Vikki Hart/Photodisc/Getty images. **8**(bl) Corbis Photography/Veer. **8**(br) Jupiterimages. **9** Onoky Photography/Veer. **10**(l) Susan Tolonen. **10**(r) Hill Street Studios/Getty. **11**(t) The Crosiers/ Gene Plaisted, OSC. **11**(c) Royalty-free image. **11**(b) AgnusImages.com. **12** Corbis Photography/Veer. **13** Digital Vision. **14**(cr, b) Royalty-free image. **14**(cl) Royalty-free image. **15** Corbis Photography/Veer. **16**(t) The Crosiers/Gene Plaisted, OSC. **16**(b) Stockbyte/PunchStock. **17**(t) The Crosiers/Gene Plaisted, OSC. **19**(bg) David De Lossy/Photodisc/ Getty Images. **20**(t) Photodisc. **20**(bl) Getty Images. **20**(br) Susan Tolonen. **21** Ocean Photography/Veer. **22**(b) Photodisc/Getty. **23**(t) The Crosiers/Gene Plaisted, OSC. **23**(b) Alexander Walter/Stone/ Getty. **24**(b) Royalty-free image. **25**(t) The Crosiers/Gene Plaisted, OSC. **25**(c) Jupiterimages. **25**(c) Rubberball/Erik Isakson/Getty. **25**(bl) Royalty-free image. **25**(br) Jupiterimages. **26**(t) Susan Tolonen. **26**(bl) Brand X Pictures/Fotosearch. **27** Phil Martin Photography. **28**(t) Brand X Pictures/Fotosearch. **28**(b) Royalty-free image. **29** Stockbyte/Getty Images. **30**(t) Susan Tolonen. **30**(c) Susan Tolonen.

Unit 2: **31**(b) Amanda Hall. **32** Amanda Hall. **33** Royalty-free image. **34**(t, c, bl) Christina Balit. **34**(br) Jupiterimages. **35**(t) Christina Balit. **35**(b) Christina Balit. **37**(b) Fred Willingham. **38**(t) Daniel Pangbourne/ Digital Vision/Getty. **39** Fancy Photography/Veer. **40–41**(b) Christina Balit. **40**(br) Courtesy of Riverside Church, New York, NY. **41**(t) Royalty-free image. **41**(b) Christina Balit. **42**(t, b) Royalty-free image. **43**(tc) Brand X Pictures/Fotosearch. **43**(tr) Brand X Pictures/ Fotosearch. **43**(cr) Anika Salsera. **43**(b) Jupiterimages. **44**(t) Brand X Pictures/Fotosearch. **44**(c) Exactostock/SuperStock. **44**(b) Katrina Wittkamp/Stockbyte/Getty Images. **45** Corbis Photography/Veer. **46–47** Amanda Hall. **48** Cultura/Veer. **49** Royalty-free images. **50**(t) Stockbyte/Groups: Children & Teenagers/CD disc. **51** Fancy Photography/Veer. **52**(t) Nana Quparadze, a Georgian iconographer. Reprinted by permission of the Holy Resurrection Orthodox Church, Singapore (Orthodox Metrolitinate of Hong Kong & SE Asia). **52**(b) Susan Tolonen. **53** Susan Tolonen. **54**(t) Corbis Photography/ Veer. **54**(b) Jupiterimages. **56**(t) The Crosiers/Gene Plaisted, OSC. **56**(c) Royalty-free image. **56**(b) Jupiterimages. **57**(t) W. P. Wittman Limited. **57**(b) Royalty-free image. **60**(bl) W. P. Wittman Limited.

Unit 3: **61**(t) Royalty-free image. **61**(b) William Thomas Cain/ Contributor/Getty Images News/Getty Images. **62**(t) St. Katharine Drexel, Robert Lentz, 2012, Courtesy of Trinity Stores, www.trinitystores.com, 800.699.4482. **62**(b) William Thomas Cain/ Contributor/Getty Images News/Getty Images. **63** Corbis Photography/ Veer. **64**(tl) Scala/Art Resource, NY. **64**(bl) Royalty-free image. **64**(br) Royalty-free image. **65**(c) Nancy R. Cohen/Digital Vision/Getty Images. **65**(b) Tom Grill/Corbis. **68**(b) Brand X Pictures/Fotosearch. **70** The Crosiers/Gene Plaisted, OSC. **72** Alloy Photography/Veer. **73** Fred Willingham. **74**(t) Susan Tolonen. **74**(c) Susan Tolonen. **74**(b) Phil Martin Photography. **75** Blend Images/Veer. **76**(t) W.P. Wittman Limited. **76**(c) Susan Tolonen. **76–77**(b) Susan Tolonen. **77**(t) Susan Tolonen. **77**(c) Phil Martin Photography. **78** Image Source Photography/Veer. **80**(c) Susan Tolonen. **80**(b) Phil Martin Photography. **81** Fancy Photography/Veer. **82**(t) Stockbyte/Getty Images. **82**(b) W.P. Wittman Limited. **83**(t) Victorian Traditions/Shutterstock.com. **83**(b) Royalty-free image. **84**(c) Stockbyte/Getty Images. **85**(t) The Crosiers/Gene Plaisted, OSC. **86**(t) AgnusImages.com. **86**(c) Phil Martin Photography. **87** W.P. Wittman Limited. **88**(t) Warling Studios. **89** Phil Martin Photography. **90**(t) The Crosiers/Gene Plaisted, OSC. **90**(b) W.P. Wittman Limited.

Unit 4: **91**(b) Mary Evans Picture Library/Alamy. **92**(t) Mary Evans Picture Library/Alamy. **92**(b) David Atkinson. **93** Wolfgang Flamisch/ Corbis. **94**(t) AgnusImages.com. **94**(c) W. P. Wittman Limited. **94**(b) W. P. Wittman Limited. **95**(t) The Crosiers/Gene Plaisted, OSC. **95**(b) Warling Studios. **96**(t) P T Images/Veer. **96–97**(flowers) C Squared Studios/Photodisc. **97**(t) W. P. Wittman Limited. **98**(t) Phil Martin Photography. **98**(b) Warling Studios. **99** IOFOTO/Veer. **100** Amanda Hall. **101** The Crosiers/Gene Plaisted, OSC. **103**(t) W. P. Wittman Limited. **104**(bd, br) C Squared Studios/Photodisc. **105** Laura Doss/Fancy/Alamy. **106–107**(grapes) Susan Tolonen. **106**(l) Susan Tolonen. **106**(b) The Crosiers/Gene Plaisted, OSC. **107**(t) W. P. Wittman Limited. **108**(b) Susan Tolonen. **109**(t) Susan Tolonen. **110**(t) W. P. Wittman Limited. **110**(br) Susan Tolonen. **111** Blend Images/Alamy. **112**(t) W. P. Wittman Limited. **112**(c) W. P. Wittman Limited. **112**(b) Larry Downing/Reuters/Corbis. **112**(bg) Jupiterimages. **113**(t) Moodboard Photography/Veer. **113**(c) Royalty-free image. **113**(b) Moon Hak-Jin, Korea. **114** Wealan Pollard/OJO Images Ltd./ Alamy. **116**(b) Photodisc/Getty Images. **117**(l, r) The Crosiers/Gene Plaisted, OSC. **118–119**(snowflakes) Jill Arena. **118**(b) Fancy/Alamy. **119**(t) W. P. Wittman Limited. **120**(cl) Blend Images/Alamy.

Unit 5: **121**(t) Roger Wood/Corbis. **121**(b) Stained Glass by Akili Ron Anderson. **122**(t) Stained Glass by Akili Ron Anderson. **122**(b) Gianna Marino. **123** Blend Images Photography/Veer. **124**(b) The Crosiers/ Gene Plaisted, OSC. **125**(b) Warling Studios. **126** Dmitry Naumov/ Veer. **127**(t) Maurizio Brambatti/epa/Corbis. **127**(b) Jupiterimages. **128**(t) The Crosiers/Gene Plaisted, OSC. **128**(b) Jose Luis Pelaez Inc./ Corbis. **129** Randy Faris/Corbis. **131** The Crosiers/Gene Plaisted, OSC. **132** Keith Levit/Corbis. **133** Christina Balit. **134**(t) The Crosiers/ Gene Plaisted, OSC. **135** Monkey Business Images/Veer. **137**(t, b) St. Louise de Marillac, Robert Lentz, 2012, Courtesy of Trinity Stores, www.trinitystores.com, 800.699.4482. **137**(c) St. Vincent de Paul, Robert Lentz, 2012, Courtesy of Trinity Stores, www.trinitystores. com, 800.699.4482. **140**(t) The Crosiers/Gene Plaisted, OSC. **141** Fancy Photography/Veer. **142**(t) Courtesy of Fearghal O'Farrell/Vincentian Family Shrine, St. Peter's Church, Phibsboro, Dublin. **143**(t) allOver photography/Alamy. **145** Royalty-free images. (h) C Squared Studios/ Photodisc **146–147**(b) C Squared Studios/Photodisc **147**(t) The Crosiers/ Gene Plaisted, OSC. **148**(br) Monkey Business Images/Veer. **149**(t) The Crosiers/Gene Plaisted, OSC. **149**(c) W. P. Wittman Limited. **149**(b) W. P. Wittman Limited. **150**(t) The Crosiers/Gene Plaisted, OSC.

Seasonal Sessions: **151** Susan Tolonen. **152**(c) Siede Preis/Photodisc **152**(f) Royalty-free image. **153** The Crosiers/Gene Plaisted, OSC. **154** The Crosiers/Gene Plaisted, OSC. **155** Warling Studios. **156** The Crosiers/Gene Plaisted, OSC. **157** Warling Studios. **159**(b) C Squared Studios/Photodisc **160** Hanna-Cheriyan Varghese. **161**(t) Private Collection/Look and Learn /The Bridgeman Art Library International. **162**(bg) Amanda Hall. **162**(r) Warling Studios. **163**(tr) Photodisc/Getty Images. **163**(cl) Jupiterimages. **163**(br) Jupiterimages. **164** The Crosiers/ Gene Plaisted, OSC. **165**(bg) Siede Preis/Photodisc **165**(c) Galleria degli Uffizi, Florence, Italy/The Bridgeman Art Library International. **166**(t) The Crosiers/Gene Plaisted, OSC. **167** The Crosiers/Gene Plaisted, OSC. **168** Ocean Photography/Veer. **169**(t) The Crosiers/Gene Plaisted, OSC. **169**(c) oliveromg/Shutterstock.com. **170** The Crosiers/ Gene Plaisted, OSC. **171** W. P. Wittman Limited. **172** Radius Images/ Corbis. **173**(cl) The Crosiers/Gene Plaisted, OSC. **173**(br) Shutterstock. com. **174**(t) Private Collection/Malva Gallery/The Bridgeman Art Library International. **176** HeQi, HeQi Arts LLC. www.heqigallery.com. **177**(l) Werner Forman/Art Resource, NY. **177**(r) Warling Studios. **178**(c) The Crosiers/Gene Plaisted, OSC. **178**(bl) C Squared Studios/ Photodisc **178**(br) Charles O. Cecil/Alamy. **180** Warling Studios.

Endmatter: **181**(tl) ©1996 Image Club Graphics. **181**(bl) Jupiteimages. **181**(br) Hill Street Studios/Blend Images/Getty Images. **183**(t) Warling Studios. **184**(t) Bibliotheque des Arts Decoratifs, Paris, France/ The Bridgeman Art Library International. **185**(br) Warling Studios. **186**(br) The Crosiers/Gene Plaisted, OSC. **186–187**(bg) Mykola Velychko/Veer. **187**(t) Warling Studios. **187**(b) C Squared Studios/ Photodisc **189**(t) C Squared Studios/Photodisc **189**(c) George Doyle/ Valueline. **189**(bl) C Squared Studios/Photodisc **191**(bl) Siede Preis/ Photodisc **192–193**(bg) Les Cunliffe/Veer. **192**(l) Corbis Photography/ Veer. **192**(r) The Crosiers/Gene Plaisted, OSC. **193** W. P. Wittman Limited. **194**(t) The Crosiers/Gene Plaisted, OSC. **194**(b) Warling Studios. **195** Greg Kuepfer. **196** The Crosiers/Gene Plaisted, OSC. **197**(tr) The Crosiers/Gene Plaisted, OSC. **197**(cr) The Crosiers/ Gene Plaisted, OSC. **197**(br) The Crosiers/Gene Plaisted, OSC. **198–199** Laura James/Private Collection/The Bridgeman Art Library International. **200**(t) Phil Martin Photography. **200–201**(b) Anni Betts. **201**(t) W. P. Wittman Limited. **201**(c) Warling Studios. **202**(t) Warling Studios. **202**(b) Susan Tolonen. **203**(tl) W. P. Wittman Limited. **203**(tr) W. P. Wittman Limited. **203**(bg) Susan Tolonen. **204**(t) Brand X Pictures/PunchStock. **204–205** Darren Kemper/Veer. **205** W. P. Wittman Limited. **208**(tr) Warling Studios. **208–209** Phyllis Pollema-Cahill. **209**(tl) W. P. Wittman Limited. **209**(tc) Warling Studios. **209**(tr) Phil Martin Photography. **211**(b) W. P. Wittman Limited. **212**(l) Corbis Photography/Veer. **213** Monkey Business Images/Veer. **214**(bl) Vie de Jésus Mafa, www.jesusmafa. com. **214**(br) RubberBall Photography/Veer. **216**(c) JGI/Tom Grill/ Blend Images/Corbis. **216–217**(b) momentimages/Tetra Images/ Corbis. **217**(t) Jamie Grill/Tetra Images/Corbis. **217**(c) Artiga Photo/Corbis. **218**(t) ArtisticCaptures. **220**(t) The Crosiers/Gene Plaisted, OSC. **222–223** Glow Images/Getty Images. **223**(c) The Crosiers/Gene Plaisted, OSC. **225** Ocean Photography/Veer. **225**(bg) Jill Arena. **226**(t) Jose Luis Pelaez/Blend Images/Corbis. **227**(b) Jupiterimages. **231** Jupiterimages. **232** Amanda Hall. **233** Yoshi Miyake. **235** Jupiterimages. **236** Thinkstock. **237** Philomena O'Neill. **238** Courtesy of Immaculate Conception Church, Earlington, KY/ photo by Ray Giardinella. **239** Amanda Hall. **240** Yoshi Miyake. **241**(b) Jupiterimages. **242** Amanda Hall. **243** Yoshi Miyake. **246** Amanda Hall. **247** photo by Greg Kuepfer. **248** Amanda Hall. **251**(t) Tony Rothberg.